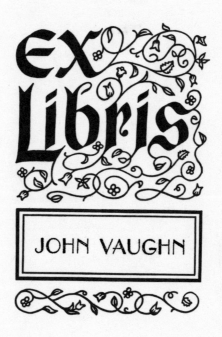

EX
Libris

JOHN VAUGHN

All About Wildfowling
in America

All About Wildfowling In America

Edited by
Jerome Knap

Winchester Press

Copyright © 1976 by Winchester Press

Library of Congress Cataloging in Publication Data
Main entry under title:

All about wildfowling in America.

    Includes index.
    1. Fowling—North America.   I. Knap, Jerome J.
SK313.A44   799.2'4'097   76-22681
ISBN 0-87691-177-7

Published by Winchester Press
205 East 42nd Street, New York 10017

Printed in the United States of America

Dedicated to
Wildfowlers Across America

Picture Credits

(pp. 3, 4) U.S. Fish and Wildlife Service; (pp. 7, 12) Rex Gary Schmidt, U.S. Fish and Wildlife Service; (pp. 17—59) drawings by Alan Munro, reproduced by permission of the Atlantic Flyway Council; (p. 63) Ontario Ministry of Natural Resources; (p. 64) Manitoba Tourist Branch; (p. 67) Ontario Ministry of Natural Resources; (pp. 69, 71) Burton J. Myers; (p. 74) Richard Rees; (p. 76) George Gruenfeld; (pp. 77, 80) Clair Rees; (p. 83) Pete Czura; (p. 87) H. Lea Lawrence; (p. 91) David Marshall, U.S. Fish and Wildlife Service; (p. 93) Burton J. Myers; (p. 94) Jerome Knap; (p. 97) Cyraine Dugdale; (p. 98) Barrymar Kennels; (p. 99) Jeffrey Kennels; (pp. 100, 101) Jerome Knap; (p. 105) Ontario Ministry of Natural Resources; (p. 106) Old Town Canoe Company; (p. 108) Mirro-Craft; (p. 109) Burton J. Myers; (pp. 114, 117) Norman Strung; (p. 120) Ontario Ministry of Tourism; (p. 122) Richard Rees; (pp. 124, 127) Burton J. Myers; (p. 129) Ontario Ministry of Tourism; (p. 132) Manitoba Tourist Branch; (p. 134) Ontario Ministry of Natural Resources; (p. 138) Burton J. Myers; (p. 139) Bob Gooch; (pp. 143, 144) Clair Rees; (pp. 146, 148)

Norman Strung; (pp. 169, 178) Jerome Knap; (p. 181) Luther
Goldman, U.S. Fish and Wildlife Service; (p. 185) George
Gruenefeld; (pp. 191, 195) Bob Gooch; (p. 199) Michigan
Department of Natural Resources; (p. 201) Ontario Ministry of
Tourism; (p. 204) Ontario Ministry of Natural Resources; (p. 211)
Peter J. Van Huizen, U.S. Fish and Wildlife Service; (p. 216) H.
Lea Lawrence; (pp. 222, 225) Pete Czura; (pp. 235, 239) Red
Wilkinson; (pp. 242, 243) Clair Rees; (p. 246) Idaho Fish and
Game Department; (pp. 251, 254) Charles C. Adams; (p. 262)
Louisiana Wildlife and Fisheries Commission; (p. 266) John
Wootters; (p. 269) Nick Covacevich; (p. 271) Norman Strung;
(p. 273) Al Tetzlaff; (p. 277) U.S. Fish and Wildlife Service;
(p. 279) Jerome Stoudt, U.S. Fish and Wildlife Service; (p. 285) Rex
Gary Schmidt, U.S. Fish and Wildlife Service.

Contents

All About Wildfowling
in America

Introduction

E VEN A MAN whose primitive senses have long been dulled by city and sophistication will instinctively look skyward when he hears the honking of wild geese. And he'll wonder. Where have they been? Where are they going? No other group of birds inspires this interest, this attraction. It is probably a vestige of ancient times when all men were hunters and waterfowl meant food.

Some men are still wildfowlers. To them, a life without misty mornings on a marsh; or without days on big waters, in a duck boat tossed about by waves, and with a wind chilling bodies to the marrow would be a life less worth living. Perhaps even a mere existence.

Certainly a world without waterfowl would be a less interesting place. Yet the future, the decades ahead, for waterfowl don't look very bright. A hungry world looks covetously at all wetlands—to them wastelands—and perhaps cries, "What is more important, wheat or waterfowl"?

Wetlands are not wastelands. They play an important role in this earth's hydrological resources. But it is probably impossible to expect reason or logic from a hungry man.

This is coming, and we must prepare against it. The only solution lies in not allowing the earth's human population to increase even more beyond the earth's carrying capacity than it already has. I am not-at-all certain how this can be achieved.

But perhaps I've been too bleak. For the present and the near future, the waterfowling picture looks reasonably bright. There are some ups and downs, of course. I certainly wish we could put our finger on what's keeping the number of canvasbacks and redheads down, but there are no major crises. Geese continue to increase, so much so that the greater snow goose has been once again added to the waterfowler's bag along the Atlantic Flyway.

And certainly the interest in waterfowl and waterfowling continues at an all-time high. Ducks Unlimited is continually expanding its operation in Canada, backed by increasing donations from hunters in the United States. The latest expansion has been into Ontario.

Sales of duck stamps have also increased. As a result, this continent's waterfowl refuges may get the rejuvenation they so sorely need.

Hunting wildlife is an ancient tradition. On this continent, its skill can be traced not only to the first European colonists, but even back to Indian hunters and their decoys of woven reeds. We modern waterfowlers are in good company. Our firearms may be superior—although a few of us are once again taking muzzle-loading shotguns into the marshes—but our techniques of calling and decoying are as old as wildfowling itself.

In a way, we may be living in wildfowling's greatest era, not because the populations of ducks and geese are even remotely like they were before the turn of the century, but because fowlers earn each bird they get. If there is a better example of hunter-backed conservation than the national refuge system and the work of Ducks Unlimited, I'd certainly like to know about it.

JEROME KNAP
February, 1976

1

Managing the Flyways

Joseph P. Linduska

W ATERFOWL ARE CREATURES of strong migratory instinct. In our hemisphere, they distribute themselves seasonally over the whole of North America, from the Arctic Circle to the semitropics of Mexico. Although some species winter as far south as Central and South America, the great bulk of the flock confines its movements to Canada, the United States, and Mexico. This calls for management on an international scale, accomplished by means of treaties between the three countries.

However, long before migratory birds became beneficiaries of international law, they had problems at the domestic level. And the reason is not hard to see. Moving as they did from province to province and state to state, there was little incentive for any one political entity to practise restraint in harvesting the birds. In the late 1800's, our states had little or no regulation regarding waterfowl. Market hunting, spring shooting, and a lack of bag limits and season restraints ravaged the great flocks. The prevalent attitude was: "If we don't get them, someone else will."

It was obvious that some national regulation, especially to curb unrestricted market hunting, was necessary. The first step came with the passage of the so-called Lacey Act in 1900. This legislation provided for national management of game birds, subject to the laws of the states. It prohibited the importation of certain wild birds and mammals except under permit; and most importantly, it invoked the interstate commerce clause, thereby making interstate shipment of any game taken contrary to the laws of the state a federal violation.

To further regulate the taking of migratory birds, a treaty with Great Britain (on behalf of Canada) was ratified in 1916. Two years later, in 1918, the Migratory Bird Treaty Act implemented the treaty. A convention similar to that with Great Britain was effected with Mexico in 1936.

The treaty of 1916 was the first step in the management of North American waterfowl. It outlawed market shooting by prohibiting the sale of migratory game birds; it ended spring shooting by limiting the season for hunting to a period not to exceed 3½ months, and closed it between March 10 and September 1; and, finally, it allowed the setting of basic bag limits and seasons nationwide by the federal regulatory authority.

Cooperation between the three countries has been very close, especially between the United States and Canada, where 85 percent of all North American waterfowl are hatched. The U.S. carries on joint surveys with Canada, cooperates in habitat preservation, and, as observers, each country participates in the other's yearly regulation-setting process. This free exchange of information and close cooperation in all phases of management have led to good understanding and reasonably considerate hunting regulations. As a result, there has been no need to establish harvest quotas for each of the three countries involved. However, as hunting pressures increase, this is something which may well become a necessity in the years ahead.

The birds themselves had a good deal to say about how we should organize our management efforts. The waterfowl of our continent segregate into groups that follow discernible patterns of migration between nesting and wintering grounds. Hunters, by returning bands they find on the legs of ducks and geese they shoot, have helped to produce this information. Although there is considerable overlapping of these flight lanes, as well as a certain amount of trading back and forth by waterfowl, studies of band recoveries have shown that the migration patterns for ducks and geese break down into four major flyways. With minor exceptions, the flyways are: the Pacific Flyway

The key factor in wildfowl management is preservation of wetlands.

from the west coast to the Rocky Mountains; the Central Flyway from the Rockies to the eastern edge of the Great Plains; the Mississippi from the Mississippi River to the Appalachian Mountains; and the Atlantic from the Appalachians to the east coast.

Before the flyway concept was developed, waterfowl hunting regulations were established on a nationwide basis. This had the great disadvantage of forcing hunting restrictions on all areas, when they were actually needed only in certain sections. The converse, when it occurred, was even more objectionable. Nationwide relaxation in regulations permitted excessive harvest in some areas and of some species that could ill afford it. Regulation of hunting by flyways not only benefits the ducks and geese, but also permits maximum hunting opportunity consistent with the local waterfowl situation.

As our knowledge of waterfowl improves, we are moving toward even more refined management within the flyways, on a flock or even a species basis. Species management is offering great possibilities for increasing the overall harvest of birds, without placing any one species in jeopardy from excessive shooting. Some waterfowl, particularly some species of diving ducks, seem to be in chronically short

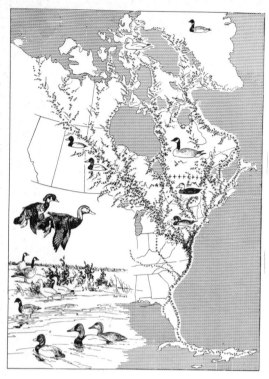

The Atlantic Flyway.

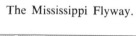

The Mississippi Flyway.

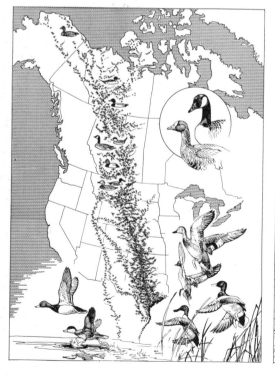

The Central Flyway.

The Pacific Flyway.

supply. Others, notably mallards and pintails among the dabblers, reach peak numbers in years of good breeding conditions. Accordingly, regulations that will permit a large harvest of species in abundance, while protecting others that need it, are good management strategy.

Species management using a point system is the latest innovation to be employed. It assigns high point values to species of low population levels and low point values to species which are abundant. The daily bag is controlled by allowing the hunter a specified number of points. The limit is reached when the point value of the last bird taken, when added to the sum of point values of the other birds already taken during that day, reaches or exceeds the specified level.

For example: mallard hens might be assigned 90 points; mallard drake 20 points; and all other ducks 10 points. If the daily point total is 100, the allowable daily bag would vary from 2 to 10 birds, depending on the order in which the birds were taken. If a mallard hen were the first bird taken, totalling 90 points, the hunter would know that he could take one additional bird of any species or sex and still be legal, including another mallard hen. If he took nine ducks other than mallards, totalling 90 points, again he would know that he could take one additional bird of any species or sex. If he took three mallard drakes (60 points) followed by four pintails (40 points), the last pintail taken would have increased his cumulative point total of 100, and he would have reached his limit for the day.

Although the point system does not require that the hunter be able to identify birds in the air before he shoots, there is a definite advantage in being able to do so. The advantage is a larger daily bag if low- or medium-point birds can be selected. On top of this, the point system allows more "challenge", with an increase in both quality and benefits from the day afield.

Another potential advantage of the point system is the ease with which varying conditions among states within a flyway can be recognized and accommodated when hunting regulations are being established. The point allocation in a state where 80 percent or more of the kill is usually mallards could be quite different from that of a state where mallards make up only 20 percent of the kill. The point system provides an effective means of shifting hunting pressure towards or away from selected species and sexes.

A major disadvantage of the point system is the inducement it can afford a hunter to "reorder" the bag. For example, with a 100-point total, a hunter might take a 90-point bird first, after which one additional duck would cause him to reach his legal daily bag limit. On the other hand, a legal bag could consist of nine 10-point birds plus a 90-point bird, providing the 90-point bird was taken last. The temptation, if the high-point bird is taken first, is to continue shooting and attempt to take only low-point birds. After the second bird is taken, each subsequent bird must be properly identified in the air before it is killed or the hunter will exceed the point total regardless of the supposed order taken.

Second, the point system provides an inducement for hunters to discard high-point birds.

Third, the point system is complicated in relation to a daily bag limit without species restrictions.

Fourth, the variable daily bag makes it difficult for a law enforcement officer to determine an illegal bag, particularly when a party of two or more persons is involved. If two daily bags are allowed in possession, the legal possession is even more difficult to determine.

Whatever the mechanism of harvest (and the do's and don'ts of waterfowling are indeed many), a herculean effort goes into data gathering to provide a basis for annual hunting regulations. Each year a systematic survey is made throughout the breeding grounds in the United States and Canada. The objective is to obtain the best possible information on the size of the crop so that regulations will be consistent with production.

In May and June, transects are flown over most of the waterfowl producing areas to get a reading on the number of nesting adults, as well as the number and condition of water areas. But counting the nesters gives no sure measure of the crop. Summer drought, widespread hail storms, heavy predation, and a host of other factors can reduce the effort of nesting hens to nought. And so in July, a second flying survey is made over the same transects, this time to get an index of brood production, and again to measure the status of all-important water conditions. Also, intensive ground surveys are made on sample areas to check on aerial data and provide a correction factor for this more extensive information.

While this production survey provides the main basis for regulation setting, a wealth of other information is also cranked in. Two additional surveys are conducted annually in the United States and Canada to determine the size, composition, and distribution of the waterfowl harvest. A Hunter Questionnaire Survey is used on randomly selected waterfowl hunters who have purchased duck stamps

Through banding, wildfowl biologists learn migration patterns and population trends.

at post offices. Following the hunting season, the participants report on the number of times they hunted and the number of ducks and geese they bagged, or lost as cripples. The adjustment and expansion of data from this survey produces estimates of hunter numbers, times hunted, and ducks and geese harvested or lost.

Hunters in another sample survey are asked to submit wings from ducks or tail feathers from geese they harvest. Plumage materials submitted provide information on the species, age, and sex composition of the sample. The survey results are then used in conjunction with the Hunter Questionnaire Survey data to obtain estimates of the species, sex, and age composition of the total harvest, and the geographical distribution of that harvest.

Approximately 56,000 persons cooperate in the U.S. Hunter Questionnaire Survey each season. Roughly 80,000 duck wings and 8000 goose tails are submitted each year. Nearly identical surveys are also conducted annually in Canada. From these two surveys, it has been found, for example, that United States hunters in recent years kill about 10 to 11 million ducks annually. The Canadian hunter kill is approximately 3.5 to 4 million birds.

The effects of drought are also readily apparent from kill figures spanning two decades, between 1955 and 1974. In this interval, the duck harvest ranged from a low of 4.2 million to a high of about 16 million, and coincided with periods of drought and good water on the breeding grounds. The goose kill, all species, during this same period averaged about 1 million birds yearly and showed a doubling in harvest from 0.8 million to 1.5 million in recent years.

All the above information, and more, is taken into account in arriving at the regulations for any one year. Immediately following the wrap-up of production surveys in late July, federal biologists of the Fish and Wildlife Service summarize all findings. Using charts, maps, and graphs, they portray the full status of waterfowl. They forecast the fall flight to biologists and other representatives of each of the four flyways. Following this, the state biologists report to their superiors, the state directors, who make up the individual Flyway Councils. In the meantime, federal biologists make a recommendation on seasons and bag limits, in keeping with the "forecast of fall flight", to their superior, the Director of the Fish and Wildlife Service. These recommendations are then reviewed individually with each of the four Flyway Councils.

As might be expected, the two groups (state versus federal) don't always view things in the same light. And so, yet another meeting is held in Washington, D.C., in early August. Here the entire review is repeated before a Waterfowl Advisory Committee, which includes two delegates from each of the four Flyway Councils, plus representatives from most of the major conservation organizations. Following a reading of the proposed seasons and bag limits, each member of the advisory committee is invited to comment. With these recommendations and counter proposals in hand, the Director of the Service then does the best he can to reconcile this information with the staff's proposals. Publication in the Federal Register follows, and another waterfowl season is in the offing.

Every waterfowler realizes that ducks and geese are subject to a multitude of mortality factors other than hunting. At present, lead poisoning is of special concern. Spent shotgun pellets ingested by waterfowl were recognized as a cause of dieoffs in North America as early as the 1800's, but serious research on the problem did not begin until the 1930's. During the period from 1937 to 1957, 34 waterfowl dieoffs attributable to lead poisoning were recorded, with losses ranging from 100 to 16,000 birds. But the greatest losses occur as unobserved attrition during fall, winter, and spring. The lead-poisoned waterfowl simply creep away, hide, and die. The annual loss of waterfowl has been estimated at 2 to 3 million birds. For purposes of comparison, United States hunters lose approximately 2 million unretrieved birds annually.

Concern about lead poisoning in waterfowl was renewed with the upswelling of environmental consciousness in North America during the late 1960's. The intensive search for a non-toxic substitute focused on "soft" steel. Laboratory and field tests reveal that although "soft" steel may not be the ultimate substitute for lead, it performs satisfactorily at shooting ranges of 40 to 45 yards. Whatever the ultimate solution, an estimated 3000 tons of spent lead shot has been deposited annually in waterfowl habitats during the past 10 years, and in some areas the accumulation ranges from 23,000 to 122,000 pellets per acre.

Another ominous threat to North American waterfowl is DVE (Duck Virus Enteritis), a disease first noted among European waterfowl, where it is known as Dutch Duck Plague. DVE was first diagnosed in North America in 1967. But initially it was confined to domestic ducks. In January, 1973, a major outbreak occurred at Lake Andes National Wildlife Refuge in South Dakota. Within a month, approximately 40,000 ducks, chiefly mallards but including other duck species and Canada geese, succumbed. The epidemic was eventually brought under control by chemical treatment of the water, collection and disposal of carcasses, and drainage of the impoundment where the birds concentrated. The mortality—representing 40 percent of the waterfowl at Lake Andes—ranks as one of the severest disease outbreaks in recent years.

DVE can be readily transmitted by contact between infected and susceptible birds, or indirectly by contact with a contaminated environment, notably an aquatic habitat. Outbreaks of DVE within captive or contained populations generally are self-limiting, with mortality persisting for 3 to 5 weeks following initial infection. Survivors of DVE outbreaks are known to acquire an immunity. However, their possible role as carriers to uninfected populations is unknown.

Another disease that can be of tremendous consequence to waterfowl is botulism. The first report of waterfowl mortality from this disease was recorded in 1876 at Owens Lake, California. In 1934, an estimated quarter-million ducks perished at the northern end of Great Salt Lake in Utah. The cause of this and other dieoffs in alkaline western marshes and lakes remained a mystery until 1934, when the causative agent was identified as *Clostridium botulinum* Type C, a poison-producing bacteria.

Botulism epidemics seem related to excess runoff in the western states, resulting in the shallow flooding of large alkaline basins and sumps. The winter and spring of 1952 were extremely wet, and an estimated 4 to 5 million waterfowl eventually perished from botulism. Approximately 125 square miles of the Tulare Lake basin in California flooded in 1941, and about 160,000 ducks died. Mortalities of these magnitudes exert a profound, but fortunately temporary, influence on local or flyway populations. Species most avidly sought by hunters are often those most susceptible to botulism. The pintail, green-winged teal, shoveller, cinnamon teal, and mallard seem especially vulnerable.

The key botulism preventive measure is manipulating water levels to deter the growth of bacteria. The treatment of sick birds is limited to their transfer to clean water or injection with an antitoxin. Countless thousands of ducks have been saved from botulism simply by altering water levels to prevent conditions conducive to the growth of the botulism-causing bacteria. In recent years, few large botulism outbreaks have occurred where wildlife managers have had a means of regulating water levels.

Avian cholera, an infectious disease caused by the bacterium *Pasteurella multocida,* has been recognized in a variety of wild and domestic birds for nearly 200 years. It was first reported in North America in 1944, among waterfowl wintering at the Muleshoe National Wildlife Refuge in Texas. The virulence of this disease differs from place to place. Sometimes whistling swans bear the brunt of the disease; at other times pintails, American widgeons, snow geese, and white-fronted geese seem particularly susceptible. Control measures are largely futile. However, sanitary practices have been employed in deterring local transmission of the disease.

How serious is avian cholera? There is some evidence that it may cause up to a 2-percent reduction in ducks and a 6-percent reduction in swans in California during the northward migration in some years.

In recent years wildlife, including waterfowl, has received the attention of biologists investigating the complex and often subtle effects of pesticides upon our environment. Mortalities of snow geese caused by dieldrin, and shell-thinning of black duck eggs, have been identified.

Studies in the mid-1960's have indicated that black ducks collected in the northern Atlantic Flyway states contained higher levels of DDT, DDD, and DDE than were found among black ducks and mallards collected elsewhere in the United States. The highest residue levels coincided with wetland areas subjected to the most intensive applications of DDT for mosquito control. The application of this insecticide for mosquito control has since ceased.

Fulvous tree duck populations underwent a sharp decline in the rice-growing region of coastal Texas after the initial widespread use of the pesticide aldrin in 1960. Similar losses were noted in Louisiana the year following the first use there of aldrin-treated seed rice. Fulvous tree duck reductions were most evident where rice was aerially-seeded, in contrast to areas where rice was drill-seeded.

Much has been written about the appearance of high levels of mercury in fish and other aquatic organisms. Waterfowl, likewise, have been found to contain substantial amounts of this environmental contaminant. Mercury compounds are a common ingredient is fungicides, widely used in the treatment of grain seed. This has provided the source of residues in both diving and dabbling ducks. Mercury concentrations in these birds in the northcentral United States were found to be similar to those in agricultural regions of Canada.

The mallard is routinely monitored throughout the United States for presence and incidence of pesticidal residues. Wings submitted by hunters comprise the analytical sample. Much remains to be learned about the short- and long-term effects of pesticides upon North American waterfowl.

Roughly one-half of the world's annual production of petroleum is transported through marine environments where oil tankers spill and leak more than 250 million gallons of oil annually. Investigations have demonstrated that hatchability of duck eggs has been reduced by as much as 60 percent when the eggs were subjected to a light coating of oil. Female ducks have stopped egg laying as a result of swallowing oil when preening oil-contaminated feathers.

The direct annual loss of waterfowl to oil may exceed 100,000 birds. Mortalities of 5,000 to 10,000 birds from a single oil spill are not uncommon. Within the past two years, the hazards to ducks of open-surface oil sumps associated with petroleum production and storage have been recognized and corrective action taken. Although off-shore exploratory and production drilling of oil wells poses great risk to estuarine and coastal waterfowl habitat, especially along our Gulf Coast, rigid precautionary standards and advanced technology have held pollution from this source to a relatively low level.

The reproductive success of Arctic nesting waterfowl, notably snow geese, brant, white-fronted geese, and several subspecies of Canada geese is largely dependent upon favorable weather or climatic conditions. These conditions, if adverse, may not always cause serious mortality; however, they are extremely important in determining whether snow and ice will vanish early enough to allow nesting water-

Geese for study are commonly captured in cannon-fired nets.

fowl to complete their reproductive cycle before autumn. Goose production for some Arctic nesters during 1971 and 1972 was poor because of delayed spring breakup and runoffs. Fortunately, ideal breeding conditions prevailed throughout the Arctic in 1973, and nearly all northern geese experienced unusually high nesting success. The vagaries of Arctic conditions during the breeding season are reflected by the following wintering populations of Atlantic brant: 1971 —151,000; 1972—73,000; 1973—42,000; and 1974—88,000. Surveys now conducted by the Canadian Wildlife Service of major Arctic goose production areas allow regulations to be set in accordance with the current year's production success.

Predation has generally been disregarded as a factor limiting North American waterfowl populations. Nonetheless, predators can cause serious local losses to nesting hens and nests, if the predator population is uncontrolled. Changes in land use, plus the removal or drastic reduction of larger carnivores from the major waterfowl breeding area, have enabled certain waterfowl predators to expand their ranges or increase their numbers. For example, the raccoon has recently moved north from the United States into important waterfowl nesting areas of southwestern Manitoba and southeastern Saskatchewan. It has become a serious predator upon duck species that nest over water, such as the canvasback, which has a relatively low reproductive capacity and high vulnerability to hunting.

The hunter, as a consumer of waterfowl, has competition of sorts from a variety of factors that cause mortality among waterfowl. Some factors, like the disease DVE, have appeared with dramatic suddenness, to exact an awesome toll before the cause could be diagnosed, let alone a solution applied. Others, such as raccoon predation, have occurred gradually, as these animals have spread northward into the major breeding grounds of waterfowl.

Our chemical world has yielded surprises and problems for many living things, on both land and water. The consequences of this over a long period are yet to be established. The accelerated search for energy sources over much of the world may likewise add burdens to the welfare of waterfowl.

Knowing that research is never at its best in a crisis, game management agencies in Canada and the United States have added substantially to their research capabilities. Perhaps, by so doing, we can avoid what otherwise might be a major impact on the natural world through ill-advised programs.

2

Wildfowl Identification

Jerome Knap

E VERY WILDFOWLER SHOULD BE ABLE TO IDEN-
TIFY ducks and geese at a glance. Having such ability not only
gives tremendous personal satisfaction, but also makes every hunter
a more knowledgeable outdoorsman. And in our waterfowling era,
there is an even more important reason for this knowledge. The sophisticated techniques of "species management" with its "point system" will only work if hunters can readily identify waterfowl. In
addition, with some species of waterfowl being fully protected, it has
become even imperative that wildfowlers be able to identify ducks on
the wing.

The ability to identify wildfowl quickly and correctly is not all that
difficult to achieve. There are a number of good bird identification
guides on the market. The old and reliable *Field Guide to the Birds*
by Roger Tory Peterson is an excellent book and certainly the best
known. The more recent *A Guide to Field Identification: Birds of
North America,* by a trio of ornithologists—Robbins, Bruun, and
Zim—is also very good. For waterfowl identification, it may perhaps
even be superior to the Peterson guide.

In addition, there are a number of identification guides which deal solely with wildfowl. Probably the best known of these is *Ducks at a Distance*, published originally by the United States Bureau of Sport Fisheries and Wildlife, and now by the U. S. Fish and Wildlife Service. In Canada, this pamphlet is available from the Canadian Wildlife Service.

More recently, the Central Flyway Council has published an excellent full-color guide on waterfowl identification. This guide is distributed by state game departments or commissions in the Central Flyway. Another fine waterfowl identification guide in full color is available from Ducks Unlimited (Canada), at 1495 Pembina Highway, Winnipeg, Manitoba, Canada R3T 2E2. Although this pamphlet is free for the asking, $1 to cover postage and handling would, I am certain, most surely be appreciated.

While on the subject of wildfowl identification guides, I must mention Frank Bellrose's *The Ducks, Geese and Swans of North America*. This is a new and expanded version of the classic work by Francis H. Kortright. This book is a must for any serious wildfowler.

However, none of these guides is good by itself. They are all simply tools. They are not substitutes for mud on your boots. Learning to identify ducks means taking to the marshes and coastlines or waterfowl refuges with a bird guide in one hand and a good pair of binoculars hanging around your neck. There is, though, a lazy man's way of learning to identify at least the more common species of ducks, and that's by means of the Super 8 mm film clips developed by the Canadian Wildlife Service. These film clips are available in Super 8 cassettes with continuous loops, or on reels for conventional Super 8 projectors. There is one cassette or reel for each species. They show ducks on the wing, in various views, and even in poor light.

The cassettes sell for $24 each, while the spools are $19 each. There are a number of dealers in both the United States and Canada. The National Film Board of Canada, located at 16th Floor, 1251 Avenue of the Americas, New York, New York 10020, or at P. O. Box 6100, Montreal, Quebec, can provide you with the name and address of the dealer nearest to you.

Again, the film clips were never designed as a substitute for field experience. They were designed to augment it.

Another good aid in teaching wildfowl identification is duck wing collections. But surprisingly few duck clubs ever accumulate wings. Wing collections are a good bet for any sportsmen's club with a division for junior members. A collection of museum-type bird skins is an even better bet. And such skins are not difficult to prepare. Anyone who has the patience to reload shotgun shells or tie trout flies can master the technique of preserving bird skins.

Ornithologists divide all North American ducks into several families. For our purposes, we will by-and-large ignore this classification and use the one that is familiar to most duck hunters. Essentially we have dabbling ducks, whistling ducks, diving ducks, sea ducks, and mergansers.

Dabbling Ducks

Dabbling ducks are sometimes better known as puddle or pond ducks. They are essentially birds of shallow wetlands, marshes, rivers, ponds, and potholes. They feed by "tipping up" to sift through silt and vegetation on the bottom, not by diving or submerging completely under water. They can dive, but usually do so only to escape danger. Dabbling ducks can easily be identified by the small hind toe and the way they spring up from the water during take-off. They are quite at home on land, and any ducks you see feeding in stubble fields will be dabbling species.

MALLARD (*Anas platyrhynchos platyrhynchos*): The mallard is, without a doubt, our most common duck. The drake's reddish-orange bill and green-purple head bordered by a white collar make him unmistakable. The female is mottled brown. Both sexes have metallic blue wing patches bordered with white. The average weight of a mallard is about 2½ pounds.

The mallard is the most abundant and most widely distributed duck in North America. It breeds from western Quebec in the east to the British Columbia coast on the west, and from Alaska south to Utah and Colorado. After courtship, the female builds a nest on the ground near the edges of ponds or sloughs in tall grass or weeds. On rare occasions, however, mallards have been known to nest in trees. The clutch averages 8 to 10 light greenish or greyish eggs. Incubation usually takes about 26 days, with the hen doing all the incubating.

The mallard feeds predominantly on vegetation, with grasses, pondweed, and smartweed being the favorite. The mallard also takes very readily to stubbles and grain fields. A wheat-fed mallard is outstanding on the table. However, along the Pacific coast, mallards have been

TIP UP TO FEED, RARELY DIVE

LEGS PLACED NEAR CENTER OF BODY

GENERALLY HAVE METALLIC SPECULUM

USUALLY SWIM WITH TAIL HELD CLEAR OF WATER

HIND TOE NOT LOBED

FOOT SMALLER THAN IN DIVING DUCKS

SPRING INTO AIR ON TAKE OFF

known to feed on spent salmon, which makes them unfit for the table.

In recent years the mallard population has declined on the prairies because many wetlands have been drained. However, during the past decade, this species has been spreading its range eastward where it has become much more numerous.

BLACK DUCK (*Anas rubripes*): Both sexes of black ducks are mot-

MALLARD
(Anas platyrhynchos)

WHITE TAIL

WHITE BORDERS
ON PURPLE SPECULUM

WHITISH TAIL

GREEN HEAD

YELLOW BILL

WHITE COLLAR

RUDDY BREAST

♂

ORANGE BILL
MOTTLED WITH
BLACK

MOTTLED BROWN

♀

tled brown with lighter brown heads, and have glossy purple wing patches bordered with black. The wing linings are white. The black duck weighs about 2½ pounds.

The black is an eastern duck. Its nesting range is limited from the southeastern corner of Manitoba to Newfoundland, and from Labrador to Delaware. It winters from Massachusetts to Florida and west to Louisiana. After courtship, the female builds a nest on dry ground, favoring wooded areas. She may also nest in fields or along streams,

(Anas rubripes)

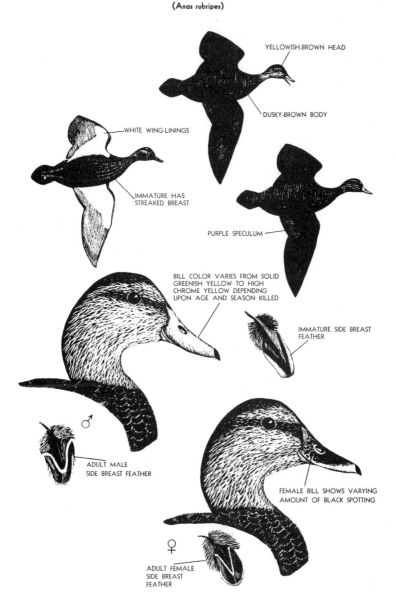

YELLOWISH-BROWN HEAD

DUSKY-BROWN BODY

WHITE WING-LININGS

IMMATURE HAS
STREAKED BREAST

PURPLE SPECULUM

BILL COLOR VARIES FROM SOLID
GREENISH YELLOW TO HIGH
CHROME YELLOW DEPENDING
UPON AGE AND SEASON KILLED

IMMATURE SIDE BREAST
FEATHER

♂

ADULT MALE
SIDE BREAST FEATHER

FEMALE BILL SHOWS VARYING
AMOUNT OF BLACK SPOTTING

♀

ADULT FEMALE
SIDE BREAST
FEATHER

and rarely even in hollow trees. Black ducks can be induced to nest in artificial nesting boxes hung up on trees or posts in proper habitat. The clutch consists of 8 to 10 pale greenish-buff eggs. The eggs of the black duck greatly resemble those of the mallard. Incubation takes 26 to 28 days and is done entirely by the female.

The black duck feeds primarily on vegetation, with grasses, sedges, and smartweed being favored. It will also take readily to feeding in

PINTAIL
(Anas acuta)

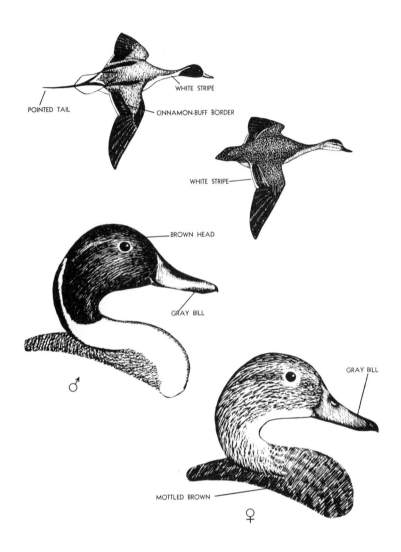

POINTED TAIL
WHITE STRIPE
CINNAMON-BUFF BORDER
WHITE STRIPE
BROWN HEAD
GRAY BILL
♂
GRAY BILL
MOTTLED BROWN
♀

grain fields in farming country. In coastal areas, black ducks like salt marshes, where they tend to eat more animal matter such as shellfish.

In recent years the black duck has been decreasing in numbers. No one has yet determined the reasons for this. It may be because the mallard is moving eastward into black duck territory, and competing with the black. But habitat and environmental contamination with pesticides may also be the culprits.

WHITE BELLY

WHITE BORDER

SILVERY BORDERED

RED IRIS

RED AND WHITE BILL

ADULT MALE HIGHLY COLORED

ECLIPSE AND
IMMATURE MALE

♂

WHITE PATCH

CONSPICUOUS WHITE EYE-RING

CRESTED

♀

PINTAIL (*Anas acuta acuta*): The pintail is hard to mistake. The drake is a striking, long-necked, long-tailed bird. It has a wing patch of metallic bronze-green. The hen has much more subdued coloring, with little or no green. She has no long tail feathers, but her neck is quite long and slim. The wing linings are mottled dark grey-brown. The pintail is a good-sized duck, weighing about 2 pounds.

The pintail has a wide breeding range. Its nesting area runs from the western shoreline of Hudson Bay to the Pacific coast, and from northern Alaska to Utah and Colorado. The bird winters in the southeastern and southwestern United States as well as Mexico. After courtship, during which the drake performs an interesting courtship flight, the female builds a nest on dry land, frequently up to a mile from the nearest water. Open fields or meadows are the preferred nesting habitat. The clutch consists of 7 to 10 pale olive-green to buff eggs. Incubation takes 23 days and is done entirely by the female.

The pintail is a vegetarian. Pondweeds, sedges, and grasses are its favored foods. Like the mallard, once the pintail learns to feed on domestic grain, it prefers this to wild plants.

WOOD DUCK (*Aix sponsa*): The male wood duck is our most spectacularly colored duck. Its head has a striking crest. Rainbow hues of metallic green, blue, and bronze predominate on its head and wings. Its chin and throat are white. The hen is less colorful, a mixture of grey-brown and green. The crest on her head is smaller than that of the drake. The wood duck is not large, weighing about 1½ pounds.

The wood duck's breeding range lies from southcentral Manitoba through New Brunswick, and south to Florida and the Gulf Coast of Texas. Wood ducks also breed in southern British Columbia, including Vancouver Island, and south into California.

After courtship, the female wood duck builds a nest in cavities of trees, as high as 50 feet above the ground. It will readily take to nesting houses put up by sportsmen's clubs and other conservationists. The preferred nesting places are woodlands near ponds, lakes, or streams, but the wood duck will nest some distance from water if there is no other choice. The clutch can vary from 8 to 15 pale buff eggs. Incubation takes 28 to 30 days and is done entirely by the female.

The wood duck is also a vegetarian, feeding on a variety of water plants as well as acorns, beechnuts, and wild seeds. At the turn of the century, the wood duck was close to extinction. Its feathers were once in great demand for the millinery trade. Also, logging at one time removed many old hollow trees, thereby eliminating places where the birds could nest. However, with legislation prohibiting the shooting of wood ducks, the protection of hollow nesting trees, and the erection of artificial nesting boxes, wood duck populations in several areas have become quite high indeed.

THE TEALS (*Anas* spp.): There are three species of teal in North America. All are small, fast flying ducks.

The BLUE-WINGED TEAL *(Anas discors)* is perhaps the best known. The drake is darkly colored with a white crest in front of its eye. It has prominent chalky blue shoulder patches, and a green speculum on the wings. The hen is dark brown in color and has the same chalky blue shoulder patch as the drake.

GREEN-WINGED TEAL
(Anas carolinensis)

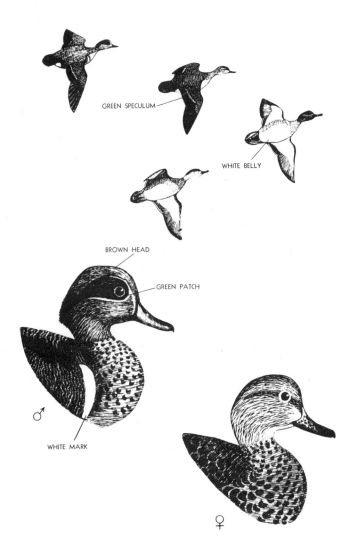

GREEN SPECULUM

WHITE BELLY

BROWN HEAD

GREEN PATCH

♂

WHITE MARK

♀

The GREEN-WINGED TEAL *(Anas crecca carolinensis)* is almost as well known as the bluewing. The drake greenwing is dark brown, with a vertical white bar separating the spotted, buff-colored chest from the grey sides. The hen is mottled brown. As the name suggests, both sexes have considerable green on their wings; the speculum is metallic green.

The CINNAMON TEAL *(Anas cyanoptera septentrionalium)* is the least known of the teals. The drake has a distinctive overall dark cinnamon-red plumage. The female is mottled brown-buff in color.

The hen cinnamon teal is virtually identical to the hen bluewing. Both sexes of cinnamon teal have chalky blue wing patches identical to blue-winged teal. All teals are quite small, weighing about 12 ounces.

The life history of the three teal species is quite similar. After courtship, the hen builds a nest on the ground, well concealed by grass and weeds. The clutch size varies from 8 to 12, and incubation takes approximately 21 to 23 days. The breeding range of these birds is, however, different. The cinnamon teal breeds in the southern, mountainous areas of British Columbia and Alberta, south to central Mexico and from central Colorado to the Pacific coast. The blue-winged teal breeds from eastern New York to British Columbia and Oregon, and from the southern part of the Yukon to central Colorado. The nesting area of the greenwing ranges from western Wisconsin to the Pacific coast in Canada, including parts of Washington, Oregon, and California, and from Alaska and the McKenzie River Delta south to Wyoming.

AMERICAN WIDGEON (*Anas americana*): The American widgeon is sometimes better known as the baldpate. The drake is easy to identify by its white crown, dark mask through the eyes, bold white wing shoulder patches, and metallic green and black speculum. The hen is conspicuously brown, with grey head, greyish white shoulder patches, and a similar speculum to that of the drake, but duller in color. The widgeon weighs about 1¾ pounds.

The widgeon nests on dry land in grassy depressions or beneath small shrubs. The clutch usually consists of 9 to 11 creamy white eggs. Incubation takes 24 to 25 days. The widgeon is primarily a vegetarian, with pondweed and grasses being the favored foods. The main breeding range of the widgeon is in the western part of North America, from western Lake Superior to western Nevada, and from Alaska and the McKenzie River Delta south to central Colorado and northern Kansas. The bird winters along the Pacific and Atlantic coasts of the United States, including the Gulf Coast, and Mexico.

GADWALL (*Anas strepera*): The gadwall drake is greyish in color with a brown head and black chest. The hen is dull brown. Both sexes have a wing patch of white, black, and chestnut, which makes them easy to identify. The average weight of a gadwall is close to 2 pounds.

The gadwall nests on the ground, but very close to water. Its preferred habitat is around prairie marshes and along grassy shores of lakes. The gadwall breeds on the prairies of Manitoba, Saskatchewan, and Alberta, and in the open country of central British Columbia, south to northern California in the west and western Iowa.

SHOVELER (*Anas clypeata*): The shoveler is a colorful duck. The drake has a glossy green head, white chest, and chestnut red sides. The female is plain brown. Both sexes have strikingly blue-colored shoulder patches. But it is the over-sized spoon-shaped bill of the shoveler

BLACK RUMP

WHITE BELLY

WHITE SPECULUM

WHITE BELLY

BILL BLUISH BLACK

♂

BOTH SEXES HAVE YELLOW FEET

BILL DULL ORANGE
VARYING SPOTTING

♀

that makes it unique. The shoveler weighs about 1¼ pounds, and breeds from Lake Superior west to central California, and from the Bering Sea south to central Colorado.

The shoveler's diet contains substantial amounts of animal matter —about 40 percent—so it is not so good a table bird as some of the other puddle ducks. The courtship of shoveler drakes is very elaborate. After mating, the female lays a clutch of 10 to 12 greenish-

SHOVELER
(Spatula clypeata)

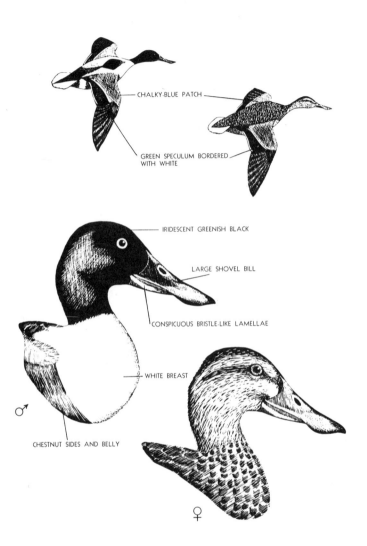

CHALKY-BLUE PATCH

GREEN SPECULUM BORDERED WITH WHITE

IRIDESCENT GREENISH BLACK

LARGE SHOVEL BILL

CONSPICUOUS BRISTLE-LIKE LAMELLAE

WHITE BREAST

♂

CHESTNUT SIDES AND BELLY

♀

grey eggs. Incubation takes 21 to 23 days, and is done solely by the female. The nest is always built in thick cover, generally close to ponds and sloughs, but shoveler nests far from water have been observed.

MOTTLED DUCK (*Anas fulvigula maculosa*): The mottled duck nests along the Gulf Coast from Mississippi to northern Mexico, to about Veracruz. In appearance, the mottled duck is very similar to the black duck or the female mallard. Two identifying features are a

(*Anas fulvigula*)

white border behind the blue speculum on the wing, and a yellow bill, which distinguishes it from the mallard. Both sexes of the mottled duck are similar in appearance.

FLORIDA DUCK (*Anas fulvigula fulvigula*): The Florida duck lives year 'round in the southern two-thirds of the Florida peninsula. In color, this subspecies is darker than a hen mallard and lighter than a black duck. In appearance, it is very similar to the mottled duck.

In fact, the mottled and Florida ducks are simply different races or subspecies of the same species.

The sexes of the Florida duck are easy to distinguish. The drake has a bright yellow bill with a black spot at the base, while the hen's bill is orange with black spots across the saddle.

MEXICAN DUCK (*Anas platyrhynchos diazi*): The Mexican duck is known to relatively few waterfowlers. This is not surprising, because the bird is found only in the Rio Grande River Valley west to El Paso and north to Albuquerque, New Mexico. Both sexes of the Mexican duck are difficult to distinguish from the female mallard. The male Mexican duck has an olive-green bill, while the female's bill has a black saddle shading to olive-green.

In recent years, the Mexican duck has been given considerable protection. In New Mexico it has been fully protected.

Whistling Ducks

Two species of whistling ducks, the black-bellied and the Fulvous, are found in the United States. These birds are sometimes known as tree ducks. This, however, is something of a misnomer, as neither species nests in trees very often. They are both characterized by long necks and long legs, giving them a somewhat unducklike appearance.

The BLACK-BELLIED WHISTLING DUCK (*Dendrocygna autumnalis autumnalis*) has a striking black breast and belly. The undersides of the wings are also dark. The outsides of the wings have large white areas which are very conspicuous in flight. The legs and feet are pink. Both sexes look alike. The black-bellied tree duck weighs about 1½ pounds.

The FULVOUS WHISTLING DUCK (*Dendrocygna bicolor helva*) has a belly, breast, and head of deep tawny yellow. The back and wings are dark, with both sexes looking alike. The Fulvous tree duck is about the same size as the black-bellied tree duck.

The black-bellied tree duck nests and winters from the southern tip of Texas through most of Mexico to Panama. It is a bird of wooded ponds and small marshes. It feeds on a variety of vegetable matter, including grains, but also grazes on grass like geese. Its nest is usually built well concealed in a clump of reeds, but sometimes in the hollows of trees.

The Fulvous tree duck nests and winters from the Gulf Coast of Texas and southern California down to central Mexico. It normally nests on the ground in weeds or grass near water. The bird feeds almost entirely on vegetative matter, including grains and grasses. It is highly regarded as a table bird.

Diving Ducks

Sometimes called bay ducks, the diving ducks are waterfowl of big waters. They feed by diving down below the surface. Diving ducks can always be identified by the relatively large-lobed hind toe. When taking off, diving ducks head into the wind and patter over the water surface until they are airborne. Their relatively small wings do not allow them to spring up from water in the same manner as the dabbling ducks. The diving ducks sometimes dive to great depths to feed, and are capable of swimming long distances under water.

CANVASBACK (*Aythya valisineria*): The drake canvasback is characterized by a dark chestnut-red head, a black chest, and a white body. The hen is brownish in color with a grey back. Both sexes have brown wings with grey patches. Another identifying feature of this duck is a wedge-shaped bill and a sloping forehead. The mature canvasback weighs about 2¾ pounds.

After a vigorous and spectacular courtship, the hen builds a nest woven of marsh plants, generally in reedbeds over water. But the nest is sometimes built on dry land. The hen lays a clutch of about 10 olive or greenish drab eggs. Incubation takes approximately 24 days and is done entirely by the hen.

The preferred habitat of the canvasback is the deeper water of marshes and deeper lakes with vegetated shorelines. During migration this duck will visit bays of salt and brackish water. The canvasback breeds from the southern McKenzie River Delta south to the Canada-United States border, and south to northern Utah in the west and central Nebraska in the midwest. Its breeding range runs from western Minnesota to eastern Washington, with a small patch of breeding territory in Alaska and the Yukon. The canvasback is primarily a vegetarian and will dive to depths of 20 or even 30 feet for its favorite foods. Pondweed and wild celery are highly favored, and because of this diet the "can" is an outstanding table bird.

(Aythyinae)

DIVE COMPLETELY UNDER WATER TO
SECURE FEED

LEGS SET NEAR REAR OF
BODY

SPECULUM GENERALLY DULL, LACKS
IRIDESCENCE

USUALLY SWIM WITH TAIL HELD CLOSE
TO WATER

HIND TOE LOBED, FOOT LARGE

ON TAKE OFF PATTER ALONG SURFACE FOR SOME DISTANCE

REDHEAD (*Aythya americana*): The drake redhead has a distinctive chestnut red head, a black chest, white breast, and dark grey body. The hen has a brownish body with a white breast. The wings of both sexes are grey-brown with grey wing patches. The redhead is also characterized by a pronounced forehead. A mature redhead runs about 2¼ pounds.

After courtship, a nest is built in reedbeds over shallow water and

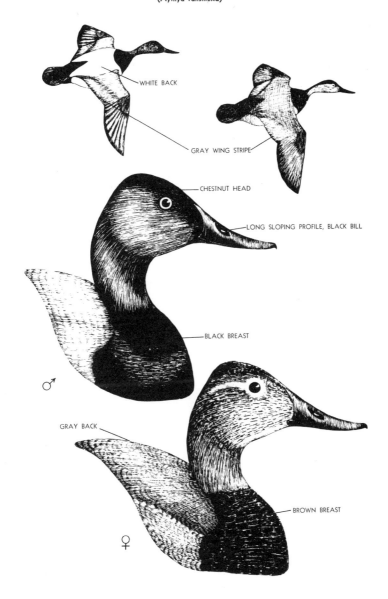

occasionally on dry land near water. A clutch of 10 to 16 pale olive buff or creamy buff eggs is laid by the hen, who is entirely responsible for the incubation of 22 to 24 days. The redhead is also known to lay eggs in the nests of other ducks.

The preferred habitat of the redhead is large lakes with shallow bays. On migration, however, the redhead, like the canvasback, will visit brackish water. The breeding range of the redhead extends from

REDHEAD
(Aythya americana)

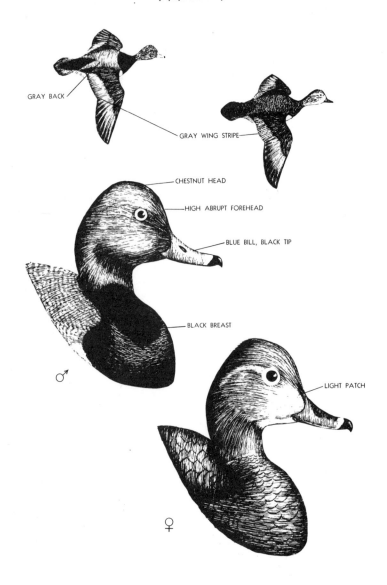

GRAY BACK

GRAY WING STRIPE

CHESTNUT HEAD

HIGH ABRUPT FOREHEAD

BLUE BILL, BLACK TIP

BLACK BREAST

LIGHT PATCH

♂

♀

northern Alberta and Saskatchewan to central Washington and Montana in the west, and southern Nebraska in the midwest. The bird breeds from eastern Minnesota to eastern British Columbia, with small patches of breeding territory in Utah-Idaho and Oregon-California-Nevada. The redhead is primarily a vegetarian, with pondweeds, muskgrass, and sedges being high in dietary preference. The redhead is as good on the table as the canvasback.

BLACK BACK

GRAY WING STRIPE

DISTINCT CREST

CONSPICUOUS BILL RING

CHESTNUT COLLAR

BLACK BREAST

WHITE EYE RING

LIGHT PATCH

♂

WHITE PATCH

♀

RING-NECKED DUCK (*Aythya collaris*): The drake ringneck is characterized by a black head glossed with purple, a black chest, and a black back glossed with green. A ring or collar of chestnut, as both the common and specific names indicate, exists around the neck. However, it can only be seen at close range. The blue bill of this duck has a distinct white band near the tip, so the duck is called ringbill on occasion. The hen is sooty brown in color with a white

GREATER SCAUP

(Aythya marila)

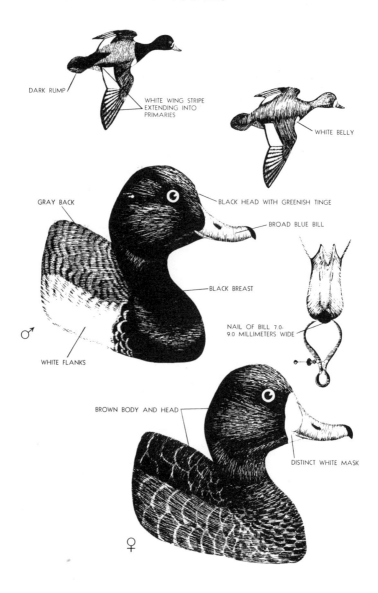

DARK RUMP

WHITE WING STRIPE
EXTENDING INTO
PRIMARIES

WHITE BELLY

GRAY BACK

BLACK HEAD WITH GREENISH TINGE

BROAD BLUE BILL

♂

BLACK BREAST

NAIL OF BILL 7.0-
9.0 MILLIMETERS WIDE

WHITE FLANKS

BROWN BODY AND HEAD

DISTINCT WHITE MASK

♀

ring near the tip of a slate-grey bill. Both sexes have grey wing patches and weigh about 1½ pounds.

The ringneck breeds from south of the Great Slave Lake to central Alberta and Saskatchewan in the west, and the western Great Lakes in the east. It also nests in New Brunswick and Maine. The diet of the ring-necked duck is about 80 percent vegetable matter, making it a reasonably good table bird.

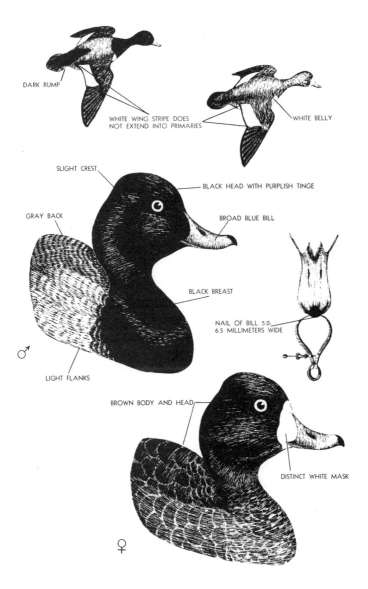

DARK RUMP

WHITE WING STRIPE DOES
NOT EXTEND INTO PRIMARIES

WHITE BELLY

SLIGHT CREST

BLACK HEAD WITH PURPLISH TINGE

GRAY BACK

BROAD BLUE BILL

BLACK BREAST

NAIL OF BILL 5.0-
6.5 MILLIMETERS WIDE

♂

LIGHT FLANKS

BROWN BODY AND HEAD

DISTINCT WHITE MASK

♀

GREATER SCAUP (*Aythya marila mariloides*): The greater scaup is characterized by a dark blue bill. The drake has a black head and chest. The back is pale grey and the sides are finely barred with black. The hen is brown, shading to light brown on the flanks and white on the breast. The hen has a prominent white patch at the base of the beak. Both sexes possess distinct white wing patches and generally run about 2 pounds.

COMMON GOLDENEYE
(Bucephala clangula)

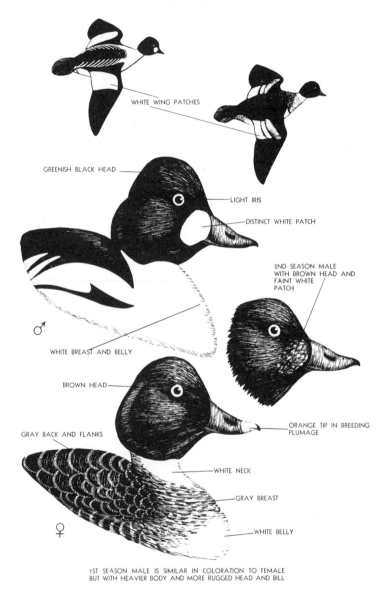

WHITE WING PATCHES

GREENISH BLACK HEAD

LIGHT IRIS

DISTINCT WHITE PATCH

2ND SEASON MALE
WITH BROWN HEAD AND
FAINT WHITE
PATCH

♂

WHITE BREAST AND BELLY

BROWN HEAD

ORANGE TIP IN BREEDING
PLUMAGE

GRAY BACK AND FLANKS

WHITE NECK

GRAY BREAST

♀

WHITE BELLY

1ST SEASON MALE IS SIMILAR IN COLORATION TO FEMALE
BUT WITH HEAVIER BODY AND MORE RUGGED HEAD AND BILL

The greater scaup nests from northern Saskatchewan right through the McKenzie River Delta to the Bering Sea. Its diet is generally about 50 percent vegetable matter.

LESSER SCAUP (*Aythya affinis*): The lesser scaup is slightly smaller than the greater scaup. However, this is hard to see unless both species are in hand. The drake lesser scaup has a purplish sheen which the greater scaup lacks. The white wing patches on both sexes of the lesser scaup are smaller than those of the greater scaup. The lesser scaup weighs about 1¾ pounds, only ¼ pound less than the greater scaup.

The lesser scaup breeds from western Ontario to central British Columbia and from the McKenzie River Delta to southern Nebraska. About 60 percent of its diet is vegetable matter.

THE GOLDENEYES (*Bucephala* spp.): Both species of goldeneyes —the common and the Barrow's—are sometimes called whistlers.

The DRAKE COMMON GOLDENEYE (*Bucephala clangula americana*), sometimes known as the American goldeneye, is a black and white bird with a black head glossed with green. It has a prominent white spot between the eye and the beak. The black wings have large white patches. The hen is an ash grey, with white body and brown head. The grey wings have small white patches.

The BARROW'S GOLDENEYE (*Bucephala islandica*) is quite similar. The black head of the drake has a purple sheen and a white crescent between the eye and the bill. This white crescent is a good identifying mark. The Barrow's goldeneye hen is difficult to distinguish from the common goldeneye hen. Both species weigh about 1¾ pounds.

Both goldeneyes have similar life histories, preferring to nest in tree cavities near water. Both, however, will nest along rocky ledges. The common goldeneye is known to readily nest in artificial nesting boxes. Clutches generally numbering 9 or 10 eggs take about 30 days to incubate. Preferred goldeneye habitat is small lakes and ponds in spring and summer, but in winter the birds prefer large bodies of open water, including rivers and the sea coast.

The breeding range of the common goldeneye is a wide strip running from the Bering Sea on the coast of Alaska southeast through the Canadian prairies and the northern Great Lakes area to the Canadian maritime provinces. The Barrow's goldeneye breeds from the southern Yukon south to central California in the west and central Colorado. Minor breeding populations of Barrow's goldeneyes are also found along the coast of Labrador, the southern coast of Greenland, and in Iceland.

Both species of goldeneyes feed primarily on animal matter such as shellfish, crawfish, fish, and insects. Thus they are not the best of table ducks. But when cooked in a flavorful sauce, they can be quite edible.

BUFFLEHEAD (*Bucephala albeola*): The bufflehead is the smallest of our diving ducks. The drake is unmistakably characterized by a large "buffled" head, comprising a white patch extending from the eye to the back of the head. The body is white with the center of the back black. The black wings have an extensive white patch on their inner half. The female bufflehead has a sooty brown body and head,

BUFFLEHEAD

(Bucephala albeola)

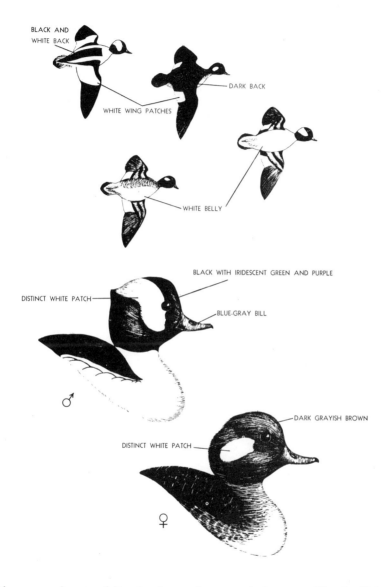

with a prominent white cheek patch around the eye. The bufflehead runs the size of a teal, about 12 ounces.

The bufflehead nests above ground in tree cavities or old stumps. It prefers open wooded habitat near marshes, ponds, or lakes. A clutch of 7 to 10 creamy white eggs is incubated by the female for 29 to 31 days.

The bufflehead breeds over a fairly wide range from western Alaska

RUDDY DUCK
(Oxyura jamaicensis)

DARK BROWN

BELLY SILVERY WHITE

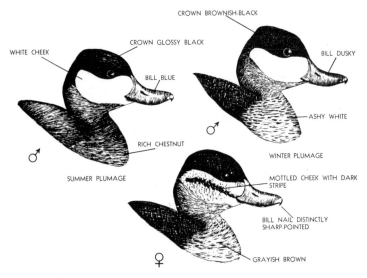

CROWN BROWNISH-BLACK

CROWN GLOSSY BLACK

WHITE CHEEK

BILL DUSKY

BILL BLUE

ASHY WHITE

RICH CHESTNUT

WINTER PLUMAGE

♂

SUMMER PLUMAGE

MOTTLED CHEEK WITH DARK STRIPE

BILL NAIL DISTINCTLY SHARP-POINTED

♀

GRAYISH BROWN

south to northern California, through the Canadian prairies to the northern Great Lakes area.

The bufflehead feeds primarily on animal matter such as shellfish, insects, and fish. It thus rates about the same as a goldeneye as a table duck.

RUDDY DUCK (*Oxyura jamaicensis rubida*): The drake ruddy duck is a rich chestnut red in color. His head has a black cap, white cheeks, and a bright blue bill. This small and attractive duck weighs only an ounce or two over a pound. The hen is mottled dark brown, with a brown cap and dullish white cheeks divided by a brown bar on her head, and a grey bill.

The ruddy duck breeds from central Alberta and Saskatchewan south to Utah in the west and Kansas in the midwest, with a minor breeding population in northern California and Nevada. The nest of the ruddy duck is constructed over water, from woven marsh grass, and is anchored to surrounding vegetation. The drake as well as the duck care for the clutch of 6 to 10 eggs, which the hen incubates for about 27 days. The ruddy duck is principally a vegetarian, and its colloquial name "butterball" suggests how highly it is regarded as a table duck.

Sea Ducks

Most hunters view the sea ducks as marine wildfowl, but biologically this is not true. Many of the so-called sea ducks nest inland, far from salt water. Some, the white-winged scoter being a good example, even winter on the Great Lakes.

But the preferred wintering habitat of sea ducks is coastal bays along both the Atlantic and Pacific coasts. It is largely because these birds are hunted on salt water that they are called sea ducks.

THE SCOTERS (*Melanitta* spp.): There are 3 species of scoters— the white-winged scoter, the surf scoter, and the black scoter.

The WHITE-WINGED SCOTER drake (*Melanitta fusca deglandi*) is black with prominent white wing patches and white crescent-shaped markings around the eyes. The hen is a dark sooty brown with white wing patches. The whitewing is the biggest of the scoters, weighing about 2¾ pounds.

The SURF SCOTER (*Melanitta perspicillata*) is also black with prominent white patches on the forehead. The hen is sooty brown with white spots at the base of the bill and sides of the head.

The BLACK SCOTER (*Melanitta nigra americana*), sometimes known as the American or common scoter, is the only duck in America with true black plumage. The drake is solid black with an orange swelling at the base of the bill. The hen is sooty brown with a

WHITE-WINGED SCOTER
(Melanitta deglandi)

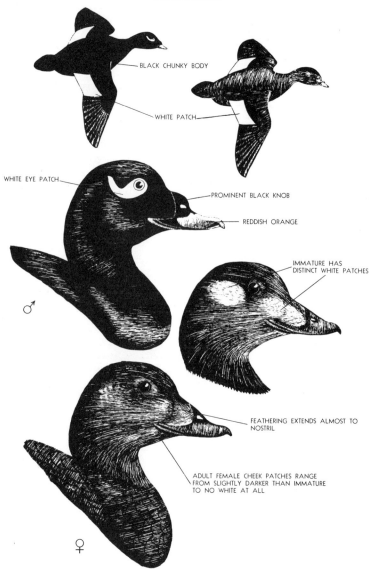

BLACK CHUNKY BODY

WHITE PATCH

WHITE EYE PATCH

PROMINENT BLACK KNOB

REDDISH ORANGE

IMMATURE HAS DISTINCT WHITE PATCHES

♂

FEATHERING EXTENDS ALMOST TO NOSTRIL

ADULT FEMALE CHEEK PATCHES RANGE FROM SLIGHTLY DARKER THAN IMMATURE TO NO WHITE AT ALL

♀

black crown and a light grey face and throat. The black scoter, as well as the surf scoter, runs about 2 pounds.

The life history of the three species of scoters is essentially the same. These birds nest on land on saltwater coasts or on lakeshores and riverbanks. The white-winged and black scoters lay from 6 to 12 eggs, while the surf scoter lays only 5 to 7 eggs. The white-winged scoter has the largest breeding range, extending from the McKenzie

(Oidemia nigra)

DARK WINGS AND BODY

ORANGE-YELLOW PROTUBERANCE

♂

IMMATURE BILL NOT
SWOLLEN AS IN ADULT

DARK BROWN CAP

LIGHT BROWN CHEEKS

♀

River Delta to northern Manitoba and North Dakota, and from Lake
Winnipeg west to western Alberta. The surf scoter breeds in the
western Northwest Territories, the northern Yukon, and parts of
Alaska. The black scoter breeds on the saltwater marshes of the
Bering and Beaufort Seas. All of these birds winter on the Pacific
and Atlantic coasts of the United States. The scoters feed primarily
on shellfish and other aquatic creatures, and are not highly regarded
as table birds. However, they are quite edible.

THE EIDERS. There are four species of eiders common to North America—the common eider, the king eider, the spectacled eider, and the Steller's eider.

The drake COMMON EIDER (*Somateria mollissima*), sometimes called the American eider, is a striking black and white duck. The black head has a greenish gloss, with a slight dip to the bill. The hen is dark brown with black bars.

The KING EIDER (*Somateria spectabilis*) is also a striking duck. The drake is white on the foreparts and black on the rear parts. The top of the head and neck are bluish grey. The hen is brown and very much resembles the common eider hen, but is somewhat brighter in color.

The drake SPECTACLED EIDER (*Somateria fischeri*) has a faded green head with large white "spectacles" around the eyes. This black-breasted bird is extremely attractive. The female is similar in appearance to the common eider, but also has the spectacles, although they are somewhat faded in color. The bills of both sexes are feathered over the nostril.

The drake STELLER'S EIDER (*Polysticta stelleri*), in its breeding plumage, is a handsome bird with unusual markings. He has a white head with a black throat. Black coloring separates the neck from the body. This black coloring overflows to the back as a black stripe. The sides, including the wings, have a fair amount of white. The female is predominantly brown. Her wing is similar to that of the mallard. Both sexes have small crests on the back of the head. The Steller's eider is the smallest of the eiders, weighing about 2 pounds. The other eiders range from 3½ to 4 pounds.

All of the eiders are sea ducks, but their life histories are somewhat different. The common eider is frequently a colonial nester, preferring low-lying rocky saltwater coasts or islands. The clutch of 4 to 6 olive-buff eggs is incubated for 28 to 29 days, solely by the hen. The common eider's breeding range extends from northern Connecticut through the Canadian maritime provinces to the coast of Labrador, as well as along the eastern and western coasts of Hudson Bay and through many of the Arctic islands.

The king eider is a solitary nester, preferring to nest on fresh water on the tundra. The clutch of 4 to 7 olive-buff eggs is incubated for 22 to 23 days solely by the female. The breeding area of the king eider stretches from the western coast of Alaska right across the top of Canada through all the Arctic islands to Greenland.

The spectacled eider breeds along the northern coast of Alaska. This eider is not abundant on the North American continent; however, it is a common sea duck along the coast of Siberia.

The Steller's eider builds its nest in a ground hollow near water, and unlike the other eiders, the male helps to rear the young. This sea duck has much the same breeding range as the spectacled eider, and again, is more common in Siberia than in North America.

All of the eiders feed principally on animal matter such as shell-fish and other marine creatures which the birds obtain by diving in deep water—down to 180 feet in the case of the king eider.

HARLEQUIN DUCK (*Histrionicus histrionicus*): The drake harlequin duck is a striking slate-colored bird with chestnut sides and an intricate pattern of white spots and stripes edged in black on the head, neck, and chest. The wings are dark slate with a tinge of blue. The female is sooty brown with white spots in front of the eyes and white cheeks. The harlequin duck runs about 1¼ pounds.

The harlequin has two breeding populations, one eastern and one western. The eastern population breeds along the shore of Labrador and northern Quebec, on eastern Baffin Island, and on the coasts of Greenland and Iceland. The western population breeds along the southern shore of Alaska, south to central Oregon and west to Montana and Wyoming.

The nest is always constructed near fast-moving streams and rivers. A clutch of 6 or 7 cream-colored eggs is incubated for 30 to 32 days by the female. When the ducklings are nearly mature, the harlequin moves to a rocky and rugged coastline where the water is always turbulent. This duck feeds primarily on shellfish and fish.

OLDSQUAW (*Clangula hyemalis*): The drake oldsquaw has two distinct color phases. In winter, the bird has a white head and neck with a dark cheek patch circling the eye. It also has two white stripes on its back near the wings. In summer, the white on the head, neck, and back turns dark brown, while the dark cheek patch around the eye becomes whitish. The drake always has long striking tail feathers similar to the pintail. The hen lacks these long tail feathers and is generally mottled brown with considerable white on her cheeks and chin. The oldsquaw generally weighs about 1½ pounds.

The oldsquaw is a maritime duck, breeding mainly on the Arctic coast from the eastern tip of Labrador to the western tip of Alaska, including the Arctic islands. The bird winters on the coast of British Columbia, the Atlantic coast of New England, and in the Great Lakes area.

The oldsquaw builds its nest on the ground in short vegetation or among rocks near ponds and lakes. Incubation lasts about 24 days for a clutch of 6 to 8 olive to yellowish eggs. This ducks feeds mainly on fish and shellfish which it catches by diving to great depths.

Mergansers

The mergansers are primarily fish-eating ducks. They can readily be identified by their long, saw-like bills. Indeed, they are sometimes called sawbills. Three species of mergansers breed in North America —the common, the red-breasted, and the hooded.

The COMMON MERGANSER (*Mergus merganser americanus*), sometimes referred to as the American merganser, is the biggest of the mergansers, weighing almost 2½ pounds. The drake has a dark back with light underside and a glossy, green-black head. The bird also has a white neck band. The feet and bill are red. The hen has a chestnut head, a grey back, and a white breast.

The RED-BREASTED MERGANSER drake (*Mergus serrator*) is similar in appearance to the common merganser, but has a striking crest on its head. Its breast is pinkish with black spots. The hen is also similar to the common merganser hen, but like the drake, she does have a crest on her head. The red-breasted merganser weighs about 1¾ pounds.

The HOODED MERGANSER (*Mergus cucullatus*) is the most handsome of the three. The drake's most striking feature is a fan-shaped crest on a black head. The female is a greyish brown duck with a white breast, and also has a crest on her head, but much smaller than that of the male. The hooded merganser is the smallest of the three, averaging about 1¼ pounds.

The diet of the three merganser species is alike. They are primarily fish eaters, but the hooded merganser eats fewer fish than the other two species.

The common merganser nests in tree cavities as well as holes in banks and rock piles. It is mainly a freshwater duck, preferring ponds and lakes near woodlands. A clutch of 8 to 12 creamy white eggs requires 28 to 32 days to incubate. The breeding range of the

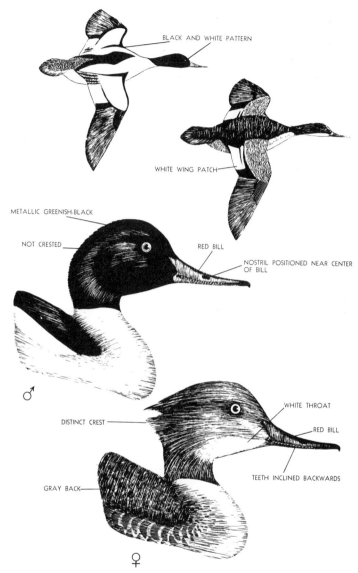

common merganser extends in a wide band across the Canadian prairies from coast to coast. The common merganser will inhabit salt and brackish water bogs in winter, but not to the same extent as the red-breasted merganser.

The red-breasted merganser is the most marine of the three species. It prefers salt water in winter, and will nest near saltwater bays. The nest is always on the ground, hidden under bushes, stumps, and logs.

RED-BREASTED MERGANSER

(Mergus serrator)

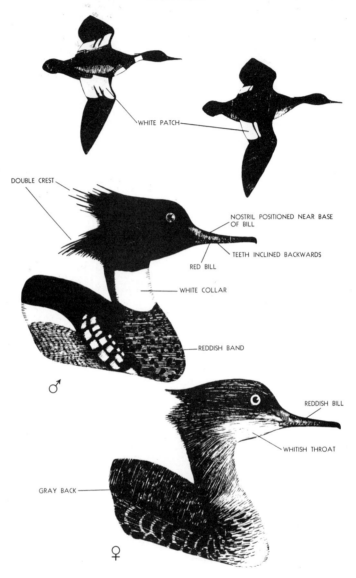

WHITE PATCH

DOUBLE CREST

NOSTRIL POSITIONED NEAR BASE OF BILL

TEETH INCLINED BACKWARDS

RED BILL

WHITE COLLAR

REDDISH BAND

♂

REDDISH BILL

WHITISH THROAT

GRAY BACK

♀

The clutch consists of 7 to 12 greenish eggs, requiring 26 to 30 days to incubate. The red-breasted merganser breeds in all of the Canadian provinces, from the eastern coast of Newfoundland through the Canadian prairies and the Northwest Territories to the western coast of Alaska.

The hooded merganser nests in tree crevices. It is primarily a freshwater duck, preferring wooded streams, ponds, and lakes. An

(Lophodytes cucullatus)

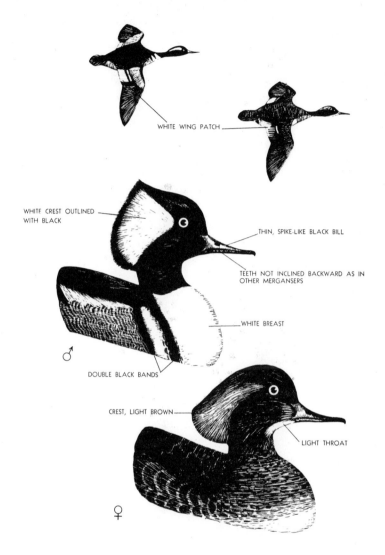

WHITE WING PATCH

WHITE CREST OUTLINED WITH BLACK

THIN, SPIKE-LIKE BLACK BILL

TEETH NOT INCLINED BACKWARD AS IN OTHER MERGANSERS

WHITE BREAST

♂

DOUBLE BLACK BANDS

CREST, LIGHT BROWN

LIGHT THROAT

♀

IN FLIGHT ALL MERGANSERS CARRY BILL, NECK AND BODY IN HORIZONTAL PLANE, GIVING THEM A CHARACTERISTIC LONG-DRAWN APPEARANCE.

incubation period of 31 days is required for a clutch of 5 to 12 eggs. The hooded merganser breeds from central British Columbia south to northern Oregon and southeast in a wide band to the Atlantic coast.

Because of their diet, none of the mergansers is particularly good as a table bird. In fact, mergansers are rarely eaten. However, if skinned out and spiced, they are palatable, particularly the hooded merganser.

CANADA GOOSE
(Branta canadensis)

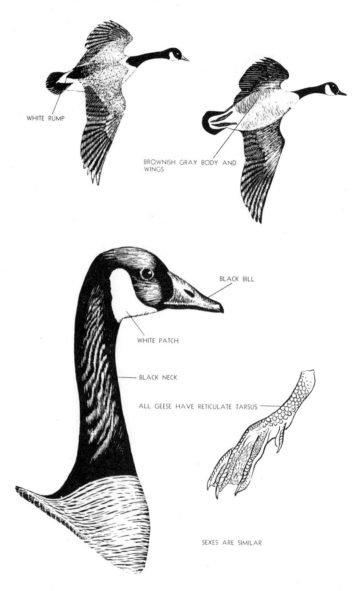

WHITE RUMP

BROWNISH GRAY BODY AND WINGS

BLACK BILL

WHITE PATCH

BLACK NECK

ALL GEESE HAVE RETICULATE TARSUS

SEXES ARE SIMILAR

Geese

Geese, regardless of the species, are the "big game" among the waterfowl. The fortunate thing about wild geese is that the populations of most species have been on the increase in recent years.

CANADA GOOSE (*Branta canadensis*): The Canada goose is so well known that it hardly needs to be described. It is a large brownish-grey bird with a long neck. The head and neck are skinny, black in color, and interrupted by an oval patch of white on the upper sides of the head and cheek under the throat. The breast is pale ash-grey. The sexes cannot be differentiated by their coloring.

The Canada goose has several subspecies or races, all of which look essentially alike except for minor variations in color. The major difference in the subspecies is in size. The largest race of Canada goose is the giant Canada, weighing up to 14 or 15 pounds. The smallest, the cackling Canada, is not much larger than a mallard.

The Canada goose, sometimes colloquially known as the "honker", flies in the familiar "V" formation on long flights. But short local flights are not usually flown in formation.

The goose, after courtship, builds a nest on land near water. The preferred sites for these large nests are tiny islets, and beaver and muskrat houses. The bird has also been known to nest in trees, particularly in old hawk nests. Canadas will also readily nest in artificial structures put up for them.

A clutch of 4 to 7 white eggs is normal, with the clutches of the northern races being slightly larger. Incubation takes from 24 to 25 days in the case of the smaller northern races, and from 28 to 33 days for the larger southern races. Incubation is done solely by the goose, while the gander stands guard, ready to fight any intruder. The gander also guards the growing goslings.

The breeding range of Canada geese extends from Newfoundland through Labrador and around the coast of Hudson Bay into southern Ontario, where breeding flocks have been established. The birds also breed from north of the Great Slave Lake south to southern Utah and Colorado, and from western Wisconsin to Vancouver Island.

The Canada goose is strictly a vegetarian, preferring to graze on grass, but also readily feeding on grain stubble.

SNOW GOOSE (*Anser caerulescens*): The snow goose is a fairly large white bird with black wing tips. The head, neck, and undersides can be a little rust colored, while the legs and feet are pink. Immature snow geese have a greyish colored head and neck, with grey wings. Both sexes look alike.

The snow goose also has a blue phase which is sometimes called the blue goose. At one time ornithologists considered the blue goose to be a separate species. Today most consider it simply a different

SNOW GOOSE
(Chen hyperborea)

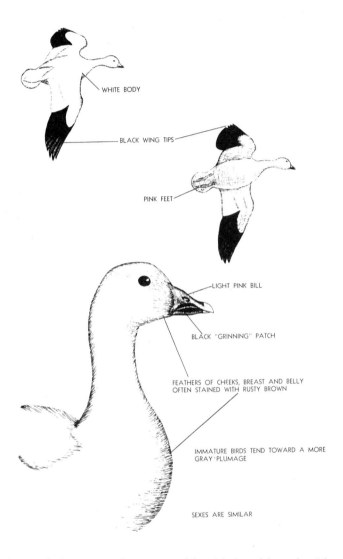

WHITE BODY

BLACK WING TIPS

PINK FEET

LIGHT PINK BILL

BLACK "GRINNING" PATCH

FEATHERS OF CHEEKS, BREAST AND BELLY
OFTEN STAINED WITH RUSTY BROWN

IMMATURE BIRDS TEND TOWARD A MORE
GRAY PLUMAGE

SEXES ARE SIMILAR

color phase of the snow. In many older bird guides, the blue goose is still listed as a separate species. The blue phase has a bluish colored body with bluish grey wings. The neck and head are white. The bill has a black "grinning patch" between the mandibles. There are two races of snow geese—the lesser snow goose weighing less than 5 pounds, and the greater snow goose weighing a pound or 2 more. Aside from size, these birds are essentially the same in appearance and have the same identifying marks. The blue color phase occurs only among lesser snows.

The snow goose, after courtship, builds a nest of moss and other tundra vegetation. The clutch consists of 3 to 5 eggs, incubated for 22 to 23 days solely by the goose. The gander, as in the case of the Canada goose, stands guard and later guards the goslings. Snow geese generally nest in colonies.

The preferred habitat for snow geese is low flat lands with ponds and shallow lakes. The lesser snow goose breeds along the Arctic coast of Alaska and the Northwest Territories to Hudson Bay, and on Baffin Island. The greater snow goose breeds from northern Baffin Island to western Greenland. The snow goose avoids forested lands, even during migration. For resting during migration, it prefers to stop on fresh or saltwater marshes and open fields. The snow goose is strictly a vegetarian, but is not as highly regarded as the Canada on the table.

WHITE-FRONTED GOOSE (*Anser albifrons frontalis*): The white-fronted goose, sometimes known as the specklebelly, is not a widely known goose. Its head, neck, back, and rump are greyish brown. The forehead is white. The tail is dark brown edged in white. The breast and belly are greyish and heavily blotched with dark brown, hence the name specklebelly. The legs and feet of the whitefront are orange. Both sexes are similar in appearance, with an average weight of a little less than 5 pounds.

After mating, the goose builds a nest of moss and grass on the ground. A clutch of 4 to 6 creamy white eggs is incubated by the goose for 27 to 28 days, while the gander stands guard. Nesting is done on the Arctic tundra on the shores of lakes or on islands and deltas of streams and rivers. This bird is also known to avoid forest land during migration, preferring to rest on marshes, in open fields, and on lakes. The whitefront breeds in northern Alaska and along the Arctic coast of the Yukon and the Northwest Territories to Victoria Island, as well as on Greenland along the Davis Strait. Again, the whitefront is strictly a vegetarian and has a reputation as a fine table bird.

ROSS'S GOOSE (*Anser rossii*): The Ross's goose is similar in appearance to the snow goose, only a bit smaller. It runs, on the average, about 3¾ pounds. Both sexes look alike, being white birds with black wing tips. The bill is pinkish, and in adult birds has wart-like protuberances between the nostril and the base. The bill of the Ross's goose is also shorter than that of the blue goose, and lacks the grinning patch.

Until recently, the Ross's goose was quite rare and in danger of extinction. It was given full protection to which it has responded very well. The bird is still protected. The Ross's goose breeds on the tundra and low islands of freshwater lakes. The nest is always built on the ground. After courtship, the goose lays a clutch of 4 or 5 dull white eggs, requiring 21 to 22 days incubation.

Until 1938, the breeding ground of the Ross's goose was unknown. It was discovered by Angus Gavin to be on the Perry River in the Northwest Territories. The bird winters in the Sacramento and San Joachin Valleys of California. Recent population surveys indicate that there are at least 35,000 Ross's geese, and very probably more.

EMPEROR GOOSE (*Anser canagicus*): The emperor goose is regarded by many to be our most beautiful goose. The predominant body color is bluish grey. The head and the back of the neck are white, but the throat is a deep brown. The feathers on the back, flanks, and breast have black, crescent-shaped markings and are tipped with white. The feet are orange-yellow, while the bill may vary from pale purple to flesh colored. Both sexes look alike.

The emperor goose breeds along the coastline of Alaska's Bering Sea and winters in the Alaska Peninsula.

The birds pair up on returning to their nesting grounds. The gander is a zealous mate and guards the female against all comers, even birds of other species. The clutch of 5 or 6 eggs is laid in early June and incubation takes 24 days. The gander does not guard the goose and nest as with most of the other geese; however, he does assume some responsibility in the rearing of the young.

Nesting is rarely done more than 10 miles from the coast. The emperor goose does not seem to have a favorite nesting site. Anything from a marshy island to a grassy hummock is fine. The nest is merely a down-filled depression in the earth.

The emperor goose is a wary bird. A feeding flock always seems to post at least two guards. The Arctic fox is an abundant predator in the emperor's breeding range. The emperor feeds on everything from eelgrass to cranberries, shellfish, and other small marine creatures. In summer and early fall, vegetation forms the bulk of the diet; while the animal diet is much more important in winter. The flesh of the emperor is affected by its diet. In summer and fall, the birds are reputed to have better flavor.

BRANT (*Branta bernicla*): The brant is a small, dark sea goose with a white head, neck, and chest. The back and upper sides of the wings are brown, while the wing tips are blackish. The rump and tails are black. The belly and sides are brownish grey. There is a narrow white crescent on either side of the neck just below the head. The sexes are similar in appearance, and the birds run about 2½ to 3 pounds.

Brant nest either singly or in colonies, and always on the ground. The nest, well lined with down, houses 3 to 5 creamy white eggs. The goose incubates the eggs for 23 to 24 days while the gander stands guard.

Brant nest on the Arctic coastal islands, deltas, wide river valleys, and well vegetated uplands along the coast from the eastern shore of Hudson Bay and Baffin Island west to the Bering Strait. The wintering habitats are saltwater bays and tidal flats where eelgrass grows, from Chesapeake Bay to the Carolinas on the Atlantic coast, and from southern British Columbia to Baja California. Concentrations of wintering birds tend to be greater at the more southerly latitudes. The Brant will also stop over in inland lakes and rivers and even fields during migration. Eelgrass and sea lettuce are the main foods of the brant. When brant feed on eelgrass, they are excellent to eat. Those that have been feeding on sea lettuce are not anywhere near as palatable.

Incidentally, in some bird guides the Pacific coast brant is called the black brant (*Branta bernicla nigricans*) because it is somewhat darker, particularly the immature birds. Waterfowl biologists generally consider the west and east coast brants to be separate races, but not separate species.

Swans

At one time the swans (family *Cygninae*) were hunted with the rest of the waterfowl, but never to the same extent as the geese and ducks. They were never particularly numerous birds, and are very shy and difficult to hunt. I have written about the swans so that no hunter would mistake one for a snow goose. Swans are almost totally protected.

Adult swans are entirely white, while immature swans are greyish on top and white on the underparts. Swans fly in stringy lines of a loose V-shaped flock. Their extremely long necks and the lack of black on the wing tips are key identifying features of swans in flight. Keeping these two features in mind, there is absolutely no way the swans can be mistaken for any other waterfowl species.

There are three species of swans in North America. The MUTE SWAN (*Cygnus olor*) is a European species, introduced to the parks of this continent. In several areas of Long Island, the Hudson River valley, and the New Jersey coast, the mute swan has established itself in the wild state. It is a large white bird with an orange bill and a large knob at the base of the bill.

The TRUMPETER SWAN (*Cygnus buccinator*) is the largest of the swans. It is totally white, with a black beak which has a pink stripe along the mandible.

Not too long ago the trumpeter was in danger of extinction, but in recent years has made a fine recovery. Although it was occasionally shot for food and feathers, it was never subjected to much hunting. The trumpeter is a shy, secretive bird. When disturbed, it moves out. It cannot live near civilization. This was the reason for the bird's downfall.

Today, national parks in Canada and the United States insure that the trumpeter will have the wilderness habitat it needs to survive. The bird breeds in Yellowstone Park, in Red Rocks Lake, Montana, and in several areas of British Columbia and Alaska. It winters along the Pacific coast, mainly in British Columbia.

The WHISTLING SWAN (*Cygnus columbianus*) is a fairly numerous swan. It breeds in the very far north of Alaska and the Northwest territories, including some of the Arctic islands. The whistling swan winters along the California coast and the Atlantic coast from Chesapeake Bay to North Carolina. Since this swan breeds in the far north, it has not encountered any serious deterioration of habitat. With recent oil exploration and mineral discoveries in the far north, what the future holds for this waterfowl species is another matter.

The whistler is also a white bird. It can frequently be heard long before its wedge-shaped flock is seen. This swan has a yellow spot at the base of its black bill.

The whistler was hunted more than the trumpeter. It was abundant, and is still found in the more important wildfowling areas such as Carrituck Sound, Black Bay, and Chesapeake Bay. But it was never a prominent game bird. It was usually shot as incidental game to ducks and geese.

(Cygnus columbianus)

ENTIRE PLUMAGE WHITE

IMMATURE BIRDS HAVE GRAY-WHITE
PLUMAGE WITH DULL PINKISH BILL

YELLOW SPOT

BLACK BILL

SEXES ARE SIMILAR

CARRIES NECK HELD ERECT

HEAD OF MUTE SWAN SHOWING
BLACK KNOB AND ORANGE BILL

Today, large flocks of whistlers migrate through the Central Fly-way. Limited hunting, by special permit, is allowed in some of the western states. Pass-shooting along a known flyroute is probably the best way to hunt this swan, but the birds do decoy to large white bleach jugs and to white pieces of cloth.

Exotic Wildfowl

Occasionally American wildfowlers bag or see exotic waterfowl species that have wandered to this continent. For example, the European widgeon makes his way across the Atlantic to our shores quite regularly. Most birds probably come from Iceland or Siberia. The European version is quite similar to our widgeon.

Another occasional straggler is the Baikal teal from Siberia. Baikal teal sightings occur fairly regularly in Alaska, but the birds have been shot as far south as British Columbia and even California. Sightings have also occurred elsewhere, but these may be birds that have escaped from aviaries.

Still another exotic teal is the Eurasian green-winged teal, very similar in appearance to our greenwing. Most hunters or bird watchers would not be able to tell the difference. Most sightings of the Eurasian greenwing have occurred along the Atlantic coast.

Yet another Eurasian duck that straggles to our continent is the tufted duck. Actually, sightings of this bird in Alaska, particularly in the Aleutians and on Amchitka Island, are quite common. Other sightings have been made in many areas of the continent.

In appearance, the tufted duck is similar to the ring-necked duck, except that it has a tuft of feathers at the back of its head. It has frequently been seen in the company of bluebills.

Not all visiting ducks are from the north, however. The masked duck occasionally straggles up from the West Indies and South America. Most sightings of this duck have occurred in Florida, Louisiana, and Texas. In appearance the masked duck closely resembles the ruddy duck. In flight, it shows a white speculum on the wings, which the ruddy duck does not.

We also occasionally play host to exotic geese. The barnacle goose, a smallish sea goose, has been a rare visitor to the Atlantic coast. It is a relatively rare bird, with a world population of some 30,000 individuals. Stragglers seen here probably come from Greenland.

Two exotic swans are seen on this continent. The mute swan I have already mentioned. This bird now nests in the east. The whooper swan, a Eurasian species very similar to our trumpeter, has occasionally been seen in coastal Alaska. Over 400 of these big waterfowl were seen in the Aleutian Islands National Wildlife Refuge in the years from 1967 to 1969.

Other exotic waterfowl species occasionally escape from aviaries. If you are interested in world wildfowl, Sir Peter Scott's *Key to the Wildfowl of the World* is a handy and interesting reference. All of the birds are illustrated in full color. This book is published by the Wildfowl Trust, a British organization similar to Ducks Unlimited.

3

___

Wildfowling Techniques

Jerome Knap

W ILDFOWL HUNTING can be described as part art, part science. It is a science because it depends on a knowledge of the habits and needs of ducks and geese. To be a good duck hunter, a man must also be a good naturalist. And to be a good naturalist requires an inquiring, scientific mind.

Yet that's not all there is to wildfowling. There's another part, and that's where the art comes in. Hunting ducks and geese requires the right eye for setting out decoys, building blinds, and swinging a shotgun smoothly on a moving target, much as an artist uses a paint brush on a canvas. These skills go beyond the reasoning of science.

To the average hunter, duck hunting means gunning mallards on a small marsh or perhaps black ducks on a lazy creek. Dabbling ducks, because they live on small waters, are more widely available to hunters than diving ducks.

Knowing what wetlands dabbling ducks are using—for feeding, loafing, and roosting—is the key to successful puddle duck hunting. The only way to find this out is either through long duck hunting experience in an area or actually going out to scout an area before the season opens.

Wildfowling is generally best on cold, windy, overcast days.

The next thing is to know how and where to set out your decoys. Too many hunters dash into a clump of reeds and throw out decoys, only to find at daybreak that they are in the wrong spot.

First, be sure to put your decoys out in a natural manner—not too close together—because ducks generally bunch up only when they are afraid. Set your decoys in two loosely spaced groups, leaving plenty of open water near your blind for the ducks to land.

A good way to set up decoys is across the wind, with the wind coming in from left to right for right-handed shooters or vice versa for left-handed ones. This accomplishes two things: it provides you with shots that allow easy swinging from left to right; and, it permits crossing shots—the most dependable for ducks because vital areas are exposed and the bird provides a big profile.

Remember that ducks will generally come onto a marsh heading into the wind. By setting your decoys on the lee side, you ensure that the ducks will see the decoys from a long way, and that they will find the lee inviting. Pond ducks do not like sitting on rough water. Also, most decoys do not ride realistically in fairly rough water.

A dozen decoys—odd numbers such as 9 or 11 are preferred by some duck hunters—is plenty. Mallard decoys are usually best because they will attract all other species, except perhaps blacks which are very wary and hard to fool. For black duck shooting, three or four decoys is enough. Flocks of blacks will not generally decoy, but pairs and singles may.

Always build your blind carefully, and out of local reeds or brush so that it is as inconspicuous as possible. Do not bring in strange reeds or grass. These will look out of place. And duck can spot "thing that weren't there yesterday" very quickly. The best blind is a thick stand of natural vegetation.

Calling is very helpful if you are good. Otherwise forget it. One bad note is all it takes. Most beginning duck hunters call much too often and much too loudly. To become a good duck caller takes practice. If you're not willing to devote the time necessary to learning it, forget it altogether.

Aside from decoying, dabbling ducks can also be jumpshot. In my boyhood, I shot my fair share of ducks by walking from one country pond to another. When approaching a pond, slip in quietly, using any trees, brush, or fence rows available for cover. Don't hesitate to crawl if that's the only way to get close. Sometimes it's possible to hear ducks quacking as they are feeding on a farm pond or livestock tank. I still bag a few this way every fall, as a sidelight during pheasant hunts.

Today, one of my favorite ways to jump-shoot ducks is with a canoe on small, slow streams. I find that small streams are usually passed up by other hunters, so I have them all to myself. Sometimes I can combine a duck shoot with a grouse or woodcock hunt. Good grouse and woodcock covers oftentimes border on streams. Other hunters find that squirrels can be taken as a side bag to a duck float.

Pass-shooting and stubble-shooting are also possible for dabblers, but more about this later.

One of the unique ways to hunt pond ducks is with a tolling dog. This is how it's done. The hunter hides on a shore of a lake or pond with ducks sitting on it. He then tosses a dummy or a rubber ball to a dog on shore, letting the dog retrieve it. As the game continues, the ducks become curious and swim up for a closer look. When they are close enough, the hunter shoots. It is imperative that the tolling dog perform in a joyful manner, and not pay any attention to the ducks. Also, there must be no other hunters nearby to frighten the ducks.

As far as I know, tolling is practised only in Nova Scotia, where a special breed of rusty, fox-like dog, the Nova Scotia tolling retriever, was developed for this sport. If more duck hunters knew about it, it might become more widely used as a technique for taking puddle ducks.

A retrieving dog is invaluable for pond ducks, more so than for any other wildfowl hunting. Many ducks are wasted every season because

The art of wildfowling is knowing how and where to set your blocks.

they fall into reeds and log-infested beaver ponds where finding a dead bird, let alone a wounded one, is hard for a hunter without a dog.

Diving ducks, of course, require different hunting techniques. I know of no other hunting sport that subjects the participants to more discomfort than hunting diving ducks. Diver shooting reaches its peak in the late fall when the marrow-chilling north winds sweep down over much of the country, and the hardy, fast-flying diving ducks move south. Divers always seem to move in with severe storms, almost as if they enjoyed riding the wind and sleet.

The cold, semi-darkness of dawn, waves breaking in the face of a north wind, and ice-encrusted decoys—lots of them—are all part of the game. Yet, as a shotgun sport, diver duck hunting has few equals. The weather can freeze the fires of hell and I'll still be out there gunning for divers.

Hunting diving ducks is a specialized, open water sport. It requires boats, motors, and large sets of decoys. The same common sense applies in hunting divers as in hunting dabblers. It is always wise to set your raft of decoys in an area where you have seen birds, or in a known feeding area. Since diving ducks fly in large flocks, you will need much larger rafts of decoys to bring them in for a look. Sets of 60 decoys are about minimum, and twice that many are better. Always set your decoys into the wind, leaving an empty space close to your blind, because diving ducks always take off into the wind to give themselves an extra lift.

When a flock of divers is looking over your decoys, watch their feet. If they are going to set down, they will start trailing their feet while still some distance away. If their feet are tucked way up, you can be sure that they will only buzz your decoys. In this case, give the birds plenty of lead when you shoot. They will pick up speed as they fly over your decoys.

I believe in well built blinds that conceal the occupants as completely as possible. Such blinds should be built or anchored out in the water before the divers come south. This tactic may not be entirely necessary for bluebills and redheads, because they generally decoy much more readily—sometimes even stupidly. But canvasbacks are a different story. They can be cagey and difficult to lure in. So you need all the break you can get for "cans". With today's low limits on canvasbacks—where they are still legal targets—any extra trouble is probably not worth it.

Bluebills are the mainstay of diving duck shooting today, with goldeneyes and buffleheads providing an extra bit of variety. Oldsquaws are sometimes included in a bag, but they are principally fish eaters, and hunters who know their ducks seldom bother with them.

Hunting "coots", as scoters are called along the Atlantic coast, has a small but dedicated following. Along with scoters, the larger eiders are sometimes taken. Scoters tend to prefer bay water, while eiders are offshore ducks. This is one reason why scoters are subjected to more hunting. Also, eiders are basically northern birds, out of reach of most hunters. The king eider winters off the coast of eastern Canada and New England, but no farther south. Scoters, on the other hand, winter from eastern Canada right down to the Carolinas, and so offer more hunting opportunities.

The sea ducks, particularly the scoters, are not overly wary. In fact, a canvasback hunter would consider them downright stupid. They will decoy to just about anything if they haven't been too heavily gunned. Wooden blocks—not even proper decoys—are frequently used. Years ago, large cork floats from fishing nets were frequently used. Some hunters use silhouette decoys—shadows as they are locally called—nailed in a row on a long board. The hunter can sit up in his boat and not bother concealing himself. All he has to do is sit still. The birds may sometimes circle and then drop in behind the gunner. Experience soon teaches the coot hunter how to handle such situations.

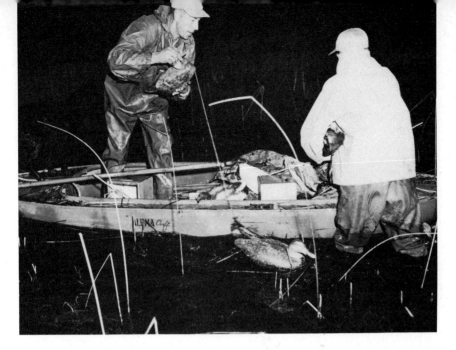

Decoys, boats, and a good retriever are all important ingredients of a duck hunt.

Scoters, however, are fast-flying birds, usually travelling in line just barely skimming the water. They rise into the air only when an obstacle—a boat or a point of land—is in their line of flight.

A good place to hunt coots is in a bay with headland thrusting out into the sea. If there is a group of hunters with boats, the boats should be anchored in a line about 100 yards apart, each with its own set of decoys. Scoters, as they pass, will decoy to one set; and as they are fired on, will generally fly to the next set instead of passing and flying away.

Almost any kind of stable boat can be used for coot hunting. Old wooden dories and skiffs are still used by some of the old-timers. The boats should be painted with dull colors. When a pair of gunners is hunting from one boat, they should sit back to back. In this way, they will have the whole field covered. In some areas it is possible to gun coots from low, offshore points. A boat is still needed, however, to retrieve the birds.

Sea ducks are hard birds to kill. A full-choked 12 gauge with a stiff load of No. 4 shot is generally best. Some hunters prefer smaller shot as the first load, or in the more open bore of a double. When gunning sea ducks, it is wise to bring along plenty of shells.

Sea ducks, likewise, are not generally regarded as our finest table birds. Most hunters eat only the breasts. There is actually very little meat on the rest of the bird. It is frequently said that you have to be born on the coast to appreciate sea ducks on the dinner plate. When the breasts are slowly simmered in mushroom gravy or a wine sauce, they can be quite tasty.

The honking of wild geese is a siren song to a goose hunter. Like the howling of a wolf or the bugling of an elk, the plaintive honk of a Canada goose is a symbol of wilderness.

Because wild geese largely nest in the far north, on land still relatively untouched by man, they have fared well in this century. All they need is some protection in the form of bag limits and seasons, and they respond. Our goose flocks have been increasing in numbers. We probably have more geese today than when my father or grandfather was hunting them. And if we can keep the remote north undisturbed, and unpolluted, we will always have geese.

Goose hunting can be full of contrasts. On the Hudson and James Bay coasts, snow geese are so unsophisticated that they will decoy to lumps of mud and sheets of newspaper folded over marsh grass. Without the expert calling of the Cree Indian guides, though, success would, of course, not be as easy. However, this is the easiest goose gunning to be had, and it loses its charm quickly. The most captivating part of a Hudson or James Bay goose hunt is the country— the wild, desolate landscape where the wild goose lives and rears its young. Every waterfowler should hunt there at least once in his lifetime.

Hunting honkers on the wheat stubbles of Saskatchewan or the corn fields of Maryland is another matter. Everything has to be perfect or it will not work. The right field has to be chosen. The pit has to be dug carefully and in the right place. No fresh earth can be left around to warn the birds. The decoys must be set just right. Finally, when the birds are flying, the calling has to be perfect, without a single false note. The hunters and dogs must be perfectly still until the geese are in shotgun range.

Goose hunting is rarely done over water; except, of course, for brant. Most goose hunting is done over feeding areas—either grassy meadows or tide flats, but more often grain fields. The technique is simple. Locate an area where the birds are feeding and be there before they arrive the following day. The only way to locate feeding birds is to be out looking with binoculars. When such a field is located, you must get the farmer's permission to dig a pit. Be sure to fill the pit in completely after your hunt, or neither you nor anyone else will ever be allowed to hunt there again.

Most goose hunting is done from pits on stubble fields.

Goose decoys must be spread out to represent a feeding flock of geese. Some of the decoys must have resting heads, others must have feeder heads, and a few must have alert upright heads. Some geese are always looking up whenever a flock feeds. A bunch of decoys all with their heads up means unrest and caution to oncoming birds.

When you spot birds on the horizon, start calling and take cover immediately in the pit. If you are not an expert, stop calling as soon as the birds are close or as soon as they head for your decoys. A single false note can easily spoil everything.

Don't shoot until the birds are within range. This can be tricky to determine for a tyro, because the birds are big. They frequently appear closer than they are. They also fly faster than most hunters realize. Be sure to lead them enough.

Pass-shooting for geese is not frequently done, largely because the birds fly high until they come down into the fields. But occasionally it is possible to pass-shoot in foul or foggy weather when the birds stay low. Geese generally spend the nights on big lakes. If you want to pass-shoot geese, this is where you should look.

Hunting brant is very specialized. It is usually done over water, in areas where these sea geese are known to feed on eelgrass. Scouting the seashore for feeding brant or stands of eelgrass is the best way to start. Brant decoys are nearly always used. Brant can also be pass-shot from rocky points jutting out into the sea. Brant do not like to fly far from shore. This is a real bonus for the pass-shooter.

A dog is not needed for most goose hunting because wounded birds almost never hide. However, I almost always use my dog because she makes the hunting much more enjoyable. Once a dog learns how to pick up and carry a big Canada, mallards are a snap.

Pass-shooting on ducks or geese is the hardest type of waterfowl gunning. The birds fly much faster than ducks settling in to decoys, and the ranges are considerably longer. Pass-shooting is a somewhat simple form of duck hunting, since decoys are not used. The hunter locates a "pass"—a local flyway which the ducks use daily, on their way to and from feeding and roosting areas. The hunter then finds some suitable cover, hides, and waits for the birds to start moving.

A good pass can be a creek, or a narrow neck of either land or water between two marshes. The shortest routes between marshes or lakes and grain fields of farm country can also be good passes. Pass-shooting can be practised in any kind of weather, even on rough, windy days. On the sea coast, reefs and breakers or points of land jutting into the water can be good passes. The birds in this case will be "trading" more than usual, trying to find a sheltered place.

The main problem with inland pass-shooting, aside from finding a good pass, is other hunters. As soon as the gunning pressure increases a bit, the ducks change their flyway or fly high. They may even learn to fly out of shotgun range or to fly early, before the legal shooting time. This is why pass-shooting is not as effective as other methods.

All pass-shooting requires a full-choked gun and heavy loads. This is where the magnums come into their own. Pass-shooting is extremely difficult. Limits are just too small for most fowlers to develop the skill and experience required to be able to consistently hit wildfowl at long ranges. Today, guns are capable of killing ducks at 60 or even 70 yards; but most of us aren't 60-yard shooters.

Sculling is yet another duck hunting technique. It is really a specialized form of jump-shooting. The scull boat is a boat with an extremely low profile. The gunner lies down in the boat and propels it forward with a single scull oar in the stern.

When a flock of ducks is spotted on the water, the sculler propels the boat slowly forward towards the rafted ducks, hoping to get within shotgun range. Some hunters mount a seagull on the bow of the scull boat to make the boat look like a large piece of flotsam. A few scullers have completely white scull boats, just for ice-festooned waters.

Any type of duck can be hunted in this way. Sculling, however, can only be practised on calm water. In windy weather, waves break over the gunwales of the scull boat, soaking the hunter and filling the boat with water. Large rivers, sheltered lakes, and bays are the best places to scull for ducks.

Ducks can also be hunted on stubble fields.

Sculling is not practised a great deal. A few devotees, however, still scull for ducks in New England and the northern seaboard states.

Geese and dabbling ducks can also be hunted on stubble fields. Ducks (particularly mallards) and geese (particularly Canadas) love grain. They will feed on grain in preference to anything else. Corn is the reason why Maryland has such fine goose shooting today. Geese have changed their migration habits because of it. On the Canadian prairies, ducks do considerable damage to standing wheat in some areas, so much so that the Canadian government is paying farmers an indemnity for damage caused by waterfowl.

Hunting Canadas over stubble can be exasperating. The technique is the same as for ducks, but you have to be sharper and a bit more clever. Fresh earth near the pit can make the geese shy away, particularly if they've been shot at. When geese are heavily gunned, they become extremely wary. They refuse to decoy. The actually avoid any "flocks" on the ground. They seldom feed in one field on two consecutive days.

Once a hunter knows where the birds are feeding, he must be there well ahead of the flight, to set up his decoys and dig his pit. Most of us prefer to dig our pits the night before. For duck stubble-shooting, it is sometimes possible to use a low blind built of straw and weeds in a fence row or on the edge of a shelter belt. Geese, however, seldom land near fences or shelter belts. They are too wise.

4

Guns and Loads for Wildfowl

Clair Rees

W HAT MAKES the best duck gun? Or, for that matter, the best goose gun? Which action type is best—slide, double, or autoloading? In which gauge? What choke? And what about shot size and charge?

These are some of the questions every wildfowler periodically asks, either of himself or of someone else. Unfortunately, there is no "right" answer. The solution depends on the type of birds hunted, the terrain, possibly the weather, and the shooting style of the hunter. And just as important is the particular taste of the man who'll be using the gun.

Thus a hunter carrying the latest in gas-operated magnum 12-gauge autoloaders isn't necessarily any more "correct" in his choice of armament than his partner, who prefers to tote a lightweight stack-barreled 20. Similarly, one gunner may dote on a long-tubed pump with a super-tight choke, while another might use an open-bored quail gun. Depending on the circumstances, either of these nimrods may have made the best possible choice. It all depends on what, when, and where you're shooting; as well as on which kind of gun *you* perform best with.

Pump guns are favored by many wild-fowlers.

While selecting a shotgun is a purely personal matter, the different scattergun types offer their own peculiar advantages and disadvantages.

One of the most popular types of shotguns among wildfowlers is the slide action, or pump. A well-designed pump gun is a rugged, thoroughly dependable piece of shooting machinery, that will keep right on functioning under conditions that could conceivably put a selfloader out of business. Even lack of proper care or downright neglect won't put a pump on the sidelines, at least not right away. As long as the action hasn't rusted solid, you should be able to get shells to feed from magazine to chamber with better-than-fair regularity. You can keep on using the gun until something breaks (and parts *will* eventually break in any gun not properly cared for).

In addition to top dependability, trombone-type scatterguns offer a single sighting plane; generally good, if slightly muzzle-heavy balance; and rapid repeat shots.

One other big point in the pump gun's favor is economy. A good slide action will typically cost from fifty to a hundred dollars less than a comparable auto, and less than half the price of an average over/under. However, you can get pumps as fancy as you like them, with prices ranging up to and beyond the $2500 mark.

Most slide-action scatterguns on the market today also offer interchangeable barrels. By simply taking an extra tube along, you'll be prepared to switch from short-range decoy work to gunning high-flying flocks. If the winter storm predicted by the TV meteorologist turns into a bluebird day, this quick-switch feature can prove to be very handy. (Winchester makes things even simpler for gunners with its "Winchoke" device—interchangeable, pocket-sized choke tubes that screw into the muzzle to vary the shot concentration.)

The autoloading shotgun is closely related to the pump. Some self-loading models are, in fact, nearly identical to pump guns of the same make; that is, from the breech rearward. Several autos and pumps share the same basic frame and action, differing only in the kind of power used to operate the bolt.

While early autoloaders had a not-altogether-undeserved reputation for malfunctioning at times, today's self-shuckers very seldom fail in the field. This is due partly to improved engineering and manufacturing, and partly to the vastly superior ammunition available today. Moisture-swollen paper hulls (a major cause of jamming at one time) are a thing of the past. The plastic shells we now use generally feed smoothly and surely.

Although the auto will fire as fast as you can pull the trigger, a good gun handler can get off as many *accurate* shots with a slide-action if he works the pump as he is recovering from recoil. The big selling feature of the autoloader is not speed of fire, but that part of the recoil energy is used up in working the action. Even more important, the energy that does reach your shoulder is felt more as a firm "push" than a sharp, hard jolt. This serves to greatly soften the kick.

I once tested a number of fixed-breech and autoloading shotguns in a laboratory, and was able to accurately compare the relative force at the moment of peak recoil in each gun. An oscilloscope tracing showed that although the total energy transmitted to the shooter was similar in each case, the peak energy felt at any given moment was up to 40 percent less when autoloaders were used. Practically speaking, this means that you can fire heavier, more powerful loads with less discomfort in an autoloader.

For this reason, my first choice for a long-range pass-shooting gun would be a tightly-choked, big bore magnum, in either a gas- or recoil-operated autoloader. (The long-recoil original Browning A-5 absorbs recoil about as well as the newer gas autos, but gives a "double shuffle" effect that some gunners find disconcerting.)

Both the selfloader and slide-action are magazine-fed guns, and usually require a wood or plastic plug to reduce the magazine capacity to a two-shell maximum for hunting waterfowl or other migratory birds. Many shooters simply leave this plug in the year around, for all their gunning chores. Consequently, some of the newer autos are

Semi-automatic shotguns also have a strong following.

being manufactured with two-round magazines (giving the gun a total capacity of three shots, counting the one in the chamber).

Autoloaders tend to be somewhat heavier than their manually operated cousins. This, too, helps dampen recoil. Pass-shooters also find that they tend to swing smoother with a weightier arm, and this has helped create additional fans for the modern "cornsheller."

Double-barreled shotguns come in two basic varieties—the traditional side-by-side, with both barrels on the same horizontal plane; and the increasingly popular over/under, with the barrels aligned vertically.

Twin-tubed shotguns typically have shorter overall lengths than the magazine guns, because there is no need for a reciprocating bolt and its attendant long action. Double-barreled guns may be had either with double triggers or selective or non-selective single trigger. Some are made with plain extractors (that merely lift expended hulls slightly for hand removal); some feature selective automatic ejectors that kick empties clear yet leave unfired shells in their chambers. Selecting among these options can make a difference of a hundred or more dollars in price.

Having two barrels available makes it possible to choose instantly between two different degrees of choke (unless the gun has a non-selective single trigger, in which case the more open tube always fires first). So if a hedge-hopping teal suddenly materializes 20 yards to port, you can turn the open-choked barrel on him. Yet you'll still be able to reach those high-flying pintails with the tighter tube.

The popularity of over-and-unders has
risen significantly among wildfowlers.

A twin-barreled gun offers, of course, only two shots before reloading is necessary. But you can restoke it faster than a magazine gun. As far as I'm concerned, the only possible disadvantage you could charge against the double is a bit of awkwardness when reloading in ultra-tight quarters. Over/under doubles are the worst offenders in this situation, because the barrels strike a larger arc when the action is opened.

As far as choosing between the side-by-side and superposed types, that's purely a matter of personal preference. Some gunners dislike the broad sighting plane offered by the side/side; others claim the wide, twin muzzles serve to catch the eye and speed up pointing. If your budget's on the lean side, you can buy a perfectly serviceable side-by-side at a lower price than you would have to pay for a comparable stackbarrel. Or you can opt for a fancy sidelock that would dent an oil sheik's income.

A few wildfowling guns are built around bulky bolt actions that are neither graceful nor fast to operate. As far as I'm personally concerned, the only reason for owning one of these guns is to have a repeating shotgun for the very lowest possible price. If you happen to be a pass-shooting addict with a yen for a magnum 10, a bolt-action arm may be your only logical choice; that is, if you want repeat firepower without mortgaging your house. Marlin's long-barreled 10-bore bolt gun is less than one-third the price of the only other domestic "big bertha" repeater (the very excellent Ithaca Mag 10 autoloader).

With one possible exception, single-shot shotguns are pretty much relegated to youthful beginners in the hunting game. That exception is the potent (at both ends) single-barreled 10-gauge now offered by Harrington & Richardson. The big 10 is for "experts only" in *any* guise.

Now, what about gauge? By far the most popular shotgun gauge on the market is the ubiquitous 12. Available in a wide range of loadings, throwing everything from a single ounce of shot to the mighty 1⅞-ounce magnum load (which all but equals 10-gauge capacity), the workhorse 12 is never a bad choice.

The 12 bore is the number one seller worldwide, and deservedly so. With modern shot-cupped loads, a properly choked 12 is capable of killing any legal waterfowl cleanly and efficiently. Many 12's come equipped with 3-inch chambers, to give the shooter the choice of regular or magnum ammunition (note that most autoloading magnums will not function reliably with non-magnum shells). And standard-length "baby magnums" will let the owner of any 12-bore in reasonable condition propel 1½ ounces of shot skyward.

Next down the line, the "sweet sixteen" was once a highly popular gauge in this country. But ammunition developments have passed it by. Consequently, the 16 is less popular than either the 12 or 20, although it tops its smaller brother's performance when both are used with standard loads. For some reason, both the 16 and the 20 throw the same amount of shot—1¼ ounces—in the magnum versions (no 3-inch ammo is offered for the 16 bore). The only thing wrong with buying a 16-gauge today is that chances are the corner store may not have ammo to fit it. This will trouble you only if you're prone to running dry in the boondocks, miles from a proper sporting goods shop.

The 20-gauge is a real comer today, with the large majority of 20 bores chambered for 3-inch ammo. Twenty-gauge guns are generally lighter and faster handling than their larger-bore brethren, and so are gaining favor rapidly with the upland crowd. Weight isn't usually a problem in a duck or goose blind, but jump-shooters can walk several miles during a day's hunt, and the light 20 offers some tempting advantages for this kind of duty.

One thing to remember, though. A light-toting 20 stuffed with 3-inch magnums can kick every bit as hard as a big-booming 12! Perhaps even harder.

While you'll have lots of company if you show up in the marsh with a 20-gauge gun, you can expect some uplifted eyebrows (and maybe some caustic remarks) if you drop a notch to the 28-gauge class. Federal makes a ⅞-ounce hunting load for this sub-bore that will kill ducks with dispatch, providing you limit your shots to the short side of 30 yards (which isn't hard when the birds are decoying well). I've eaten my share of mallard dinners collected with the use of a pet 28, but I'd never depend on it for day-to-day wildfowling. Under the right circumstances it'll do the job just fine. But circumstances tend to get out of hand in the marshes I usually hunt in, so I generally opt for heavier armament.

As far as the diminutive .410 is concerned (actually, a 67-gauge), I'll label it a show-off gun for egotistical experts (or tyros who don't know any better), and be done with it. It has no business in the hands of a serious wildfowler.

At the other end of the scale lies the mighty 10. This potentially potent round has, for years, suffered under the handicap of outmoded components—paper hulls, felt wads, and uncupped shot. Now that interest is being directed at steel alloy shot (required now at some federal refuges and eventually scheduled for mandatory use nationwide, unless policy changes), interest in this largest of legal gauges has re-awakened. Steel shot, lighter than lead, make less efficient projectiles and are required in greater numbers than comparably sized lead shot to do the job. Even when larger numbers are used, the poor flight characteristics of this new shot means fewer sure kills at long range.

To get anything like a full-range load of steel alloy pellets, a shell with a big capacity is required. And that's where the 10-gauge shines.

Three separate manufacturers have produced new 10-gauge guns (the aforementioned Marlin bolt gun, the Harrington & Richardson single shot, and the recoil-absorbing Ithaca autoloader). And at least one manufacturer—Remington—now offers truly modern 10-gauge ammo, complete with plastic shot cups. At this writing, no steel-shot loads are being manufactured in 10 gauge, but it's only a matter of time before such fodder becomes available (unless programmed restrictions on the use of lead shot are lifted).

A word about choke. Most scattergunners use too much constriction, and I'm including wildfowlers in this category. Full-choked guns with maximum loads are intended for long-range pass-shooting only. At close range, they're difficult to score with, and the birds you *do* hit are going to be too mangled to masticate without armor-plated dentures.

The ponderous 10-gauge magnums are favored by some for long-range wildfowling.

Over decoys, a modified choke is better. In fact, an improved cylinder may be the best choice of all. Put your decoy spread some 30 yards from your blind and shoot only at the ducks between you and the decoys, and I'll guarantee you'll have better luck with an open-choked gun. My duck-gunning doubles wear modified and improved cylinder chokes, not the "full" and "full" tubes so many nimrods dote on. Shotguns are *scatterguns,* and the wise shooter will let them live up to their name.

Which gun to select for *your* waterfowling needs? If you're buying your first shotgun, talk your friends into letting you try theirs, until you've had a chance to shoot several different types. Then pick the one you like best. It's that simple.

If I had to limit my waterfowling to a single shotgun, I could probably get along just fine with my pet 12-bore pump, with either a single modified-choked tube, or preferably a selection of barrels. Or I wouldn't complain if I could use my favorite over/under 20 with its 3-inch chambers. I'd have to hold the range down a bit when gunning honkers (my magnum 10 auto lets me indulge my pass-shooting fancies, but it's just too much gun for "all-around" use), but I wouldn't feel overly handicapped.

Pump, auto, bolt, or double—take your pick. Any will do the job, and each has its own set of advantages and disadvantages. As far as gauge and choke are concerned, anything between (and including) 20 and 12 should do the trick, and the smart gunner will opt for something more open than a tight full choke.

Use 5's or 6's on ducks over decoys (4's are all right too, and 7½'s will do the job this side of 30 yards); and rely on 2's and 4's for geese. Remember that the larger, heavier shot will carry farther and have more punch at the longer ranges.

5

How to Hit Wildfowl

John Wootters

THERE ARE SO MANY WILDFOWLING techniques and environments, and so many different kinds of shooting available across the continent, that generalities about guns and loads are likely to be misleading. The weaponry which well serves a midwestern river-hunter may or may not suit a Louisiana marsh-hunter, and certainly will not be the thing for the hardy New England gunner of sea ducks. I live in Texas and frequently use a 20-gauge on geese with good success. But a recent excursion to Maryland's eastern shore for some tremendous pass-shooting on greater Canadas saw me crouching in a pit blind, clutching a 3-inch magnum 12-gauge and still feeling a bit undergunned.

American duck-shooting can be broken down into three basic types of gunning. The first is classic pass-shooting, where ranges are apt to be long and the birds in full flight. There is only one optimum moment in which to trigger the shot at each passing duck, and never a second chance.

The second type is on decoying ducks, but this doesn't necessarily mean that every shot is within 30 yards, and at a bird with its wings

Wooters thinks that most wildfowlers use too long a barrel on their guns.

set and feet dangling. Not these days! If a flock swings enough to give you a low pass before going on, that qualifies as "decoying". Gunning over decoys, then, may offer shots varying from skeet ranges on slowly-moving birds, up to some which do not differ markedly from pass-shooting, except that the targets will rarely be straight overhead.

The third kind of duck gunning is jump-shooting. This may take place while floating a river in a canoe, walking the marshes, or stalking small stockwatering ponds in the arid southwest. If the gunner's tactics are sound, most of his shots will be within very reasonable range—probably less than 40 yards—at towering birds which really aren't traveling very rapidly (that is, for ducks).

The requirements for guns, ammunition, and techniques for these three basic forms of shooting vary so widely, that any effort to define a "duck gun" or proper "duck loads" is fruitless. The same is true of the two basic types of goose-gunning—pass-shooting and shooting on decoyed birds. Jumping geese just isn't a viable technique, although I suppose that most youngsters who grew up in good goose country have belly-crawled up to a resting flock a few times. The usual result of such sneaks, however, is not wingshooting, at least not for the first shot; it's called sluicing.

A few situations occur in which the hunter is about equally likely to have shots at either ducks or geese or both, which poses additional problems in the selection of armaments.

Having belabored the point that the vast variety of American wild-fowling precludes the formation of general rules, I shall, in the mysterious manner of gun writers, proceed to attempt to do exactly that. My first rule is that the vast majority of waterfowlers use too long a barrel. Regardless of your shooting style, a barrel longer than 28 inches is almost invariably a handicap; one longer than 30 inches is always a handicap. With modern shotshells, the velocity increment arising from an extra couple of inches of snout on a shotgun is, for all practical purposes, nil. Barrel length, of course, has nothing to do with patterning. A full choke is a full choke, whether the tube is 20 inches long or 40 inches. For very long-range shooting, there may be some minor advantage in the longer slighting plane, but probably not one gunner in a thousand is expert enough to notice and make use of that theoretical advantage. The oft-quoted bonus of a smoother swing-through with a long barrel is far more often than not offset by the fact that the gun loses dynamism and most shooters cannot point it as well or move it as freely as necessary. On the whole, I'll call 28 inches the longest *practical* barrel for wildfowling, and personally regard even that as a couple of inches longer than needful.

Rule Two is that most shooters use at least one degree too tight a choke. The full choke (or so-called "extra full") is sort of standard for ducks and geese. But I have talked many gunning friends into trying a modified or improved-modified bore for a day or two, and they're astonished at the improvement in their shells-per-birds-bagged ratio. Admittedly, for very long-range pass-shooting, a full-choked barrel is the one feasible constriction. But that is very specialized shooting and requires a very specialized gun, not to mention very specialized (and rare) skills on the part of the man behind the gun. The gunner who has that sort of skill probably can't learn anything from me, anyway. The other 98 percent of us are well-served by a modified choke for almost all our duck shooting and probably 50 percent of all goose gunning. If you don't believe me, try it for yourself. For decoy- and jump-shooting, you may actually halve the number of shots fired for a limit, and will very likely get cleaner kills and fewer "sailers" to boot.

This strongly suggests that the double-barreled shotgun, whether side-by-side or over-under, choked modified and full, has wildfowling virtues largely unrecognized in this, the land of the pump or semi-auto repeater. When I'm hunting over decoys or jumping tanks, I often use a fast-handling side-by-side, choked improved-cylinder and modified (actually the same gun I carry when after quail and doves), and I get my share of ducks, even without the largely mythical "advantage" of a third shot.

The third rule is that the average shotgunner tends to select shot for waterfowling which is one size too large. Again, for the longest-range pass-shooting, No. 2 pellets are the ticket, simply because they carry enough energy out at barrel-stretching distances to knock down geese. But most hunters who regularly buy No. 4's for ducks would be better off with No. 5's, even if they had to handload them. For most shooting under about 45 yards (which is most of the shooting that cleanly kills ducks), 6's are even better, and for jump-shooting puddle ducks in a 3-inch chambered 20-gauge, I've found No. 7½'s to be even deadlier.

It's merely a matter of pattern density. *Pattern* is what kills; pattern and pattern alone. The gunner who blazes away hoping for a one-pellet hit in the head or neck or a broken wing is a mindless butcher, wounding untold numbers of magnificent birds. Day in and day out, multiple hits are what brings ducks down consistently and humanely. Tests have proven that a minimum of about four to five pellets of adequate energy is required for reliable kills on mallards. Geese need more hits, teal fewer; but multiple hits—which is to say *pattern*—are what make a shotgun an effective tool for waterfowling. And, of course, the smaller the shot size, the more pellets in the pattern. Note the following numbers:

AVERAGE NUMBER OF PELLETS

Shot charge		No. 2	No. 4	No. 5	No. 6	No. 7½
1	ounce	90	135	170	225	350
1¼	ounces	112	168	212	280	437

The above are the two most commonly used shot charges for ducks, in 20- and 12-gauge. Observe, for example, that in the 1-ounce 20-gauge charge, dropping down from No. 4 to No. 6 increases the number of pellets in the load by more than 60 percent. This provides a much better chance for the necessary number of hits on a winging mallard (assuming that the gun in question produces equally dense patterns with both shot sizes and that the bird is equally well centered with both charges). Since No. 6's carry adequate *energy* for ducks out to any practical gunning range, pattern *density* is the key, and this size shot should, as noted above, put more than half again as many pellets in the pattern as No. 4's. The choice shouldn't be difficult to make, and it is nearly always in favor of smaller shot. The exceptions exist, but they are very specialized.

Rule Four is related to Rule Three, and it is that the majority of wildfowlers (even the experts) of my acquaintance do not really *know* how their guns pattern with various loadings. They may not even realize that the nominal choke stamped on a shotgun barrel can, at best, describe that gun's performance with only one size of shot. I've seen barrels marked "modified" throw patterns which counted out every level from "skeet" to "full" with different loads. And with handloads, it's fairly easy to produce this range of patterns from any socalled modified tube. It's crucial to gunning success, regardless of the game, to take the time and trouble to pattern a barrel on paper with a variety of brands of ammunition, and various shot sizes. This means doing it right—firing at least five rounds of each different loading at a 4-foot-square plate or piece of paper at a *measured* 40 yards; drawing a measured 30-inch circle to enclose the bulk of the pellet holes; and tediously counting those holes. Not only can the percentage of the original total shot charge which struck within the circle be converted to a realistic choke designation, but a great deal about the evenness and uniformity of the patterns can be deduced. When it's all done, the gunner may be astonished to learn that his pet gun simply doesn't like a certain size shot, but that it performs like a dream with another size. Such information can make an enormous difference in field results, not to mention the boost in that all-important confidence it offers the shooter. Rule Four, then, is "pattern your gun." It's a nuisance, but it's worth it!

Rule Number Five takes us away from the technical aspects of guns and ammunition and into the marsh. It is, "lay off the longrange shots". Yes, I know there are days when the birds seem to be operating on oxygen and the long shot is the only shot you'll get. But consider the ballistic problems involved in a long shot. To begin with, there's the matter of accurate estimation of range, a feat for which human optical mechanisms are quite poorly adapted. The simple truth is that very, very few hunters can reliably guess the distance to a flying bird, within an accuracy limit of 5 yards; and only the uncommon shooter can get within plus or minus 10 yards. Yet 5 to 10 yards makes a tremendous difference in the amount of lead necessary. A day or so spent in the field with an accurate rangefinder can be an eye-opener even for a veteran gunner. In fact, just pacing off distances to downed birds will produce a lot of surprises.

Differences in angles, lighting, and sky conditions help to make duck gunning difficult.

If a hunter guns only one or a few species of wildfowl, he sooner or later learns to make valid judgements of range on that species, based on apparent size. But size differences between species, some of them very subtle, make range estimation in mixed-bag areas very risky. For instance, if you think it's a baldpate and it's really a gadwall, you're likely to try the bird about 5 yards too far out and miss, or even worse, cripple. I'd like to be able to impart some secret formula for solving this problem, but I'm afraid I don't know one. Differences in angle, lighting, and sky conditions can confound any rule or formula ever invented. The one and only way to be fairly sure most of the time is to refuse all shots on which you find yourself speculating about distances. When the bird's within sure-kill range, any hunter of even moderate experience will *know* it. If you're trying to convince yourself it's in range, it's probably not.

There are other problems with 60-yard-plus shots. One is wind-drift, a thing most of us have seen and been surprised by when we tried to kill a cripple on the water in a stiff cross-breeze. Even at a modest 40 yards, a strong wind can blow a charge of shot far enough to fringe, or even completely miss, a stationary target. True, a duck on the wing is subject to the same moving air currents as the shot, but a duck has a different ballistic coefficient from that of shot pellets, and isn't affected to the same degree. The longer the range, the more radical the wind-drift of the shot swarm.

Similarly, the longer the range, the greater the drop. Few shot-gunners pay much attention to *trajectory,* a subject of intense interest to riflemen, but shot pellets drop much faster than any rifle bullet. In long-range pattern tests with a 10-gauge magnum throwing a 2-ounce charge of No. 2's, I've seen patterns drop between 2 and 3 *feet* at 75 yards. Naturally, the more a gunner must elevate his muzzle to swing on a bird, the less apparent drop his charge has. But on a long, low, passing shot, it can cause mysterious misses.

Finally, there is the problem of pattern density itself. There are a few shotguns made which can deliver killing patterns beyond 60 yards, but not many. Most of those marked "full choke" won't do it beyond 50 yards. The best bet is to actually test yours, with the ammo you've found it handles most efficiently. The very best bet is to shoot patterns at the long ranges about which you're curious. But if you already have pattern data for the standard 40 yards, you can estimate that you will lose an average of about 8 percent for each additional 10 yards. Assuming your barrel delivers 65 percent patterns at 40 yards (in the low end of the full-choke range), you can figure that you'll be lucky to be throwing decent improved-cylinder densities at 65 yards. And thin patterns mean crippled and losts ducks and geese, something nobody who calls himself a sportsman would willingly risk.

All of the problems of long-range gunning combine to form a single complex which requires the mental abilities of a computer within a shotgunner. Sure, there are such people, but they comprise about one-tenth of one percent of active wildfowlers these days. Seasons are too short and limits too low to permit us to gain the intuitive skills of our market-hunting forefathers. The net conclusion is simply that long-range shots rarely pay off in birds in the bag, and many of those kills are pure accidents.

This, then, is the fifth rule, which is guaranteed to help you hit more ducks and geese: learn your own "sure-kill" range (it's probably about 40 yards; 40 *real* yards, that is, like mine) and stay within it. A corollary benefit is the sense of superiority you'll feel as you watch those sky-busting idiots in the next blind blasting away at out-of-range birds.

Five easy ways to increase your birds-per-cartridge ratio, put more duck dinners on the table, lose fewer cripples, and enjoy your water-fowling more:

> switch to a shorter barrel
> switch to a more open choke

use a smaller shot size, within limits

learn your gun's actual performance characteristics by pattern shooting

limit the ranges at which you attempt shots to those at which you *know* the shotgun/load/shooter combination is reliable

Then, all you have to do is remember to keep your head down, follow through, lead enough, swing from the hips, and time the shot for the optimum instant of angle, distance, and swing. It's just as easy as that!

In truth, there is nothing easy about hitting ducks and geese consistently, taking the shots as they come. If it were easy, I'd carry a better average than I do on wildfowl, and so would you. The five rules, though, will help make it a *bit* easier. If it were too easy, it wouldn't really be fun.

6

Duck Dogs

Jerome Knap

N o DUCK HUNTER CAN DENY the value of a good retriever. There has never been an excuse for wasting game, not even
in the halcyon years of the last century when the autumn skies were
alive with waterfowl. Today, every lost or wasted duck is crucial. Indeed, it is a black mark against the sport of hunting.

The fact that a good retriever promotes conservation and ensures
a heavier game bag, by retrieving all birds that are shot, should not,
however, be the sole reason for owning one. Today, a man should not
go hunting simply to bring home meat for the family larder. The
aesthetics of the sport are far more important.

To see a big-chested retriever leap into ice-festooned water after
a fallen bluebill, or crash through a stand of cattails after a winged
mallard are thrills that elevate hunting beyond the mere killing of
birds. Certainly there are those to whom a difficult retrieve by a dog
is a far more noteworthy event than a double on a pair of teal riding
a strong north wind.

The actual killing of a duck is an anticlimax; proof to our predatory
souls that we have indeed been hunting, a way of reliving our racial

origins of times when all men were hunters. The memories that many wildfowlers treasure are not those of ducks or geese shot, but rather of special things accomplished by their dogs. If these aesthetics were removed from hunting, the sport would become butchery.

Retrievers, as a group of sporting dogs, are not very old. Their history spans just a couple of centuries, certainly less than three. It can be traced to the time when fowling pieces became good enough to make wingshooting a practical sport. Prior to that, there was no need for retrievers. Other breeds of sporting dogs—pointers, setters, spaniels—all have longer histories. These dogs were used to "spring" game for hawks; to "set" game birds so that nets could be cast over them; or to point hares for coursing greyhounds.

But an efficient shotgun and the new sport of "shooting flying" changed all that. Bird hunters suddenly discovered that a dog which would retrieve game was a valuable asset. The old cliché about necessity being the mother of invention is certainly true with respect to dog breeding. When a need for reliable retrievers became established, men strove to fill that requirement.

The early origins of retrievers are obscure. There is no doubt that some of the spaniels, particularly the old and extinct breeds such as the Tweed water spaniel, were among the early dogs used for retrieving both upland and wetland game. In fact, spaniels were probably the first group of sporting dogs to be used as gunning dogs.

The black Labrador retriever is *the* duck dog in the minds of many hunters.

The water dogs, or ship's or fishermen's dogs, were the other early breeds used for retrieving, particularly waterfowl. The notable dogs in this group were the now-extinct St. John's, the water pudel (actually a German dog that was taken over and modified in France), and the Newfoundland.

All modern retrievers stem from either of these avenues, and in some cases perhaps from both. For example, the St. John's dog became the Labrador, while Chesapeakes have Newfoundland blood in their veins. The golden retriever came from the old Tweed water spaniel.

Among the lesser known retrievers, the Irish water spaniel probably has some "pudel" in his background. But the base of the breed was the now-extinct South Country dog, sometimes known as the Shannon spaniel. The beautiful curly-coated retriever may also have some pudel, but according to Stonehenge, the great English dog authority, the curlycoat was developed from the St. John's dog and the Irish water spaniel. The flat-coated retriever has St. John's bloodlines, as well as Gordon setter. And last but not least, the neglected American water spaniel probably has some Irish water spaniel in its genes, and perhaps even a bit of curly-coated retriever.

No one, of course, will ever know the true background of these breeds. Many of the early breedings were haphazard. In cases where a single individual created a breed, the crosses originally made were rarely revealed. The only exception is Sir Dudley Majoribanks, Lord Tweedsmouth, who left a written record of how he developed the golden retriever. These dogs did not come from a strain of Russian circus dogs, as legend claims.

Advising someone as to what breed of duck dog to get is a perilous task. Much depends on the type of wildfowling done, where, and even when (late season or early). Such things as kennel space, family dictates, and even preferences and prejudices enter into the selection process.

As an aside, let me say that long before a man gets his first duck dog—his first pup—he should get several books on dogs and dog training. No one can train a gun dog of any sort unless he understands dogs and how to train them.

Very few hunters actually do this. They usually acquire a pup first, and get a book only after they've run into problems. By then, the dog may be beyond the stage of making him into a useful duck dog.

For retriever training, I would recommend the following books:

The Chesapeake Bay retriever is a big dog, bred for big waters.

Training Your Retriever, by James Lamb Free; *Water Dog*, by Richard Wolters; and *Charles Morgan on Retrievers*, by Ann Fowler and D. L. Waters.

Free's book is now something of a classic. For a long time it was the bible of retriever trainers, pro and amateur alike. But in the light of modern knowledge of dog behavior, the book is rather conservative in its approach. For example, it recommends that no serious dog training begin until a dog is a year old. Yet the book contains much pragmatic advice, all given in the slow, humorous, and highly readable James Lamb Free style. No retriever man can afford to be without this book.

Wolters' book is at the other end of the pole. It would have you believe that you can have a finished retriever by the time the dog is 12 months old. Yet it was this book that fermented much of the new thinking about retriever training. *Water Dog* has a different perspective on training retrievers. The true course, in my opinion, lies somewhere between this book and the one advocated by Free.

Charles Morgan On Retrievers is, in my opinion, the best advanced book on the subject. Morgan certainly has few peers as a retriever trainer. This is not an "ABC" book for beginners, yet I would consider it as essential reading for anyone deeply interested in retrievers. Morgan advocates early, natural training of retrievers, backed by sound discipline as the dog turns from puppyhood to adulthood.

For those who believe that the springer may be a better bet for their type of waterfowl hunting, I would recommend two books: *The Complete Springer Spaniel*, by Charles Goodall; and *Springers for Sport*, by Talbot Radcliff. For those who use one of the European versatile gun dogs, I recommend my own book, *Training the Versatile Gun Dog*.

For general knowledge on dogs, John Falk's *The Practical Hunter's Dog Book* and Jeff Griffen's *The Hunting Dogs of America* are good bets.

While on the subject of retriever training books, let me state that training a retriever, or any other gun dog for that matter, is a time-consuming task that requires a fair amount of patience and a high degree of specialized knowledge and experience. Dog training books are a good source of knowledge, but time and temperament are frequently not so easy to acquire.

If you don't have the time or patience to train a retriever, you might be better off buying a pup and sending it to a professional. It's just as expensive to feed and provide veterinary care for a poorly trained gun dog as a well trained one. Although professional training

The golden retriever is a handsome dog, best suited for inland ponds and marshes.

doesn't come cheap, when you consider a duck dog's working life—say 10 years—that basic training works out to less than a dollar a week. To me, it's a good investment for a well-trained duck dog.

The logical place to find a retriever trainer is in the *Retriever Field Trial News,* 1836 East St. Francis Avenue, Milwaukee, Wisconsin 53207. This is also a good place to find a puppy of any of the retriever breeds.

To make a choice about which retriever to get, one must have facts. One must know exactly what a retriever is able to do and for what he has been bred. One must know a little about each of the breeds of retrievers, how they work, their characteristics and temperaments, their strong points, and their weaknesses.

Retrievers were developed primarily, though not solely, for retrieving ducks. Ducks are their real forte. A serious duck hunter should consider no other type of gun dog. During the last two or three decades, some retrievers have also been asked to fulfill the role of spaniels—to flush upland game. They handle this task with varying degrees of efficiency, but only rarely with the same dash, spirit, and abilities of the springer spaniel.

In my opinion, the flushing of game by retrievers should be viewed solely as post-graduate work. The retriever should know his specialty first and the handler should have his dog in full control before allowing him to act as a flushing dog. If the retriever is allowed to flush and hunt before he is fully trained in retrieving, he will be harder to control and harder to train in the fine points of decorum expected of a retriever. After all, a retriever must spend many hours sitting quietly and patiently in a duck blind or boat. And when he's sent out to work, he must obey his handler to the letter.

The Labrador retriever is the most popular of our retrievers, in numbers of dogs registered. It totally dominates the field trial scene in wins and number of dogs entered. The Labrador is a fast and stylish performer who puts everything it has into the game. It is a dependable retriever from both land and water.

In disposition, the Labrador is generally quite gentle. Most Labs make good house dogs. It has been my experience that Labs can take a surprising amount of mishandling by tyro trainers without being ruined or without any marring of personality. Labs, though, seem to be something of hobos. They like to wander.

The Chesapeake Bay retriever is a big, burly dog with an independent or even stubborn streak down its back. The Chessy was developed by market hunters as a heavy-duty water retriever. And that's still the Chessy's bag. Chesapeakes can retrieve over 100 ducks a day from ice-cold water. Since our duck limits will never again be more than 5 or 6 birds per day, this breed's forte is wasted.

In my book, the Chesapeake has a sort of "macho charisma" about him. The Chessy is a dog for real wildfowl specialists, who have a nostalgic streak for things of yesteryear. It is too independent to handle well enough to make field trial wins a specialty.

Because the Chessy is a big dog, it is happier where it has a bit of room. Some Chessys have a reputation of being somewhat of a bully with other dogs. The Chessy makes a good watchdog. It is a homebody who protects what belongs to it.

The golden retriever is an attractive dog with a mild disposition. It is not a dog for a trainer who might blow his cool. Lose your temper but once and you may mar a golden's character or even ruin it. The golden has done well in obedience trials, showing that it has plenty of intelligence. But it's had a difficult time competing against the Labrador in field trials because it doesn't have the dash or the drive.

The golden seems to be a popular dog with women handlers. This could be because of its good looks or its mild disposition, which responds to gentle and unpressured training. The golden is not a good choice for retrieving on big, open waters. Its forte is prairie potholes and small marshes.

There are also a number of other retrievers such as the Irish water spaniel, the curly-coated retriever, the flat-coated retriever, the American water spaniel, and the Nova Scotia tolling retriever. All of these are relatively uncommon in North America.

The American water spaniel should be more popular and better known than it is. It was bred as a small duck dog, to work out of boats in the wetlands of the American midwest. For this reason, it is classified as a retriever.

Actually, the American water spaniel is a very versatile dog. It is a good flushing dog in the uplands, as well as a good retriever. It is a solid bet for a hunter who goes out after a little of everything. Because of its small size, it's not an ideal dog for big waters or thick marshes. It is not as spirited as the springer spaniel, and for this reason it is generally easier to train and handle.

The flatcoat is one of the oldest retrievers, if we are to go by official recognition of breeds. The first flatcoated retriever registered was Wyndham in 1860. The breed was then called the wavy-coated retriever. Until the early 1900's, this was the most popular of the retriever breeds in England.

The flat-coated retriever is one of the rarer duck dogs.

Actually the flatcoat is still common in England, where it is frequently considered a "gamekeeper's dog". In temperament, flatcoats remind me much of golden retrievers. They are fairly soft. In general, they lack the speed and style of Labradors and have difficulty in competing well in field trials, but some individuals have made good showings. During the past decade, there has been a bit of resurgence of interest in the flatcoat.

The curly-coated retriever is actually even older than the flatcoat. It received its recognition in 1859. Certainly the curlycoat is a handsome dog with a thick coat of tightly curled hair.

English wildfowlers claim that the curlycoat is the best dog for cold water and cold weather fowling. Certainly its coat must give it much protection against the elements. In temperament, the curlycoat is also mild and gentle. But it does have a reputation for determination when it sets out on a retrieve. It is known for endurance and a soft mouth.

Curly-coated retrievers were much more popular before the Civil War than they are now. But among waterfowlers in Australia and New Zealand, curlycoats are still the most popular duck dogs.

The Irish water spaniel has an ancient history. According to the Irish, it dates back to the Irish Laws of 17 A.D. But in its present form, the dog goes back to about the 1850's.

The Irish water spaniel is the largest of the spaniels, but is classified as a retriever (and hence is eligible to compete in retriever trials). It is best characterized by a long, bare tail—a rat tail—and a

The first duck dog to be officially recognized was the curly-coated retriever.

poodle-like head. Indeed, the Irish water spaniel possesses the gay, quick movements of a poodle. It also has a reputation of being very intelligent.

At one time the Irish water spaniel was a highly renowned gun dog. Even up to the early 1920's, the Field Dog Stud Book registered more Irish water spaniels than any other retriever breed. Today, it has a small but faithful following. A number of old waterfowlers swear by the Irish water spaniel.

The Nova Scotia tolling retriever is perhaps this continent's least known duck dog. But it is probably no longer the rarest. There are a number of dedicated breeders in Canada, and a few in New England as well. Thus far, the Nova Scotia tolling retriever is recognized only by the Canadian Kennel Club.

In appearance, the Nova Scotia tolling retriever resembles a golden in a vague sort of way. It is an attractive, alert-looking dog of foxy red color. It was bred not only to retrieve waterfowl, but also to toll or lure ducks within shotgun range.

The way ducks are tolled is simple. A hunter locates a lake or river with ducks on it, and hides near the shore. The dog then runs back and forth along the shore near the hunter. Ducks are curious creatures. They will swim close to shore to see what is going on.

In Europe, largely before the advent of firearms, ducks were tolled by dogs into large tunnel-shaped traps made of netting. Dogs of no special breed were used for this purpose. The idea of hunting with

Nova Scotia tolling retrievers were developed in eastern Canada for tolling and retrieving ducks.

a tolling dog is an old one. It probably stems from someone watching a fox hunt ducks, by tolling them close to shore and then pouncing on them. I have personally seen a coyote try this trick while I was filming ducks on a Saskatchewan pothole.

Thus far I have written solely about retrievers, as if they were the only dogs capable of retrieving ducks. Certainly, according to most waterfowl hunting books, they are. But that's not true. For example, the springer spaniel is a capable little duck retriever. Springer field trials even call for the retrieve of a duck.

No one can legitimately expect a springer to be in the same retrieving class as a Labrador, or perhaps even an American water spaniel. But a springer can still do a yeoman's job on small marshes, potholes, and beaver ponds.

One problem with springers is that, in recent years, small and lightly built dogs have come into vogue because they look more lively and attractive in the field. For duck retrieving, the bigger, heavier dogs are a better bet. They are generally stronger swimmers. A drake mallard is a big mouthful for a small dog to handle. The small dogs also find busting through reeds and cattails a more difficult task.

The European gun dogs, frequently now called the "versatile hunting dogs", can also be useful duck retrievers. Versatile gun dogs are divided into three classes—short-haired, wire-haired, and long-haired. The Brittany spaniel is the only commonly encountered European gun dog with long hair.

It may come as a surprise to many Brittany owners, but at one time

The springer spaniel can be a useful retriever on small marshes and ponds.

the Brittany was expected to retrieve waterfowl. The dog developed as a French farmer's hunting dog. It was expected to point pheasants in hedgerows and retrieve ducks from Brittany marshes, all in a day's work.

Most Brittanys on this continent have been turned into bird dogs, sort of miniature setters. This, I think, is a pity. As a result, many Brittanys are too active, too highly strung to have the patience to sit in a blind on a duck hunt. But I have encountered Brittanys in Quebec that still hunt ducks on beaver ponds and grouse and woodcock in woodlots, all in one day's hunt.

The short-haired gun dogs from Europe are best characterized by the popular German shorthaired pointer. Two other breeds are weimaraners and vizslas. The problem with all of these breeds is that they've suffered the same fate as the Brittany. Originally they were versatile dogs who were expected not only to point upland game, but also to retrieve from water under moderate climatic conditions.

But water retrieving is not required by present bird-dog field trial rules. And so many of these short-haired versatile gun dogs don't like water. But it is still not difficult to find a German shorthair, a vizsla, or a weimaraner that likes water and can make a good retriever.

The short-haired dogs have another limiting factor for water retrieving—temperature, of both water and air. Retrieving bluebills

The European versatile gun dogs can also be effective wildfowl retrievers.

along the Lake Michigan shore when ice forms on everything that water touches is not for them. They are much better suited for retrieving ducks on mild October days and from small, relatively warm waters.

In this regard, the wire-haired breeds—the German wirehaired pointer, the wirehaired pointing griffon, and the relatively rare pudelpointer—are far superior. There is no question that the thick coat of wiry hair and the undercoat of fine woolly hair make these dogs much better duck dogs. They certainly are hardier in both cold water and cold weather. They may perhaps be equal to a golden retriever in this respect, but certainly not the equivalent of a Labrador or a Chessy. But then, it's likely that nothing will equal the Chessy in this department.

There is no doubt that most of the wire-haired versatile dogs have a deep love for water, perhaps equal to that of any retriever. They are good, strong swimmers. Many will also leap into the water after a duck with a fury that would do credit to a Labrador.

This does not mean that these breeds are as good, let alone better, for duck retrieving than retrievers. They are not.

For example, it's very difficult to teach them how to take a line for a blind retrieve. This should be of no surprise to anyone. After all, they have been bred to show independence; to go out on their own and search for birds. To suddenly ask them to forget all this and handle like a Lab, who is always told what to do, would be too much.

But on small wetlands, where they can mark most of the birds that fall, the wire-haired versatile dogs can be as good a duck dog as any of us wants. That's certainly true in my case. I don't even own a retriever now. Most of my duck hunting is confined to puddle ducks —mallards, woodies, and the occasional black—on beaver ponds. I also get in a little open-water shooting late in the season for divers— bluebills, goldeneyes, and buffleheads.

For one type of duck shooting, my German wirehaired pointer is all I need. For the other, I don't need a dog at all. I use the boat to retrieve my birds.

This perhaps brings out another point. When should you get a retriever? For this, I have kind of a stock answer—when you want one and your wife will let you keep it. This is not meant to be as facetious as it sounds. I feel that a man should own a gun dog for reasons aside from the dog's being useful.

But perhaps more to the point is the following formula:

If you are a shotgunner who divides most of his hunting time be- tween upland bird shooting and waterfowling, and you can keep two or more dogs, you'd be wise to have a bird dog and a retriever. On the other hand, if you can keep only one dog, the choice would depend on the type of hunting you do most. If 50 percent or more of your hunting is for ducks in marshes, then you need a retriever. If it's less than 50 percent and the rest is made up by upland game gunning, then you may be better off with one of the European versatile hunt- ing dogs, a springer, or an American water spaniel. This is particularly true if most of your waterfowl gunning is on small wetlands during the early season, when the water is still warm and air temperatures are moderate.

On the other hand, if most of your waterfowling is for geese on the Maryland corn stubbles or for sea ducks and divers on open water, you really don't need a retriever at all. A dog in a boat can be a nuisance, and a boat is a better tool in retrieving lightly crippled ducks on open water than any dog. A lightly crippled diving duck can generally outswim and outdive any retriever going.

Wounded geese never seem to make much of an effort to hide. A dogless hunter generally has no problem finding them. This, of course, doesn't mean that you can't take your dog on a goose hunt. We do all the time. It simply means that a dog is not absolutely needed unless you're hunting geese in a marsh and have no boat.

But then, of course, we've gone right around in a circle to our earlier tenet that a dog brings new dimensions to the sport of hunting.

That's why we take ours. The day that our German wirehair retrieved 36 geese—all that our party shot—in a day on the desolate coastline of Hudson Bay will never be forgotten. It was the dog's determination and hard work that made the day so memorable. How these geese were shot is all but forgotten.

That's what hunting with a retriever is all about.

7

Boats for Wildfowling

Malcolm Hart

V OLUMES OF LITERATURE have been devoted to such topics as duck guns, decoys, duck calls and calling, blinds, and, of course, duck hunting techniques. Yet relatively little has been written on boats for duck hunting. This seems a major oversight, for aside from gunning small potholes on the prairies, the boat is as essential a piece of equipment as a rig of decoys.

During the market hunting years of the past century, duck hunting was big business. An entire flotilla of highly specialized boats was developed by professional wildfowlers, with such romantic names as Barnegat Bay sneakbox, Merrymeeting Bay grass boat, sink box, and skull boat. Today, these highly specialized duck boats play a much smaller role in waterfowling. Some, like the sink box, have been outlawed by the Migratory Birds Treaty Act because they were too lethal. Others were too specialized.

Before going into the subject in more detail, perhaps we should define what a duck boat is. To some hunters, a "duck boat" means any boat used for waterfowling. But this is not correct. Duck boats are specialized boats, developed and used exclusively for waterfowl-

Duck boats are craft developed especially for wildfowling.

ing. By this definition, any of the prams, runabouts, cartoppers, or even airboats that are frequently used by waterfowlers are not "duck boats". They might correctly be called "boats for duck hunting".

Much of our waterfowling today does not require a highly specialized craft, because the boat is, more often than not, used simply as a means of transportation across the marsh to the blind. The boat is then hidden in nearby reeds and not used until it's time to head home. In some cases the boat might also be used to retrieve downed ducks.

If you use the boat for gunning, a specialized design might be needed. But not always. For example, duck hunters on the Great Lakes frequently use a floating blind that is nothing more than a grassed-in or camouflaged frame. The blind is anchored out on the shooting ground. The hunters simply run a boat into the blind, tie it up inside, and use the boat as a shooting platform.

For this purpose, any conventional runabout or cartopper is a good choice. Actually, some of today's punts, prams, and johnboats can make fair duck hunting boats to shoot from, if painted a dull color and grassed-in. But their real advantage comes in being more versatile. They can be used during the off-season for other water-based forms of recreation such as fishing or even family boating. The true duck boats, on the other hand, are suitable only for duck hunting.

Let's go into the components of a good, serviceable boat for duck hunting. There are several. And unfortunately, there is no single boat that will fill the bill under all duck hunting conditions.

If you are going out on big water—a saltwater bay or the shores and marshes of a large lake—where the seas can build up, a stout boat with plenty of freeboard is a must. It should be able to carry two men and a dog easily without submerging the Plimsoll or load-line mark. It should also be able to accommodate a motor of at least 10 horsepower. For this, a 14-foot length is about minimum.

For small ponds, marshes, and rivers, a smaller and lighter boat is adequate. Such waters will not be rough. But again, the boat should be able to accommodate two men and a dog easily. It should also take a motor of up to 5 horsepower. A 10-foot boat may be big enough. Since the craft will be used in shallow or reedy water where it may have to be poled or even dragged, it should be fairly flat-bottomed. The boat should be easy to maneuver and handle, because such waters as beaver ponds tend to harbor many partially sub-merged logs. If the boat will be used for jump-shooting, it should also be easy to row.

The material from which the boat is made is relatively unimpor-tant as far as the effectiveness of the craft is concerned. Wood is still a good boat-building material, but it is almost impossible to buy a light wooden boat today. This means making one yourself, or having it made. On top of this, the maintenance of a wooden boat is con-siderable. If the boat is out of water for any considerable length of time, the wood tends to shrink and the boat leaks. For these two reasons, I don't view wooden boats as the best choice for duck hunting.

This "Old Town" duck boat is one of the few that is made commercially.

Aluminum can make a good, light boat for duck hunting, but in its natural color it's worse than useless. It is impossible to camouflage a natural aluminum boat well enough, even where vegetation is very thick. Ducks can see it a long way off. Thus, an aluminum boat for hunting wildfowl must be painted a dull-grass or camouflage color.

Unfortunately, aluminum also tends to be somewhat noisy. This is something of a handicap for both duck hunting and fishing. There are aluminum boats available that have been spray-painted on the interior with a rubber-based material that makes the craft quieter, but again such treatment adds a great deal of weight to the boat.

Fiberglass is a good choice for a duck boat. It may not be able to withstand as much pounding against rocks or logs as aluminum, but this is a relatively minor criticism. Getting a fiberglass cartopper is no problem. The only unfortunate thing is that fiberglass tends to be a bit too shiny. On sunny days, it can flare ducks. However, maintenance on a fiberglass boat is almost nil, and that's a fine feature indeed.

The color of a duck hunting boat is, of course, extremely important. In fact, the only acceptable colors are dark to mid-green, dark brown, or khaki. These can be camouflaged relatively easily with vegetation. Brightly colored boats or natural aluminum are very poor choices. The best color for a duck boat is a camouflage, such as is found on canvas used for military purposes. Fortunately, many manufacturers of aluminum boats and canoes are now offering their craft in duck hunting colors, to cash in on this specialized market.

The second criterion for color is that it not be shiny. A dull finish is definitely best. It should not glare, even in sunlight.

To be perfectly serviceable, a duck boat must be rigged with two anchors; one in the stern, the other in the bow. Both anchors should be fairly substantial, so that the boat can be kept from swinging about. I also find a couple of sheets of canvas very handy. These can be spread over the boat, breaking its outline and covering the motor. Thus the craft is less conspicuous in the reeds or blind, or even when being rowed while jump-shooting. The canvas also keeps a great deal of water out of the boat on rainy days.

But what about the specialist duck boats? These are, of course, the best choice—in fact, the only choice—for some types of duck hunting. The serious wildfowler should consider no other kind of craft. The choice of a duck boat is, of course, determined by the type of wildfowling.

Any dull-colored cartopper or runabout can be used for duck hunting.

A duck boat meant for general duck hunting must get the hunter to the shooting ground comfortably and safely. Then it must help to hide the hunter there, and at the same time offer a fair amount of protection from wind and rain. It must also, of course, be easy and safe to shoot from. On top of this, it should be able to carry two men, a dog, and a pile of duck decoys with a fair degree of comfort and safety.

This means that a duck boat must have such features as a full deck, to make it more seaworthy in rough waters. The deck also helps to keep out wind and rain; to keep you warm and dry. In fact, a fully decked boat with a catalytic heater, or even better a propane heater, will keep you snug even when the temperature plummets close to freezing and the north wind is whistling more than just a Yankee version of Dixie.

The deck, of course, also helps to hide the gunner. But for camouflage purposes, the boat's profile is very important. It should be as low as possible. The sides should be low and the deck curved so that when the boat is run into a reedbed, the grass is pushed out and over the boat. The sloping slides and curved deck also, of course, help to shed rain and surf much better.

The boat should be fairly light so that you can push it into the reeds with oars or paddles. And, of course, it must be light enough to trailer well, even with a pile of decoys inside. A one-man duck

The layout boat is commonly used for diver duck gunning.

boat shouldn't weigh much over 120 or 130 pounds. Such a boat can be cartopped easily. A two-man boat shouldn't go more than 200 pounds.

Another necessary feature is a 3-inch coaming around the cockpit. This, again, makes the boat safer and more seaworthy in stormy waters. It also helps to keep waves from washing over the deck into the boat. Ideally, the cockpit should have hatches which can be closed when the boat is moored or stored outside, so that rain and snow can't get in. The hatches should have hasps to padlock the boat so decoys and other gear aren't stolen.

The hull should be flat, so the boat planes when pushed at a fairly good clip. A flat bottom on a duck boat has other virtues. It is good in shallow water, and it slides fairly well over grass and mud.

If the duck boat is made of wood, fiberglass the bottom, even at the expense of the extra weight, to protect the wood from rocks and ice. The fiberglassing should come up the sides, a good 6 inches above the water line.

The color of any duck boat must be drab (except one meant for gunning on ice flows, which should then be white). The finish should be flat to avoid glare.

The old-time wildfowlers of the Atlantic coast invented and used a whole fleet of specialized duck boats. These included such craft as big cabin johnboats, which actually accommodated hunters for several days at a time. Then there were assorted gunning barges, other johnboats, and dories of various kinds. Sneakboxes of one sort or another were also used. And most of our commercial duck boats are patterned after sneakboxes.

Canoes can be useful for jump-shooting ducks on streams and rivers.

Coffin boxes, in which the gunner laid on his back (he sat up to shoot), were also popular. These were generally towed to the gunning area and anchored there. Their low profile made them very effective for diving ducks and sea ducks. Indeed, coffin boxes are still used by some gunners.

The most specialized of duck boats were the sculling boats, propelled by a single sculling oar in the stern of the craft. Sculling is a form of jump-shooting, and is still practised to some extent by wildfowlers along the Atlantic seaboard.

Canoes are also used by some waterfowlers on small marshes and beaver ponds, but their real forte lies in jump-shooting ducks on streams and rivers. This is becoming an increasingly popular way to hunt dabbling ducks. Any canoe can be used for this, but, again, it should be painted a drab color and perhaps even grassed or brushed in a little for maximum effectiveness.

The very wide-beamed canoes such as the Sportspal are good for this type of waterfowling, if the current isn't too fast. They are stable enough that a dog can even work out of them.

The pirogue is still used by waterfowlers in the bayous and marshes of Louisiana. The original pirogue was a form of dugout canoe, made from a single log. But modern-day pirogues are crafted of plywood or even fiberglass. They are excellent for shallow marshes. They can also be used for jump-shooting ducks on channels and bayous, much like a canoe.

Another type of duck hunting craft used to transport hunters to and from blinds in shallow swamps and marshes is the airboat. Certainly an airboat can go where no other form of craft can follow. Airboats are used mostly in Florida, but they've also been used by biologists in the northern states and provinces to chase down molting, flightless ducks for banding.

The subject of duck boats is a fascinating one. In the old days, with long seasons and no bag limits, there was a need for specialized duck boats. That's why they sprang up. Today our need is much less intense, and many of the old duck boats are seldom seen.

Every autumn I read several stories about duck hunters drowning. The stories make me wonder how many hunters meet an untimely death in this manner. I suspect that the number is greater than we think.

Actually, in late season the unfortunate duck hunter who falls overboard runs two hazards. One is drowning. The other is what medical men call immersion hypothermia, or lowering of the body temperature by external cold. In this case, the culprit is freezing cold water.

It has been calculated that a man falling into water of about 32° F has about 15 minutes before cold and exhaustion set in. Since salt water is about 30° F during late fall or winter, a sea duck hunter wouldn't have that long to live overboard. It's possible that warm duck hunting clothes may prolong the exhaustion a little, but what's a few minutes? Once your body temperature becomes lowered by 20 degrees, your chips have been cashed in.

If you ever have a hunting partner fall overboard in cold water, get him out of the water and out of his clothes as soon as possible. Lend him some of your dry stuff, even your underwear. Build a fire, or even better two small fires—one in front and the other in back. If there is no firewood, use the gas from your outboard gas tank. Wring out his wet clothes and dry them over the fire.

Most duck hunters drown because they don't wear life preservers, and at the same time they are heavily clothed. Their pockets are frequently even loaded with shot shells. The old-style life preservers are too bulky to shoot with, but the new ones made especially for canoeists are not. Even better are the new flotation duck-hunting jackets. These are not only warm, but keep you afloat, without being bulkier than any other duck hunting jacket.

One other tip. Don't keep your shells in your pocket. I have a canvas bag for that which I hang in the blind or keep in the bottom of the boat. If I wade out where I can't see the bottom, I push my boat ahead of me in case there's a sudden drop-off, or I use a wading staff such as is used by trout fishermen for wading streams. Actually that's what I bought mine for originally, but it now serves a dual purpose. Being of Scottish ancestry, I find that kind of thrift rather appealing.

But the biggest thrift, of course, is saving your life. You only have one to lose.

8

The Lure of the Decoy

Norman Strung

COAXING WILDFOWL into gun range through the use of decoys is very special sport. The decoy hunter, the artist among outdoorsmen, creates an imitation of nature so well-wrought that a wise wild bird is made to seek the company of patent fakes. It is not, however, simple sport. No other form of hunting requires more knowledge, dedication, or patience; or involves so many variables—vagaries of migrations, winds, whims of the birds themselves, and weather.

If it sounds like you're opting for no small amout of work when you become a decoy hunter, you're right. But the rewards of the sport are on par with the investment. You become what you do—a part of the marsh and the wings that whisper above.

Selecting Your First Decoys

A decoy spread can come from any number of sources. You can make your own, stumble across a few bags of stool in a relative's

Luring ducks within shooting range is, to many, the epitome of wildfowling.

attic, buy someone else's rig, or purchase brand new blocks. Making your own decoys is an exercise I strongly endorse, but if you're a beginner, I'd recommend some other route. Decoy construction has subtleties you'll only appreciate after long hours in the marsh. Without knowledge of those subtleties, you'll likely turn out inferior stool.

Your first decoys then, should be someone else's. When buying either second-hand or new blocks, there's a whole raft of things to keep in mind.

Duck decoys, like ducks, are divided into two categories: diving duck models and puddle duck types. In nature, puddle ducks and diving ducks seldom mix. Their habits, food preferences, and migratory routes keep them apart. Within each group, however, species mix quite freely. Teal are ready companions to a flock of feeding mallards, and canvasbacks regularly mix with rafts of scaup. So the first consideration when selecting stool is that they all be of the same type—either divers or puddlers. The type you choose should fit into your hunting plans. If most of the hunting in your area is around marshes, pick puddlers. If there are vast stretches of open water, choose divers.

Because species mix freely within the limits of type, it's fine to select one species of duck decoy. In fact, most professional rigs you'll run across will have one species in plain majority, with perhaps one or two blocks of a different species, as "confidence" decoys, to add a touch of realism. On the Atlantic Flyway, black ducks are the preferred puddler decoys. Central and Mississippi Flyway gunners favor mallards; and on the Pacific Flyway, it's a toss-up between mallards and pintails. Scaup are close to universal in their use as a diver decoy.

Divers and puddlers exhibit yet another difference. Puddlers are usually found in small groups; divers in large rafts. A dozen to 18 decoys will thus be a good spread for puddlers. If you're rigging for divers, I'd put an acceptable minimum at 30, with the outer limits determined only by your ambition. When hunting over open water from a large tender with five other gunners, I've set up to 250 broadbill.

Decoy appearance and construction are important too. A long and close relationship with the products of both commercial manufacturers and home craftsmen has demonstrated that there's a wide difference of opinion about what a duck looks like. My experience has indicated that ducks and geese don't really care, *so long as all the decoys match*. I've hunted over home-made blocks that looked like they were carved with an axe. I've also hunted over rigs carefully fashioned with intricate feather detail. In all candor, the lovingly-hewn decoys seemed to interest more ducks, especially at that moment of truth when the wings either cup, or the birds flare. But both rigs were far better attractors than piecemeal spreads I've encountered —a variety of block shapes, painting patterns, and sizes gleaned from old attics, spring shorelines, and mantles.

Although ducks and geese don't especially care about certain construction features, you will when you're afield. It's important that decoys be self-righting; that is, keel-weighted, so they'll turn upright when thrown into place, or tipped over by a strong wind. I also favor low-profile stool, that are wide at their base. This conformation discourages tipping over and rocking (something that never happens with real, live ducks). Another thing I look for in a truly fine decoy is a breast that swells above the waterline. This design feature dampens the unnatural, frantic yawing that will occur with a strong tide or river current. It also deters ice-buildup in bitter weather, a phenomenon you're bound to encounter if you get the least bit serious about waterfowling. "The worse the weather, the better the gunning" is a provable rule-of-thumb.

While I can get pretty lyrical about owning and using handmade stool of cork, hollowed pine, or cedar, unless you've got a duckboat, you'll find toting all that weight across a marsh a literal and figurative pain in the neck. Today's average duck hunter needs mobility as much as a full load of No. 4's, and in that department, the lightness of styrofoam or molded plastic decoys excels. Pleasantly enough in these days of economic uncertainty, they're also the cheapest decoys to buy (with the exception of papier-mâché, which simply will not stand up, even to gentle hands and weather).

The final agonizing decision you'll have to make when choosing a rig of any sort, is whether to buy oversize or life-size decoys. An oversize duck decoy is roughly twice the volume of a natural-size decoy, the correct assumption being that real ducks can spot the big decoys from farther away.

However, ducks look for a lot of company. Undeniably, the more decoys you have out, the more ducks you'll attract. Oversize decoys limit the total numbers of blocks you can lug around. I much prefer to carry as many natural-sized stool as I can pack, and satisfy the "distance" appeal with a few Canada goose decoys.

Rigging Decoys

The destruction that wind and weather can wreak upon a decoy line is one of the subtleties of wildfowling. When you see tarred, 80-pound-test line chewed through in five hours by a modest 20-mile-an-hour wind and a 1-pound decoy, you can hardly help but be humbled by the power of natural forces. I have yet to find the perfect decoy line, knot, and anchoring system. But my best answer so far is 200-pound-test nylon parachute cord, threaded twice through the decoy's eyelet, and tied off 6 inches below the eyelet with a bowline knot. Observe the same procedure on the anchor end of the decoy. Burn the end of the cord so it creates a knob of plastic that also resists slipping the knot. And choose the cord in a color that matches the bottom you'll be hunting over. Be sure to check the condition of your knots each time you set your stool.

The most practical decoy anchor is made of a fist-sized ring of heavy wire cast in a mushroom-shaped hunk of lead. This type of anchor digs into the bottom as it's worked by the wind, and slips over the head of the decoy to hold the wrapping firm.

Decoy Placement Patterns

Setting an attractive rig, or "stooling out" as fowlers of a bygone era called it, requires cognizance of a number of factors. First, there's the type of duck you're hunting. A workable puddler rig is set in a very different pattern from a diver rig.

Generally, puddler duck hunting is a shore-blind proposition.

Big spreads of decoys are needed for diving duck gunning.

Spend a lot of time looking over a prospective marsh before you ever toss a decoy, and identify favored feeding and resting areas. When you're sure a place is attractive to birds, look for some sort of natural shelter from wind and waves, with a shoal bottom, from 6 inches to 3 feet deep. Ideal spots are coves, cuts, sloughs, river backwaters, and tide- or rain-flooded meadows. Stay away from large expanses of open water; that's diving duck territory.

Next, choose your blind site considering wind and camouflage. Even though a flat-grass hay meadow might have mallards galore, you'd be foolish to set up a brand new blind there and expect to hunt from it the same day. It takes time for birds to become accustomed to new features of the terrain. If you're building a blind to be hunted from that day, select, instead, a place with natural cover. Waist-high willows, cattails, bullrush or beach plum are ideal. Don't, however, go overboard when sizing up cover. Tall, dense vegetation shies birds away, as they come to learn that hunters can easily hide there. Build your blind out of vegetation native to the area. But don't take materials from the immediate blind site. Leave it natural-looking with plenty of standing cover, even to the point of sticking to a narrow path as you enter and leave the blind.

The blind should be situated so the wind is blowing from a direction within a half circle, the 90-degree mark of the circle falling squarely in the middle of your back. There is an old saying that a man who hunts with the wind on his face should be hunting with someone else. And I've found this true 95 percent of the time.

My favorite wind position is 45 degrees from my back, right or left. This leaves incoming birds looking at natural marsh rather than the hole in my 12 bore. (Ducks always land into the wind.)

The pattern you set your decoys in is determined by weather conditions. When winds are down and temperatures moderate, set the stool in a "C" configuration, with the back of the "C" close to shore and the legs leading away from shore. Keep the decoys 3 to 6 feet apart, and in loose groups of two to five blocks. If all things go well, most of the ducks should land in the center of the "C", so keep this area in good gun range.

The "C" pattern imitates what puddle ducks do in relatively pleasant weather; they spread out and loll about. When the wind blows hard and temperatures plummet, however, puddlers bunch up in a tight group to take advantage of the wind- and wave-breaking effects of each others' bodies.

Under these conditions, the best decoy pattern is an "I" shape, leading away from a lee shore. Space the decoys closely—1 to 2 feet apart. Again, set them in groups of two to five birds, with open water between each group. Incoming waterfowl will tend to land in these holes, usually choosing the one closest to the center of the "I".

Setting a shore rig for diving ducks involves some of the same rules as those prescribed for puddlers. Watch for areas of bird activity, around a spot where you can construct a natural-looking hide, that affords some degree of protection from the elements. But there the similarity ends. You've got to set up on open water for diving ducks; a place that is approachable from a large expanse of water. Unlike puddle ducks, divers are most reluctant to pass over any land mass.

By far the best location for a diving duck shoot is on a point jutting out into a lake or bay. With water on three sides, it's easy to engineer a spread that offers over-the-water access and egress. The most attractive set to a diving duck will be one that has him looking at open water as he attempts to land.

For this reason, I like to find a point with a crosswind blowing from a quadrant between 45 and 0 degrees to my back, right or left. Although such a wind might tend to kick up a chop, the bars leading off points usually dampen heavy breakers. So it's still possible to find relatively calm water even in a crosswind. Then, too, divers aren't quite so bothered by rough water as puddlers are.

In such a situation, no decoy patterning is more effective than the old market gunners' "fish hook". This configuration assumes a fish hook or tadpole shape, with the tail of the hook leading seaward.

Divers have a proclivity to follow leads and lines—the edge of a sheet of ice, the edge where shoals drop off into deep water, conflicting lines of tidal currents, and so forth. The "tail" of the fish hook pattern will lead the birds into your spread, and it can be set so it stretches well out to sea and beyond gun range. Ducks will pick it up and follow it to the main body of decoys, usually landing inside the bend of the hook.

Shore gunning for diving ducks depends a lot on weather. As a rule, you'll find the hottest action in the worst weather—storms, cold, and ice. It takes these kinds of conditions to drive the birds to protection afforded by land masses.

For this reason, no hunting technique is so regularly productive as "open water" or "layout gunning" when you're after the diving species.

This form of wildfowling involves the use of a low-profile flat-bottomed boat, painted either gray to match the water, or white when there is ice around.

Under the watchful eye of a larger tending craft, the layout boat is anchored near a popular feeding or resting area, or along one of those edges the birds love to follow. Decoys are rigged either in a fish hook pattern, or a "V", with the boat at the apex of the "V" or at the bend of the fish hook.

Because divers are so attuned to the safety afforded by open water, they come to this kind of rig freely, and pay no attention to the layout boat whatsoever, so long as the hunter stays out of sight. It's cold sport, requiring extensive equipment, and involves real danger. But no other form of bird hunting, upland or wetland, packs the pure action that comes with a lay-out rig. Given today's liberal limits on divers (most notably broadbills), it's possible and probable for four gunners, taking turns, to shoot between 20 and 30 birds.

While that kind of excitement provides a tangible reward for the decoy hunter's investment, you won't find shooting like that every day you go out. Even after you've slogged enough miles through marsh mud to classify as an expert, there will be many days when you'll witness only two or three tolls; and if you shoot as well as I do, will go home empty-handed.

But never empty-minded. I cannot think of one day spent hunting over decoys that I didn't enjoy. Beauty abounds on the marsh, from the explosion of sunrise to the shimmering reflection of your stool on a still pond, and in this respect, wildfowling has no seasons and no limits.

Wings from previously bagged snow geese are favorite goose decoys among the Indians.

9

Calling Wildfowl

Burton J. Myers

T H E F I R S T T A S K a prospective caller faces is selection of a call. Proper selection of that first call is the cornerstone upon which future calling success depends; no small task, considering the myriad of calls that now flood the market.

Almost all of the duck calls found on the shelves of sporting goods stores today are mallard calls, designed to imitate the voice of a talkative hen mallard. With a few possible exceptions, most puddle ducks will respond to a well blown mallard call. Although rare, there are times when this same call has also been known to pull in geese and diving ducks.

Surprising as it may seem, duck calls weren't in common use at the beginning of this century. Although no one knows for certain, it's widely accepted as fact that a Frenchman by the name of Glodo was the father of the modern call. Indeed, the calls which he crafted around the turn of the century are prized pieces of wildfowling memorabilia on today's collector's market.

From his original concept, two slightly different types of calls emerged, which are generally referred to as the Arkansas call and

The duck call is essentially a reeded instrument which the hunter must learn to "play".

the Louisiana call. But I'll pick this up later. Before going into these differences, it's important to understand the mechanics of a call (which is, in fact, a reeded musical instrument).

The call is composed of five basic parts: the barrel which channels the sound towards the keg; the keg which fits into the barrel and holds the inner working parts; the trough which acts as a sound chamber; the reed; and the wedge which holds the reed in place.

In the Arkansas call, the keg and trough are formed from one piece; while in the Louisiana call, each is separate. There is, however, one other major difference between the two—the size of the opening at the end of the keg. In the Louisiana call, there tends to be a fairly large opening which results in a loud, raucous high-pitched call that carries for a considerable distance. In the Arkansas call, this hole tends to be somewhat smaller, resulting in a low-pitched call with more mellow tones. While the latter call is often more pleasing to the ear, it doesn't carry well across vast distances.

The experienced caller probably has one or more of each strung on a cord around his neck as he heads out into the marsh. Experience has taught him that conditions change—weather in particular—and ducks will often react differently from day to day to various calls.

The high-pitched, far-reaching Louisiana call might be better used on a blustery, rainy day when it takes a noisy call to be heard by distant passing birds. On the other hand, when the air is dead calm and the slightest of sounds seems to echo in a waterfowler's ears, the raucous sound of a Louisiana call might frighten rather than attract passing birds. At such times, the more subdued tones of the Arkansas call would probably be more suitable.

While you may think I've gotten a little off-track on the subject of selecting a first duck call, it's important to know these differences before venturing to your local sporting goods dealer. If you frequent big, wide-open marshes, you'll want to concentrate your selection on the Louisiana calls, with their greater volume. On the other hand, if you hunt backwoods potholes and beaver ponds, you'd probably be better off selecting one of the Arkansas type.

Now that you know what to look for, your next step is the selection of your call.

Begin by asking to see a selection of calls by various manufacturers in the style you have chosen. Nothing less than three will do. If the store doesn't have at least that many, shop somewhere else. You can't choose wisely if you don't have a good selection to start with. Give each call a serious workout and decide which one comes closest to producing a tone which satisfies your expectations and which seems comfortable to blow.

Now ask to see a half dozen or more identical calls to the one which you've just selected, and give each of these a good workout. You'll be surprised to find that each one has a slightly different tone. The reason for this is differences in tuning, and in the structure of the wood from which the calls were crafted.

If you're inclined to think that all of these shenanigans aren't necessary, you're wrong. I've watched some of the best callers I know go through more than two dozen calls before deciding on one. Of course, the stores where they shop have become accustomed to these actions; accept them without questions; and carry a small bottle of disinfectant under the counter to clean all unpurchased calls after each session.

Now that you've purchased your call, it's time to make a second purchase—a good duck calling instruction record or tape cassette. For most beginners, this is almost as important as the purchase of the call.

Produced by various duck call manufacturers, these duck calling instruction aides are a godsend to the beginning caller who cannot take advantage of the expertise of a successful, seasoned caller for

Duck calls are essentially composed of three parts—a barrel, a reed, and a wedge.

help. These recordings provide the neophyte caller with the sound of "duck talk" at its best. With practice, a caller should be able to reproduce similar calls of his own.

Yet notice that I said similar; not exactly alike. No two callers will ever produce identical sounds, even on the same duck call. But since no two ducks sound exactly alike either, slight variations in pitch between different callers doesn't alarm the birds. More important than the degree of pitch of a call, however, is the consistency of its user. Herein lies the biggest difference between the sound of an experienced caller and a newcomer to the game. The sound produced by the veteran could be likened to the voice of a church elder in the Sunday choir; the newcomer's call to that of a teenager in a back pew, whose voice falters back and forth between that of a tenor and a baritone. It only takes one off-key note in an otherwise flawless performance to send incoming birds cartwheeling over each other as they beat a frenzied retreat.

Keeping this in mind, it's now time to seek a secluded spot and begin practising. As you'll soon learn, any spot where you practice soon becomes secluded.

While there are probably no less than a dozen various calls a wildfowler could utilize, most hunters would be wise to concentrate on the four basic calls: the highball, the greeting call, the feeding chuckle, and the comeback call.

The most useful of the four, and the simplest call to make, is the highball. This call is used to attract the attention of distant passing birds.

Begin by placing the keg of the call, where it joins the barrel, firmly between the base of the thumb and index finger. When relaxed, the remaining three fingers should form a shallow cup over the opening.

Now place the opening of the barrel firmly against the upper lip, so that it covers about half of the opening. The position of the call against the upper lip never changes, since only your lower lip and jaw are movable. The lower lip is pressed against the bottom rim of the barrel, so that any air which escapes must pass through the call.

Now, say the word "quaCK" without using your tongue. Notice that when doing so your diaphragm will contract. Repeat this again, only midway through the "quaCK" use the three fingers of the cup to seal off the opening in the keg and trap the escaping sound. The result should be a clear, crisp sound.

Once you've mastered this, make five successive calls in a row, starting loud and finishing low over a three- or four-second interval, with each "quaCK" a little shorter than the one which preceded it. Sort of, "quaaaaaCK, quaaaaCK, quaaaCK, quaaCK, quaCK." You've just blown the highball.

Next, learn the greeting call, which is used when the ducks are approaching and close enough to be spotted by feeding ducks represented by your decoys. In essence, it's little more than a speeded-up highball, but less sharp and with the quacks blending in to each other.

Now, with the ducks beginning to cup their wings, it's time to break into the feeding chuckle. This is performed by saying the words "tucka, tucka, tucka" over and over again. When doing so, your tongue should flap back and forth over the opening.

Should the ducks be a little nervous and swing away from your blocks for another pass, it's time to break into the comeback call. It is similar again to the highball, but lower and more pleading, with the first few quacks more drawn out.

Learning to blow a duck call is no different than learning to play any other musical instrument. It takes practice and plenty of it to become good. However, all of this practice becomes pointless, if sooner or later you don't put your skills to the test in front of a critical audience, in this case the ducks themselves. Play the wrong note to some of these wary critics and you'll find yourself playing to an empty marsh.

If, after a few practice sessions alternately blowing and listening to your recording, you've convinced yourself that you are capable of producing a reasonable facsimile of the calls on your record, it's time to head out into the marsh.

Being able to blow a duck call and being able to call ducks may seem like the same thing. But to the veteran waterfowler, there is indeed a big difference. Many callers have mastered the mechanics of blowing a duck call, but far fewer know when and when not to blow it. Few duck hunters have the ability to identify and interpret the behavior of birds on the wing. Those who do are the good callers.

Beyond this group is an even smaller, elite group of callers—masters at the craft. Besides having the ability to perform a flawless, awe-inspiring display of duck talk and being able to think like a duck, they add that little bit of uncanny wildfowling savvy that can make the difference between being two birds shy and bringing home a full count.

The average weekend waterfowler isn't likely to ever achieve the lofty status of "elite". He or she doesn't have enough day-to-day contact with birds. The few such callers with whom I've had the honor of sharing a blind were all professional guides, whose abilities had been honed to a fine edge by more than a score of seasons in the marsh. While it's unlikely you'll ever become a master caller, a few of the tricks they use could help to put roast wildfowl on your table.

As I've mentioned, calling ducks requires that a fowler know when to use a call and when to leave it alone. The basic rule-of-thumb is to call only as much as is necessary and no more. Excess calling only increases the chance of making that one off-key note, which is often all that is needed to turn even the greenest of birds away from your spread. When the birds are coming your way, stop calling; when they show the slightest sign of drifting off, start calling again.

On your first few attempts, stick to the highball. Use it to attract the attention of passing birds. When you think they've got your spread spotted, stop calling and depend on your decoys to do their thing. Calling errors are easily disguised by distance and the closer the birds come, the more chancy calling becomes.

A word of caution at this point. Don't nullify the effect of your calling by blowing directly at the birds. By doing so, you tend to make it easier for birds to pinpoint the source of all the commotion (in this case, you). Call into your blind, at the floorboards of your boat, or towards the ground. This tends to make the sound echo or bounce. All the calling in the world won't do you a bit of good once your "cover", so to speak, is blown.

Next to the highball the feeding chuckle is the waterfowler's most useful call. It's a low-key call used when the birds are at close quarters. Wisely used, it brings shortstopping puddlers that last few yards that puts them in range. In heavily gunned areas, puddlers often develop the infuriating habit of landing 40 or 50 yards outside of a spread to survey the situation. A relaxed feeding chuckle will often allay their fears, and the birds will drop their guard and paddle right in.

The greeting call is used once the birds have shown an interest in your spread and are close enough to be seen by birds on the water. Using this call adds a natural order to the series and tends to excite the birds.

The comeback call, a pleading highball, is particularly effective with wary birds like the black duck, and is often sufficient to convince the birds to have one more look. A trick often used by veteran callers in conjuction with this call is to splash water. Doing so when the birds have their backs turned simulates the ripples created by feeding dabblers, so that when the birds return it's to a more life-like spread.

Another trick often used by good callers is to have two hunters use their calls at the same time, creating an effect of a multitude of happily feeding birds. Easy does it though! When the birds get in close, rely on one caller. Don't fall into the competition pitfall that sets one caller against the other. The only winners in such competitions are the ducks.

Last, but not least, learn to identify ducks on the wing and to interpret their behavior. You should know that a wavering head on a passing bird means it is looking for company; and those high straight-flying formations aren't likely to pay the slightest heed to your finest efforts.

It also pays to know that blacks are less talkative than the gabby mallard, and that a low-key performance would probably be more

Pintail whistles are a form of specialized duck call.

appropriate when birds of that feather are on the wing. Teal talk almost as much as mallards, but as befits their smaller size, their voice isn't nearly as loud as a mallard's. Pintails and widgeon, although drawn by the sound of a mallard call, don't quack. They whistle, a sound easily duplicated by a dog whistle with its bead removed.

As I have said, almost all puddle ducks will respond to a mallard call. Almost all. Like everything else in waterfowling, there are no hard and fast rules. The magnificent wood duck is one of the exceptions. I've never seen it mentioned in any of the duck calling articles I've read, but my experience in the field has led me to the conclusion that the woodie doesn't respond particularly well to the sound of a babbling mallard. Orvis markets a wood duck call. To my knowledge it is the only company that manufactures such a call.

What about caring for your calls? You wouldn't abuse a good violin by leaving it in a damp closet nor play with its carefully tuned strings. Calls require reasonable care if they are to perform up to snuff.

String calls on a lanyard tied around your neck, not in your pocket with cookie crumbs and tobacco strands. And unless you're an expert, leave the reeds alone. The Mylar reeds found in most modern calls tend to take a set and can easily be damaged by tinkering hands. If for some reason your call fails to work properly, take advantage of the services offered by almost all call manufacturers and send it back, to be retuned at the factory by the call makers.

If, as occasionally happens, your call becomes waterlogged, let it dry slowly in a corner away from intense heat. Although not a problem with the highly popular hard-rubber calls produced by Olt, the traditional wooden call could crack if dried too fast.

Until now we've discussed only duck calls. But ducks are far from our only North American waterfowl species. The wise wildfowler always prepares for the unexpected, which often comes as an impromptu appearance by a gaggle of geese. No matter which flyway you frequent, there's always the chance of seeing geese on the wing— a thrilling, spine-tingling event. The geese probably won't come in if you're not geared up with goose decoys, but if you have and know how to use a goose call, there's a chance that you could draw the birds in for a closer look and a quick shot.

Goose calls are easier to use than duck calls, because a hunter need only know one or two basic notes. Remember that feeding geese call sparingly when on the ground (unlike their brethren in the

Some wildfowlers can call without the aid of a mechanical call.

sky), and pick up their gabble as a flock filters down amongst them.

Select a call to match the predominant species you see—Canadas, specklebellies or, snows—though you can't go wrong with the two-note honk of the Canada, the wary royalty of the goose kingdom.

Out of the marsh, there are calling contests. Calling for the ears of judges instead of waterfowl is becoming an increasingly popular event throughout the United States and Canada. But nowhere does it reach such peaks of excitement as in Stuttgart, Arkansas, for a week in early December, when the town becomes alive with hopeful callers from all over the continent. Contestants display their ability before three judges, who can't see the identity of individual callers. A caller is generally required to display an example of a highball, greeting call, comeback call, and feeding chuckle, and to follow this up with a complete performance containing all four calls in a natural sequence.

The ability to blow a duck call does not a duck caller make. But don't be disillusioned into thinking that the winners of such contests aren't superb callers of ducks. Most were good long before they ever entered calling competitions, and most are more than willing to give short, off-the-cuff lessons in the parking lot between heats in competition.

No, calling isn't easy to learn. But until you've mastered this fascinating bit of wildfowling trickery, you'll never know all of the thrills that wildfowling has to offer.

10

Blinds for Wildfowling

Burton J. Myers

M Y FIRST DUCK BLIND didn't cost me a cent to build. It fit neatly into my game bag, and for the six years it lasted was very nearly perfect for the type of hunting I did. The blind consisted of nothing more than two potato sacks, sewn together into one long bag.

In those days, most of my wildfowling was confined to an area dotted with small, hardwood-rimmed beaver ponds, where wildfowl feasted on bountiful annual crops of acorns. Prior to opening day of each season, the birds would be spread evenly throughout the area. But following the barrage which took place on the long-awaited October morning, the birds tended to concentrate on one or two ponds. Since the particular pond at which waterfowl activity intensified varied from year to year, or even from week to week, a permanent blind was out of the question.

During those days I would head out at dawn, in search of a pond holding feeding birds. When it was located, I'd saunter up, flush the ducks without firing a shot, and quickly set up.

Time was critical. Having scattered the birds in residence on the

Hiding in natural vegetation frequently makes the best blind.

pond, I often had no more than 10 minutes to prepare for the blacks, mallards, and teal that would begin drifting back in small groups.

Three to six decoys would be set in a likely looking opening, 10 to 15 yards from shore. Then I would hastily slip into my potato-sack duck blind and wait for the birds to return.

My first blind offered portability, adequate camouflage, and most important of all, it worked and worked well. The system taught me a lot about ducks and their behavior. And though I've hunted from far more elaborate blinds since, the lessons I learned have made me a far more cautious blind builder than I might otherwise have been.

A blind should meet three important criteria: it should conceal the hunter from the birds; it should not, in itself, arouse the suspicion of the birds; and it should not unnecessarily hamper the gunning of its occupant.

The best duck blind ever made need be nothing more than the clothes on a hunter's back. Too often hunters forget this basic point and depend solely on their blind for total concealment. This is something akin to building a house without a firm foundation. Sooner or later, it's going to cause you problems.

A duck's first line of defence is its incredibly acute eyesight, which is far superior to that of any wildfowler. The slightest movement can send an incoming flight of ducks off for greener, safer pastures.

Camouflage starts from the skin up. Even longjohns are better dyed a dull green or tan than left a glaring white. Take a close look at the garb of your hunting companions and you'll soon begin to realize my point. If they've been slugging through heavy, waist-deep marsh grass, they will invariably have opened the collars of their shirts and unzipped the fronts of their hunting coats, exposing a slight, but highly visible triangle of white at the base of the throats.

Over their inner underwear they'll often wear a heavy cotton shirt in a red or blue checkered pattern. Birds aren't color-blind. They'll spot such an unnatural hue as though it were a neon sign on Broadway saying, "Trouble awaits you here." Buy drab shirts in a marsh-blending color, so that if you should get a little warm, you're not sacrificing concealment for comfort. For the same reason, pants should be of a corresponding tone.

Most of the jackets sold for waterfowling are of a suitable shade. However, be wary of the increasingly prevalent nylon-skinned coats. They may be more durable and water-repellant than the traditional khaki hunting coat, but they are noisy, particularly when the mercury drops to the freezing mark or below. Pass up any coat with a red lining, especially if the red is also inside an attached parka.

Under many conditions a hunter wears chest waders over his coat. This is fine, since waders are normally of a dead-grass shade. However, be wary of noisy nylon waders and be sure to dab a coat of concealing paint over the shiny buttons and fasteners which hold suspenders in place.

On top of this mountain of garb should be a good hat with a long, wide peak and ear flaps. The hats which waterfowlers too frequently wear serve as little more than toques, and aren't nearly as warm. A long, wide peak keeps the sun out of your eyes. And if you wear glasses, it prevents reflection from the lenses. On days of inclement weather, it also keeps stinging rain or sleet out of skybound eyes.

More important is the concealment which the wide peaks of such hats provide. They cover the revealing glare of a pale face (which, incidentally, should be given a slight dab of charcoal-colored face make-up). If you are lazy like me, the growth of a beard left unharvested from the day before provides adequate facial concealment.

Don't overlook other gear. Thermoses should be green, not crimson red. And after you've eaten your lunch, put the tin foil back in your lunch bag where it won't reflect light. Keep track of spent shells. The mirror-like finish on their brass bases can, at times, be spotted from a long distance. It is best to pick up all empties. A good blind often accumulates more than a case of shells fired from within its confines over the duration of an entire season.

To be effective, a blind must do more than conceal a hunter. It must, in itself, be inconspicuous. This isn't a hard-and-fast rule for all waterfowling though, since some of the contraptions used successfully for diver duck shooting stick out like sore thumbs. But in such cases the blinds have been in place a long time, and the ducks are used to them. For puddlers and geese, however, it's a cardinal sin to build a blind that doesn't blend with the landscape.

Don't abuse the site of your blind. Caution must be taken during its construction not to trample nearby vegetation. The ground which surrounds a blind often ends up looking as if it had been attacked by a massive horde of rampaging muskrats. Pick a route to and from the blind which does the least amount of damage to the surrounding flora. Remember, the site may look unobtrusive from a low-water angle, but from the high vantage point of passing birds, the crushed cover which surrounds the blind could give it the appearance of a meteorite crater.

Though often overlooked by blind builders, a blind must be comfortable to be effective. If it isn't, its occupants will soon become overly fidgety. This destroys the main purpose of the structure—to conceal the slight movements of hunters.

The addition of a small catalytic heater can serve to warm hands

Permanent blinds must be built early so that ducks become accustomed to them.

and feet, or to toast a sandwich, and is extra welcome when the weather turns unreasonably sour. Windbreaks of heavy canvas, burlap, or polyethylene placed behind exterior natural cover are also useful.

I well remember my first attempt at constructing a permanent blind. My able hunting companion, Manfred Duenisch, and I were the epitome of two frustrated engineers. There never was, nor will be, a blind more carefully built, with such loving care and attention to detail, as that first duck blind we built on the shore of a backwoods pothole.

Its frame was carefully constructed of aged 2-by-2 spruce strapping, mitered and cut to fit exactly. Its floorboards were salvaged from an old, weather-beaten shed. Onto the frame we nailed 1-inch-mesh chicken wire, into which was woven a matt of bullrushes, rush by rush and without missing a single hole. It was 6 feet long, 4 feet wide, and 4 feet high; featured a hinged door, a gun rack, an inner windbreak of heavy burlap, a stoop for our Lab retriever, and two treasured wooden shell crates to give it that unmistakable touch of class.

Trouble was, it was totally useless. We had followed every rule in the book—built it early to accustom local ducks to its existence; used natural materials so that it blended in with surrounding topography; and designed it for maximum shooting comfort and maximum concealment. Every rule, except one. We hadn't reckoned on the fact that puddle ducks never had, and probably never would, land (or for that matter pass) within shooting distance of it. We had assumed that birds passing along a traditional flight path 400 to 500 yards away would, upon seeing our spread, ignore tradition and pile into the middle of our blocks.

Tailor your blind location to the natural flight patterns of the birds. And unless the blind is to be used solely for camouflage while pass-shooting, plunk it alongside the best feeding ground you can locate. If you're hunting in a spot in which the birds are customarily feeding, you've got half the problem licked.

Besides feed, your chosen spot should provide protection against the prevailing winds. In my hunting territory, most of the weather fronts move in from the north or northwest. Thus, my blind is almost always located on the south or east side of a point of land that juts out into the marsh or lake. Failing the availability of such topography, I'll use the north or northwest corner so that I have the shoreline vegetation as a backdrop and protection against the wind. Your blind should be positioned so that stooling birds can land against the wind (which, if at all possible, they'll always do).

Also to be considered is the departure route the birds will take once they've been shot at. They will take off into the wind to provide lift. A properly placed blind takes advantage of this so that the birds must stay within range for a few moments as they leave.

In the cramped quarters that prevail throughout a large portion of North America's marsh and backwoods pothole country, successful wildfowling often depends on mobility. Small marshes and ponds often don't provide enough hunting opportunities throughout a season to warrant the time-consuming task of constructing a permanent blind.

To capitalize on the ever-changing patterns of wildfowl, many hunters devise portable blinds. If there's enough strong, standing cover in the area in which you intend to hunt, a simple sheet of burlap or a tarpaulin stretched between upright branches will often provide all the protection necessary against the wary eye of wildfowl. The camouflage netting sold in most sport shops and army surplus stores is also excellent for this purpose. It is light, durable, and inexpensive. However, it doesn't provide protection against cold winds; and unless well anchored, it tends to flap in a blow.

In areas where existing cover is sparse and wouldn't adequately support canvas, netting, or even burlap; the camouflaging material can be stretched between pieces of heavy dowel, sharpened on one end so that it can be pushed into the ground.

One of the most ingenious set-ups I've ever seen was used by two hunters who worked the shoreline along the edge of the Great Lakes. It consisted of the cut-down frame of a baby's crib, over which burlap had been stretched. It was light (less than 10 pounds total weight) and assembled in a few seconds.

There are a number of portable blinds for sale today by a variety of manufacturers, one of which is certain to meet the needs of wildfowling in your area.

Another form of portable blind, the sheet blind, is used when snow covers the waterfowling scene. As its name implies, it is simply a white sheet draped over the crouched form of a motionless hunter, blending him into a landscape void of contrast.

Most blinds in use today fall into the category of the box or piano blinds, and vary from semi-permanent structures designed to last through a single season, to concrete and metal fortresses that will last well into the 21st century.

Box blinds are four-sided affairs, with a floor and back or side entrance. Piano blinds are somewhat the same, except that they have the added feature of a roof or partial roof which conceals hunters from above. Those with a complete roof covering generally have a forward-facing opening, providing room for shooters to swing their guns.

Correct placement of such blinds is of prime importance, since most are close to immovable once construction is completed.

Steer away from complex structures that provide nooks and crannies for critters to hide. More than one sleepy southern hunter has slipped into his blind at dawn to find, only too late, that a cottonmouth has taken up residence within its comfortable confines.

When building a box or piano blind, consider your dog. Too often a dog is relegated to a hidden corner, and every retrieve made is a blind one. The wise hunter treats his dog as a third man and includes a stoop or raised platform in the blind's design, so that the dog can sit high enough to view the action. Besides simplifying the retriever's task, the dog will learn to spot ducks, often before the hunters themselves. A keen-eyed dog can make a handy sentinel when hunters turn their attention to pouring a cup of soup or unearthing an extra shell or two from their gear.

In almost all cases, box or piano blinds must comply with the rules of concealment and should blend into natural cover. However, when they're used for diver duck shooting, this can become impossible. The blinds found along the gravel shorelines of big, open waters are certainly not inconspicuous. Often covered with dense cedar or possibly burlap, they stick out like sore thumbs. Yet they work, so long as they conceal the movements of the hunters inside.

An oddity sometimes found in flooded timber is the tree blind. Besides lifting hunters out of the water, it often provides cover which would otherwise be non-existent at water level. Tree blinds also put hunters closer to incoming birds approaching at tree-top level.

At the opposite end of the spectrum are the pit blinds. They're often damp, and of necessity hastily dug, providing cramped below-ground quarters that leave a hunter stiff and sore after a few hours of use. If they weren't so successful, I'd hate them with a vengeance.

The use of pits is widespread throughout North America, wherever birds feed in stubble fields. However, pits see maximum use on the Canadian prairies. The common practice here is for hunters to spot in the evening for fields being actively used by feeding birds, and pit-in just before dawn the following morning. The soft texture of western soil makes digging a pit relatively easy.

Decoys are place upwind so that landing birds pass over the heads

After digging a pit, the soil must be spread far away from the site.

of the hunters; and far enough away so that they don't draw attention to the pits. The pits themselves must be deep enough to hold the hunter's whole form below ground level, and narrow enough to cut down the viewing angle of its contents from circling birds.

Great care must be taken to assure that the site of the pit retains a natural appearance. The soil removed tends to be darker than the surrounding stubble, hence it must be spread evenly around the area or carried to a distant point where it won't frighten incoming birds.

A common error is for the hunters to drive right to the pit site to unload their equipment, before parking their vehicle in a distant field. The result is often highly visible tire tracks in the dew-ladden stubble, pinpointing the location of the waiting hunters.

It's also a wise procedure to have only one hunter call the shots. This practice decreases the chances of a bobbing head being spotted by the birds. At the right moment, the spotting hunter yelps "now", and everyone pops up to shoot simultaneously.

As a footnote, show respect for the landowner and fill in your pits after the morning shoot, or you will likely never be allowed to shoot there again.

Similiar in concept to the pit blind is the sunken blind, used in marsh areas or on tide flats, in which part or all of the blind rests below water level. Because of this, the blind—a barrel or box constructed of wood, metal, or cement—must be watertight and anchored so that it doesn't float up out of the muck when in place. Anchoring is usually accomplished by the use of a foot that juts out at a horizontal angle on each side of the blind's base. Placement of such blinds requires no small amount of physical exertion. At its worst, it's like trying to empty the ocean with a water bucket.

In areas where shoreline installations are impractical, a wide variety of floating blinds are used. Most are designed as sheaths, into which a boat is slipped. The boat then becomes the shooting platform. In more complex structures, the above-water portion of the blind rests on pontoons or drums (which support the weight of the hunters) and the boat is either tied alongside or slipped below the floorboards. Most of these structures are used for diver ducks. However, in some open-water areas, they can and do fool respectable numbers of puddlers and geese.

Why the ungainly looking contraptions known as stilt blinds are so effective, even on occasion for puddle ducks, is a mystery. They defy the most basic rule of blind construction, that of blending with the landscape. Basically they are a box blind on stilts, usually placed a goodly distance from any available cover. And yet they work. On more than one occasion, I've had diver ducks like scaup and bufflehead pass beneath the floorboards of the stilt blind I was using.

Unquestionably, the most successful hunting blind ever devised was the sink box. It consisted of a watertight box, sunk to within a

Sink boxes are the most effective blinds ever devised.

hair of waterlevel. Around its edge was a curtain that rose and fell with the waves, thus preventing spilling into the box. The hunter was completely below water level, except of course when rising to shoot. The sink box was an invention of the east coast market gunners, and was so deadly on waterfowl that its use is now illegal.

Waterfowlers are an inventive lot. Just when you think you've seen every blind ever designed, you run across something a little different. Like the doctor I once met who had a telephone installed in his blind, so that his duty to his patients didn't interfere with his early morning forays into his private marsh. I'll bet that more than one harried mother has found herself on "hold" while he dumped a mallard into his spread!

11

The Wildfowler's Garb and Gear

Norman Strung

WHILE I'M SURE no waterfowler will ever make the nation's best dressed list in his native attire, duck and goose shooters may rate as the "Beau Brummels" of the hunting fraternity by the variety of clothing the sport demands.

Take my situation for example. I regularly hunt waterfowl on both coasts. I've also hunted them as far north as The Pas, Manitoba, and as far south as Teacapan, Mexico. That involves temperatures from 10 to 100 degrees, under conditions that include northeastern gales, western snowstorms, and south-of-the-border sunburns. Then there's the camouflage factor, involving background colors from jungle green to solid white (in winter), and touching virtually every natural shade in between.

Even though your hunts might not include such extensive travel, you still need a wide selection of clothing if you plan to do a lot of wildfowling. The normal progress of a season anywhere encompasses marked changes in temperature and surroundings. These conditions are comparable to my wanderings, though perhaps on a smaller scale.

But before you go off the deep end and either decide to forget about wildfowling altogether, or take out a second mortgage on your house to pay for your wardrobe, rest assured that it's eminently possible to dress for both ducks and the weather without making a big investment.

When selecting clothing for duck or goose hunting, two requirements must be met. Your outerwear must help hide you, while outer and underwear must protect you from the elements. Let's take a look at the camouflage question first.

The human body is unique in nature. No other creature walks erectly, with stick-like arms. Nor does any other animal have a bright, flat face set in the middle of a round head. We have been the ultimate predator for so long that all forms of wildlife, ducks included, are quick to recognize our outline and flee.

One function of your wardrobe should be to break up that outline —to blend into whatever background you're hunting against. For all the territory I've covered, I find one of five garments will do just that, no matter where I'm at:

> A jungle camouflage pattern of basic greens is the shade to choose when hunting in lush climates or early in the season when plants are still green.
>
> That same camouflage pattern in rusts, tans and browns will conceal you when frosts have turned fall marshes gold.
>
> Black or dark brown clothing masks your presence around plowed fields of emerging winter wheat, or when hunting from rock jetties on either coast or the Great Lakes.
>
> Gray garb blends best with ice or when hunting over open water in a layout or scull boat.
>
> White should be used for hunting around solid snowcover. The spottier the snowcover, the more seriously you should consider one of the other shades.

It's important, to the point of being critical, that you use the right shade for the given condition. I once had a neophyte goose hunter show up at my snow-covered pit in jungle camouflage. To him, camouflage was camouflage. He couldn't grasp the principles involved. On a more subtle scale, but nearly as revealing to wildfowl who are looking at things from above, that same jungle camouflage will contrast with the golden brown of late fall bullrushes, as will tans and browns against the greens of conifers or early-season brush.

It's also important that you be covered entirely. From a bird's-

Appropriate wildfowling garb can range from jungle camouflage in warm weather to whites in winter.

eye vantage aloft, blue jeans are easy to spot by their contrast, even though you may be wearing a jacket and hat of perfect hue.

By far the easiest and most inexpensive way to satisfy these changing conditions of color is through the use of light, unlined coveralls. Traditional camouflage patterns are available at any sporting goods store. You can find a full set of whites by talking to anyone involved in the dairy industry. Grey and dark brown coveralls are standard items in auto supply stores.

When buying these garments, remember the kinds of weather you'll be using them in, and size them according to temperature. Buy your warm-weather gear to fit over minimal clothing, and get things like white and grey coveralls large. More about what goes under those coveralls in a moment.

Although few of us take the trouble, some sort of facial camouflage is really a big edge. If you tone down your face, you can watch incoming birds without fear of being spotted. Otherwise, you're re-

Proper duck hunting apparel is the first line for a good, effective blind.

duced to peering out from under a lowered hat brim, or from behind a screen of bullrushes. This limits your view to a point where you frequently fail to notice a toll, and often puts you in a bad position for a shot.

The two most workable forms of facial camouflage I've used are: the makeup variety (available in most stores that cater to bow hunters), or a mask made of the same material you're wearing. By far the most ingenious mask I've encountered has been a full hood, like a skier's balaclava, with a pair of lensless eyeglasses sewn to the eye slits. This anchors the mask firmly to your head, so when you turn, the eye slits turn with you.

Matching your background is a necessary ingredient in successful wildfowling. You'll seldom creep within, or lure birds into, gun range if your presence is obvious. But personal comfort is part of the recipe too. When you're cold, wet, or otherwise uncomfortable, you're bound to fidget and flare birds away, or end up outside the blind stamping your feet when the flock of mallards tips toward your stool.

The most logical way to take a look at the kind of clothing that will keep you comfortable lies within the framework of a typical season. Opening day across the nation usually dawns cool—perhaps even frosty—but the weather turns warm by noon. These conditions are best met by a combination of several garments that includes: cotton underwear to absorb perspiration; denim pants and a wool shirt; plus a wool sweater. Camouflage overalls and a hat account for outerwear.

With this combination of clothing, you can remove layers at a time, ending up with nothing more than camouflage coveralls and skivvies if it gets warm enough. This is just the outfit I wear when hunting in Mexico.

This arrangement of clothing also illustrates some important principles of dress worth remembering, whatever conditions you're hunting under. First, layered clothing will keep you warmer than an equivalent-weight single garment. Trapped air is what really insulates your body from the cold, and the more layers of clothing you wear, the more air you trap.

Second, the moisture of perspiration is usually at the bottom of a chilled body or numbed feet. If you're going to stay warm, you must take pains to avoid excessive sweating, and to absorb into clothing whatever body moisture does occur.

Point number three: there are certain kinds of clothing that resist the chill of moisture; most notably, wool and Dacron Fiberfill II. If you wear garments made of these materials, you'll eliminate about half the chill you'd otherwise experience from body moisture.

This arrangement of garments is suitable for temperatures at the freezing point and above. When the thermometer drops below freezing and stays there for most of the day, you'll need a different type of garb to keep your body warm. Some sort of windbreaker, worn just under camouflage outerwear, is ideal. It increases the insulatory capabilities of your clothes. An unlined jacket of tightly woven synthetic cloth eliminates the wind/chill factor, so your clothing retains nearly all of the heat your body generates. We're all different in the amount of heat we give off, but the addition of a windbreaker keeps me comfortable down to the low 20s range.

When the temperature dips into the teens, I add a set of Dacron II underwear, tops and bottoms, worn over full cotton underwear. I seldom find the need for more clothing than this. When the temperature drops to single figures, birds take the clue just as you should, and remain bottled up to keep warm.

The great part of duck hunting is soggy sport, centered around

Waders are a must for any wildfowler.

marshes, potholes, rivers, and bays. Although I've heard manufacturers claim otherwise, I have never worn, nor heard of first-hand,
a truly "waterproof" leather boot. The only way to keep outside
water away from your feet is with rubber. But this creates a problem
on the other side of the boot. Rubber doesn't breathe, and consequently, it's awfully easy to build up moisture that originates from
the inside of the boot.

There are, however, a few things you can do to at least temper
the effects of foot moisture. Always put on dry socks. If you're in a
duck camp or recvee on a several-day hunt, keep one or more
sets of socks hanging near the fire. Every time you return to home
base, put on a dry pair. If your blind is a long walk away, wear
leather hiking boots to get there, and carry your waders (if practical).

It's wise to avoid rubber boots that lace tight. Boots that stay open
at the top allow some moisture to escape.

There are three styles of rubber boots that could conceivably be
useful to the wildfowler. If you know you'll only encounter soggy
marsh conditions, with water no more than ankle deep, the calf
high "pac"-type boot will make for the easiest walking, because it's
the lightest footwear.

If you know water will not be deeper than your knees, hip boots are preferable because they're lighter, and to some extent more comfortable to wear than chest waders. However, let me issue two warnings. I have found that 99 percent of the water I hunt over restricts a man in hip boots. Lively cripples, drifting decoys, and setting that last block on the tail of a fish hook invariably finds water sloughing over the top of them. Hip boots are also potential death traps when coupled with duckboats. If you go overboard in a deepwater crossing, they fill with water immediately, and are impossible to remove quickly if they're snapped around your calf.

This is not true of chest waders. Chest waders are heavy, bulky, and hot in warm weather, but they're usually of sufficient height to get you where you want to wade. I've also tested their safety on the water, and found that they'll actually act as a life preserver if you keep your wits about you and a bend at the waist to trap air around your legs. In this attitude, you can slip out of them easily, then buoy yourself by laying over the crotch of the boots. I strongly recommend chest waders if you'll be shooting around deep water.

A significant amount of wildfowling, though, is done on dry land (primarily mallard and goose hunting). The footwear best suited to this aspect of the sport is made of leather. Leather "breathes", allowing some transfer of moisture from your feet to the air, so your feet stay reasonably dry and warm. Even the coldest goose shoot will be comfortable if you wear a good pair of insulated leather boots.

Whenever I'm gunning in cool or cold weather, I bring two kinds of gloves—one set to keep me warm, the other to keep me dry. My "warm" gloves are green wool gloves with a reinforced palm and trigger finger. When the weather really gets cold, I slip them inside a set of shooting mittens, with a slit palm. Fingered gloves just can't keep your hands warm in frigid weather. There's too much finger surface exposed to the cold air. By encasing your gloves in a second covering, you create a buffer between fingers and cold.

My "dry" gloves are a piece of equipment often overlooked by gunning buddies. No matter how careful you are, when you're hunting around water, you're going to get your gloves wet. This usually happens when setting or winding up decoys, or when retrieving a cripple. Even a few drops of absorbed water renders gloves worthless. To keep my hands warm and my gloves dry, I carry a pair of thick rubber gardener's gloves in my shell box and don them whenever I have to go into the water. In fact, I've got two pairs of "dry" gloves. My other set is a pair of armpit-high electrician's gloves. I

For safety in case you fall in, ammo should be kept in bags or metal boxes, not in your pockets.

wear these when picking up or setting stool from a boat. Their gauntlet length means I don't have to worry about waves or sea spray wetting the arms of my clothing.

The best duck days usually come with inclement weather. Thus rain is frequently part of the wildfowler's world. It's surely been a part of my blind time, and only one arrangement of raingear has been capable of keeping me bone-dry. The principle is easiest to understand if you've ever shingled or roofed a house. The top "shingle" drains water to the second, to the third, and finally to the ground. The first shingle should be a rubberized rain jacket, with a hood, that reaches a point just below your buttocks. Wear the bottom of the jacket outside a pair of chest waders, and the cuffs of the jacket outside a pair of rubber gloves.

A baseball-type cap with a long brim rounds out the rainsuit. If you don't wear one, rain will bead and drop from the center of the hood, hitting the tip of your nose. It's also wise to choose a jacket that has a drawstring to cinch the hood down around your face. If you wear a loose hood, every time you turn your head you'll be looking into the inside of the hood, rather than at what caught your interest.

While that rounds out the kinds and vagaries of apparel I find useful in the course of a season, let me point out a few of the things I don't wear and why; as well as a few other things that aren't exactly worn, but are sure to help keep you comfortable.

Shell vests and/or shell belts are dangerous around deep water. Should you go in over your head, they'll pull you to the bottom and anchor you there. That also goes for the practice of keeping shells in your pocket. Instead, carry shells in a waterproof 50-caliber ammo case, available as war surplus material.

Big, bulky parkas may look warm, but as I pointed out earlier, the same weight of several layers of clothing will, in fact, insulate you better. Then, too, parkas virtually must be *the* outergarment. Buying four or five parkas in the camouflage colors required during a season would mean quite a chunk of cash. You're far wiser—and richer—to buy several inexpensive coveralls and pack clothes under them.

Down-filled garments are the most efficient insulators of all, but at least for wildfowling, I steer clear of them. They lose their loft as they become damp; another way of saying they won't stay warm when wet.

To end on a more positive note, here are a few accoutrements that might not be classified as "garments", but they have proven their usefulness to me:

On a cold day, a decoy bag can do more than just carry decoys. Make sure you keep it dry, and once the stool is set, cover your legs with it like a blanket. Just that little bit of a windbreak will warm the air around your legs by 10 degrees.

Bring along a small piece of styrofoam, or a similar synthetic substance to sit on. I don't know how or why, but this stuff seems to generate its own warmth, and prevents transfer of moisture from seat to body. When lying down in a slit trench or a layout boat, a body-sized piece of styrofoam is the most comfortable way to wait, for the same reason. It's almost needless to say that the styrofoam must be painted, or covered with some sort of material, to match the color of your surrounding (unless, of course, you're hunting on snow).

A small handwarmer, tucked in a breast pocket, supplements body warmth and quickly takes the numbness out of cold, wet hands.

A Thermos of some substantial hot liquid—bouillon, soup, or hot chocolate—will provide quick energy and warming internal heat faster than a steam bath. One traditional warmer-upper to stay away from is liquor-laced coffee. Coffee has no food value, and liquor's effect finds internal warmth transferred to surface skin. You might feel warmer for a while, but you're actually losing heat in the process. Then, too, mixing gunpowder and alcohol is bad practice under any circumstances.

Still another way to stay warm is with a small heater. You can fashion one at home out of a coffee can that's used with charcoal, or tote one of the modern catalytic heaters. Both provide external heat, and a means to enjoy the feast of a lifetime. Place a foil-wrapped sandwich (I'm addicted to ham and cheese) on one of these heaters, turn it once after five minutes, and three minutes later you'll savor a meal no gourmet will ever duplicate unless he has some unlikely spices; gunpowder, duckfeathers, and savory fall marsh.

12

After the Shot

Malcolm Hart

I N T H E O U T D O O R P R E S S, stories on how to hunt water-fowl are about as abundant as ducks on Manitoba's Delta Marshes during migration. But stories on what to do with the birds once you've shot them are much less common. Even books on wildfowling tend to dsmiss this topic with a few niggardly paragraphs.

Every competent hunter knows that for game to reach the kitchen at peak flavor, it must have proper care and handling after the shot. If a hunter neglects or mishandles an animal after it is shot, he cannot expect to enjoy fine eating. Much of the strong, unpleasant, "gamey" flavor that can occur with big game is the hunter's fault. Game birds are harder to mishandle, but it can happen.

In the case of big game, most hunters know that the first rule for finely flavored meat is to open the carcass so that it can cool as quickly as possible. The same rule applies to birds. They, too, must cool as quickly as possible.

For this reason, I view the rubberized game bag in the back of most hunting jackets as an invention of the devil. It's convenient, but that's all. A duck stuffed into the back of a game pocket retains its heat much longer than a bird that is exposed to the open air.

A similar situation occurs when ducks and geese are allowed to sit piled up somewhere in the sun. The proper way to deal with birds is to hang them individually, so that air can circulate around them. If hanging is impossible, as it frequently is in the marsh, then lay the birds down, spread apart, in the shade.

The next steps are laden with controversy. Should the birds be dressed—gutted—right after shooting or should they be left whole? Should the birds be hung, or should they be plucked and drawn and frozen or cooked as soon as possible?

No two wildfowling experts agree on this. For example, Grits Gresham, author of *The Complete Wildfowler*, belongs to the dress-and-eat-as-soon-as-possible school. On the other hand, Zack Taylor, in his book *Successful Waterfowling*, recommends hanging birds in cool weather and refrigerating in warm weather, at least for a few days.

Who is right? The hanging of game is traditional with European wildfowlers. But does this mean that Taylor and the Europeans are right? Or are both men right? Perhaps it's just that waterfowl, indeed all game birds, can take a lot of mishandling before they become unpalatable, let alone ruined for the table. Gresham does most of his waterfowling in the south, where the weather is mild and perhaps downright warm. Taylor, on the other hand, does his along the Atlantic tidewater, and much of it in cold weather. That may partially explain the differences of opinion.

But it could be that the issue is more fundamental. I consider grass-fed beef far superior to the beef produced in feedlots where the steers have been fed a high protein diet to accelerate their rate of growth. I think range beef has a far superior flavor. But this flavor is markedly different, and some people don't care for it.

The same applies to chickens. Today's chickens, from modern chicken farm-factories, are insipid birds in comparison to the old-fashioned farm birds that were fed largely on whole grain, plus grass shoots and insects that they picked up on their own. Yet farm chickens taste "wild" to some people.

If the thought of hanging birds repels you, don't do it. On the other hand, if you think it enhances their flavor, then by all means hang them. After all, you're the guy who's going to sit down to the duck or goose dinner.

Some years ago I read an article in a restaurant management magazine about an experiment conducted by a restauranteur, to see if hanging did or did not improve the flavor of game. Pen-raised mallard ducks and pheasants were used. The reason the study was conducted with pen-raised birds was not only because they were easily and legally procurable, but also because all the mallards and all the pheasants were likely to have been fed the same diet. Wild birds would almost certainly have been feeding on different things, which could have accounted for a flavor difference. Also, some birds would have been more shot up than others, and this too could have affected the flavor.

The birds were treated in the following manner. One mallard and one pheasant were killed, hung for 10 days at 34 degrees, and then frozen for 30 days. One mallard and one pheasant were killed, dressed, and frozen for 30 days. One mallard and one pheasant were killed and hung for 10 days at 30 degrees, and then cooked. Finally, one mallard and one pheasant were killed, dressed, and cooked immediately. All birds were cooked on the same day, with one chef doing the honors on the mallards and another on the pheasants. The birds were coded by the restauranteur. Neither of the chefs knew which birds were which, so they had no reason to give any bird special treatment.

A taste panel of four gourmets was assembled to sample the results and make a choice as to which of the birds had better flavor, texture, and were more tender. The panel unanimously chose the mallards and pheasants that had been hung and then cooked without freezing. The second choice was birds that had been hung and frozen before cooking. The birds killed and cooked immediately without hanging were third, while the birds that had been killed, dressed, and frozen before cooking ranked last.

All this says something about hanging game birds before eating them. But what? All it seems to prove, or at least indicate, is that game birds, like venison, should be aged. In fact, all meat should be aged. Any butcher will agree that aging meat enhances its flavor.

This is because the natural enzymes in meat have a chance to work and increase flavor. Also, alterations occur within the muscle fibre, making the meat more tender. Wildfowl are birds with large muscle masses in the breast. The meat is dark and richly supplied with glycogen. This is one reason why aging is particularly effective for wildfowl. Old birds—adults as opposed to juveniles of that spring —especially benefit from aging.

Yet I question whether the aging has to be done by the traditional method of hanging whole birds. Geese and puddle ducks that have been feeding almost entirely on grains and other vegetable matter, or diving ducks such as canvasbacks and redheads, can be hung whole in cool weather. But they can also be dressed and left to age for a few days in a refrigerator or other cool place, before they are eaten or frozen.

However, other ducks—bluebills, whistlers, buffleheads, sea ducks, and mergansers are another matter. These species all feed primarily on crustaceans, mollusks, and fish. For this reason, they should be fully dressed as soon after shooting as possible. Animal matter, particularly fish, in a bird's stomach imparts a strong flavor to the meat, especially if shot has penetrated the bird's abdominal cavity. The same is true for brant that have been feeding on sea lettuce, because this plant tends to give the bird a strong and rather unpleasant flavor.

I prefer to dress any badly shot-up bird—whether wetland or upland fowl—as soon as I can. I generally carry plastic bags with me in the field.

I suspect that most of the theories about the hanging of wildfowl were developed with birds that eat a largely vegetable diet; not on birds that feed on assorted crustaceans, mollusks, and small fish. But more about this later.

There is no question in my mind that hanging is a must for old birds—adult birds as opposed to juveniles of the year. Most experienced waterfowlers can tell juvenile birds from their plumage early in the season. With geese, size can also serve as an age guide. In fact, the lead birds in a skein are frequently older geese. The goslings usually trail behind.

One certain way of telling the young of the year is by the Bursa of Fabricius. This is a sort of blind pouch that opens into the cloaca. The pouch is large in young birds, but very small or non-existent in adults. Biologists use the Bursa to date all game birds, when plumage does not offer any reliable indication of age.

One thing I am against is opening the birds to field dress them and then hanging them. Either hang them whole or dress the birds completely and let them age wrapped in freezer paper or plastic bags. Opening up birds to draw them in the field is fine if you're going to finish the task of dressing by plucking or skinning later that day.

Opening up a bird actually hastens spoilage because it allows bacteria to get into the body cavity. The only exception is if you use a bird-gutting hook to eviscerate ducks. A bird-gutting hook makes only a small hole in the bird's abdominal cavity, which quickly seals itself with loose skin and down. I can't understand why bird-gutting hooks aren't more popular among upland bird hunters and wild-fowlers. I wouldn't be without one.

Purists claim that wildfowl should be dry plucked, but plucking them after scalding is much easier. And, of course, to a purist, skinning a duck is almost like committing blasphemy.

Again, I tend to view all definitive pronouncements on this subject with a jaundiced eye. Plucking—wet or dry—or skinning are all relative.

I think that any duck or goose that will be roasted should be plucked. Roasting a skinned bird dries the meat out too much. Also, from the aesthetic point of view, a skinned duck or goose never takes on that rich, golden color so characteristic of roasted wildfowl.

On the other hand, if the bird is to be cooked or smothered in a sauce, or covered with some sort of coating, it may be skinned or even breasted out or filleted.

I generally pluck all mallards, pintails, teal, canvasbacks, and red-heads. Yet such divers as goldeneyes, bluebills, and sea ducks, I usually skin or fillet. The latter birds are generally cooked in sauces or gravies, while the former I prefer to roast.

Skinning has one other feature in its favor, aside from being faster. Much of the "fishy" flavor in the diving ducks lies in the fat just below the skin. By removing the skin, the fishy flavor is largely eliminated. Even mergansers, if fully dressed, drawn, and skinned right after being shot, can be made quite good to eat, especially if they've been marinated.

One tip about skinning. The task is much easier when the birds are warm. Wildfowl are not as easy to skin as upland birds. The skin of pheasants, grouse, or quail just slips off like a glove. However, with ducks, you have to pull and cut.

Plucking waterfowl is never much fun. The only reason I put up with it is because I love to hunt ducks. A friend of mine bribes his wife, an old-fashioned farm girl, to do it. But not all of us are lucky enough to have married a farmer's daughter!

I generally pluck my wildfowl dry, not because I'm a purist, but because setting up a scalding bucket is too much trouble. I pluck the birds in the garage, or on cold days in the basement. To keep the mess to a minimum, to keep the down feathers from floating around, I hold the bird inside a large paper bag.

Here's my procedure. First, I behead the bird, and cut its wings and feet off at the first joint. I then wrestle out all the primary feathers off the wings, followed by the tail feather. After that, I hold the bird inside the bag and pluck the feathers from the breast and back. Pluck by taking "pinches" of feathers between the thumb and the first two fingers, and pull them with the grain (the direction in which the feathers lie). Don't pull against the grain or you'll tear the skin. Don't take pinches that are too large or you'll also tear the skin.

The down can be plucked the same way, but if you have a bunch of birds it's worthwhile to have a bucket of melted paraffin handy, and quickly dip the birds into the paraffin. Be sure to do this quickly so that you don't sear the skin. Or, you can brush the hot paraffin on with a wooden ladle. Once the paraffin has cooled and hardened, simply peel it off and the down, feathers, and even the hair come off as slick as a whistle.

If you don't use the paraffin method (I seldom do), then you still have the fine hair on the birds to cope with. The easiest way to get rid of it is to singe it off with a candle. Again, be careful not to burn the skin.

What about plucking the birds wet? After all, you've heard it is so much easier and faster. Well it is, but I don't think there's much of a time saving unless you're at a duck club with lots of birds to pluck and a whole team to help. Or unless you and your hunting partner have been blessed with extra good gunning and each has a couple of days' worth of bag limits to cope with.

To scald birds, you must set up a metal bucket or tub with water that is about 145 degrees. Keeping the water at that temperature is not always easy. The best way is to have a hotplate below the tub. If the water gets overly hot, you must regulate it by adding cooler water.

You immerse the duck completely in the hot water for about 20 seconds, and then try pulling out a pinch or two of feathers. If the feathers come out easily, pull the bird out and hang it by its feet on two ropes, spreading the feet apart. (By this time you've probably scalded your hand.) Let the bird cool a little and then begin plucking.

Once the bird has been plucked, you must then draw out the viscera. Simply cut around the vent, stick your hand in, and pull the insides out. If you have used a bird-gutting hook, there won't be much left inside.

Be sure to keep the livers, hearts, and giblets. Duck and goose livers make outstanding pâtés and rumaki.

Then cut off the oil gland and clean any feathers from shot holes. Finally, wash the bird in cold water and it's ready for the oven. Again, purists are generally against washing dressed ducks, claiming that water draws out the juices from the bird. They recommend wiping the bird with a dry rag or paper towel. I always wash my birds.

In some wildfowling areas such as Stuttgart, Arkansas, or down at Horseshoe Lake in Illinois, there are operators who custom dress ducks and geese on a piece-work basis. That's the easiest way I know of to pluck ducks. The only problem is that your birds frequently get mixed up with someone else's, and Murphy's Laws will see to it that you get someone else's badly shot-up birds.

To make sure that you get your own birds, have some metal tags made with your name and address on them. Wire or tie these tags to the feet of your birds. This way, you're pretty sure of getting back the same birds you shot.

If you are going to freeze the birds, you must, of course, wrap them carefully. When I leave dressed birds in the refrigerator to age for a few days, I always keep them in a plastic bag to prevent them from drying out. This same bag can be used to wrap the birds for freezing, but only as a first wrapper. For freezing, double-bag the birds, making sure that all the air has been expelled from the bag before tying. Only by double bagging can you avoid freezer burn.

An even better way of wrapping ducks for the freezer is with a layer of aluminum foil followed by two plastic bags, the heavy type that are sold as "freezer bags". Old-fashioned freezer paper is good too, but it's harder to work with. For the past couple of years, we've been wrapping waterfowl in a freezer wrap produced by Alcan. This is a two-ply freezer wrap of aluminum, coated with a film of polyethylene. Wildfowl wrapped in this material and placed inside a single plastic bag can easily be kept frozen until the next duck season.

Before freezing ducks or geese, be sure to label them well as to species, date, and whether the bird has been plucked or skinned. The date is important so that you don't keep the birds frozen too long. Freezing over a long time doesn't enhance the flavor of anything.

Wildfowl, to me, are among the finest creatures on this earth. I love to see them on the wing and on water. I love to see them pitch into my decoys. Even after I've filled my limit, I stay in my blind just to watch the birds. I also love them on the table, and that's why I think it's very important that they get the care they deserve, after the shot.

13

Wildfowl Cookery

Alyson Knap

W ILDFOWL CERTAINLY have a distinctive flavor, yet the flavor varies quite a bit between groups of ducks or geese. The diet of the birds is partially, or perhaps wholly, responsible for this. One certainly cannot expect a merganser to taste like a mallard. And a duck that has been feeding on small invertebrate creatures and fish will certainly have a stronger, and to many people more disagreeable, flavor than a bird which ingests primarily plant life.

Puddle ducks feed largely on vegetable matter. But even here, diet makes some difference. Ducks and geese that feed on grain and seeds generally have a finer flavor than those which feed largely on grasses, algae, and other aquatic vegetation.

For this reason, the Canada goose generally rates higher on the table than the snow goose. Brant, on a diet of eelgrass, are quite tasty. But when they've been feeding on sea lettuce, they're not nearly as good. Wheat-fed mallards or pintails are probably the most favored birds among wildfowlers. But when these birds have learned to feed on spent and rotting salmon along the rivers of the Pacific coast, even a starving man might turn up his nose at their flavor. Ducks that feed heavily on wild celery are excellent table fare. That's why redheads and canvasbacks make such fine eating.

Oil pollution affects the flavor of ducks. Wildfowlers along sea coasts and on the Great Lakes occasionally have the misfortune of bagging birds that have been contaminated by oil. Serious cases of oil contamination are, of course, lethal to ducks; and we lose thousands of birds this way every year. But even in minute quantities, oil affects the flavor of ducks because the birds ingest the oil as they preen their feathers in an attempt to get rid of it.

If there is a secret to cooking wildfowl, it's knowing when to enhance the flavor of the bird and when to disguise it. Unfortunately, there are no hard and fast rules. All depends on the palates of the people who are going to eat the birds. If the diners don't like the taste of wildfowl, you'd best disguise it. It's not difficult to have people come around for a second helping of duck gumbo and never know what they're eating. Other spiced and peppered dishes serve the same purpose. But do persons who don't appreciate the taste of waterfowl deserve to be fed it?

If you're feeding a bunch of people who like ducks and geese, cook the birds in a way that will enhance their flavor. My remarks here are meant primarily for vegetable-feeding waterfowl. I generally recommend that all ducks which feed primarily on animal matter be cooked in a way that will tone down their flavor. For mergansers, this is an absolute must. Bluebills, on the other hand, may be an exception because at times their diet may contain up to 60 percent plant life.

An entire cookbook could be written for wildfowl. There are myriads of wildfowl recipes—for many different species, with many different flavors, from many parts of the world. I have well over one hundred waterfowl recipes on index cards, and I haven't even scratched the surface. The following are among my favorites.

Roasted Mallards

Grain-fed mallards are probably the epitome of waterfowl on the table. Mild of flavor yet rich to the palate, stubble-fed mallards can be cooked like any domestic duck.

For a really easy recipe, salt and pepper the birds, inside and out, and place them in a roast pan at 400 degrees for 15 minutes.

After that, prick the skin of the bird with the prongs of a fork (to drain away excess fat under the skin), sprinkle with a teaspoonful of celery seeds and sesame seeds, and continue roasting at 300 degrees until the birds are tender and juicy. A little water may be added to the pan if necessary. But make sure that the water is warm. Nothing toughens breast meat faster than throwing cold water on it when it's hot!

When cooked, the bird can be carved. But a better way of serving it is the traditional European manner: cut the bird into sections (quarters for teal; sixths or eighths for larger ducks) with poultry shears. Gravy made from the drippings in the roast pan is excellent served over brown rice and onions.

Roast Duck Stuffed with Wild Rice

A delightful staple which can be purchased for an exorbitant price in specialty markets or collected free-for-the-taking in many fresh-water marshes and streams in eastern North America, wild rice naturally complements the rich flavor of grain-fed waterfowl.

For the stuffing, brown 1 cup chopped onions, 1 cup chopped celery, ½ cup chopped sweet pepper, and ½ cup cubed ham until golden. Then add ½ teaspoon rubbed sage, ½ teaspoon thyme, 1 teaspoon parsley flakes, ½–1 cup bread crumbs, 1½–2 cups cooked wild rice, enough light cream (10 percent butterfat) to moisten a bit, and salt and pepper to taste. Stuff this mixture into the body cavities of the birds and roast in a moderate oven until tender.

Roast Duck with Fruit Stuffing

The rich flavor of vegetarian wildfowl, whether ducks or geese, goes naturally with fruit. Almost any stuffing recipe, supplemented with fresh, canned, or dried apricots, peaches, apples, prunes, raisins, or other fruits can be used to stuff ducks (or geese). Or the fruits may be used alone.

One of our favorite recipes involves chopping up 1 cup of presoaked dried prunes, ½ cup of presoaked dried apricots, and 1 cup fresh apples. To this, add 1 cup coarsely chopped onions and 2 tablespoons lemon juice. Before stuffing the duck, liberally salt and pepper the body cavity. Then roast the bird slowly until tender and juicy.

This fruit-stuffed duck is best served with brown or long-grain white rice; or better yet, with European bread dumplings and braised red cabbage.

Roast Duck à l'Orange

My background is, for the most part, French. My ancestors came to America early in the 17th century, settling in the St. Lawrence River Valley of Quebec. I have always had a small, warm spot in my heart for French cooking.

To make my favored version of the famous "rôti de cunard à l'orange", peel three Florida juicing oranges and stuff them, in halves, into the cavity of a big mallard. Skewer the bird and roast in a moderate oven until tender. Transfer the bird to a clean roasting or serving casserole dish. Section if desired.

In a small saucepan, combine ⅓ cup sugar and 2 tablespoons wine vinegar. Add, while slowly heating, ½ cup orange juice and ⅓ cup white wine. Then add 3 tablespoons grated orange rind and the drippings from the roasted duck (it's wise to ladle the excess fat from the drippings first). Slowly bring to a boil, adding 1 tablespoon of cornstarch and ⅓ cup brandy or cognac. A few tablespoons of cointreau or benedictine can be included, if you really like the orange flavor. Pour thickened orange sauce over the sectioned duck and serve hot.

If you really want to impress company, set this duck with sauce (it must be hot) on the table. Warm ¼ cup of cognac, and light the cognac with a match. Pour flaming over the oranged duck. Very impressive, but be careful. I did this once with French cognac that left a sizeable mark on the ceiling!

Duck on a Spit

If you have a barbecue chef in your house, you can produce the most superb results with young, tender ducks on the spit. There are two ways of doing this: on the outdoor barbecue, which takes some time but produces delicious results; or in the kitchen oven. If you choose the latter, it's wise to have a self-cleaning oven.

I once had a pintail barbecued in an oven and basted every 15 minutes with a commercial barbecue sauce from a bottle. I am not, myself, much in favor of store-bought cooking concoctions, but this one was superb. So if you have a favorite bottled barbecue sauce, by all means try it on a duck.

If you'd like to try mine, proceed as follows. Clean two large onions and 2 large stalks of celery and pass them through a meat grinder. To this, add 3 large chopped tomatoes, 1 finely ground clove of garlic, ¼ cup malt vinegar, ½ cup brown sugar, ¼ teaspoon cloves, ¼ teaspoon cinnamon, ½ teaspoon Worcestershire sauce, and salt and pepper to taste. Blend all ingredients in a blender for a few seconds. Use this to baste the wildfowl throughout barbecueing.

If you really enjoy the flavor of wildfowl, you may find this sauce too strong. Try, instead, basting the bird with melted butter (corn-oil margarine if you have cholesterol problems), salt and pepper, and a touch of lemon juice or wine vinegar.

Ducks in Pieces

Ducks don't have to be cooked whole, by any means. A good butcher knife and a sturdy pair of poultry shears will give you about any size and configuration of fowl that you'd wish to cook with.

Pieces of waterfowl can be braised, roasted, fried, glazed, broiled, baked, stewed, or just about anything else you can imagine. If you're in a hurry, try one of the commercial chicken coating mixes for baked chicken. They're good, but one shouldn't really ever be in a hurry with wildfowl.

For a superb dinner of grain-fed ducks with little or no fat on their bones, try marinating the pieces in dry red wine for an hour. Then drain, and coat with a mixture of ½ bread crumbs and ½ grated parmesan cheese, spiced up with a little thyme, marjoram, and oregano.

Place the pieces in a shallow casserole, cover with ½ cup melted butter mixed with ¼ cup dry vermouth, and bake (covered) in a moderate oven until the bird is tender.

Pieces of ducks can also be deep-fried with great success. For instance, take teal in quarters. With a coating of corn meal and flour, mildly spiced with salt and pepper, paprika, and garlic, they are delicious deep-fried and served with scalloped potatoes, candied yams, and a fresh salad.

The flavor of grain-fed ducks is so fine, that the birds lend themselves to the most marvelous of epicurean delights.

To describe the procedure of boning a mallard for an eight-jewel duck would take half this chapter. But to those who enjoy gourmet cooking and wild fowl, this laborious and expensive task is well worth the final result.

Indeed, the Asians have a great many recipes for waterfowl of many species. Ducks rubbed in ground peppercorns and shallots, ducks basted with honey and ginger, and ducks heavily herbed and floating in mandarin orange sauce are but a few treats. The possibilities are endless.

But what about the ducks that aren't grain fed? What about those mergansers that insist on eating fish and those buffleheads and scoters that seem to love shellfish and other varied invertebrates? These can't be treated like a mallard, a Canada goose, or for that matter, a canvasback.

The sea ducks and mergansers are generally considered less palatable by most duck hunters, because of their strong fishy flavor. And there's no question that this is true if the birds are prepared for the table in the same manner as the puddle ducks. As a result, such birds as mergansers are generally not brought home for the family larder. If they are shot, they're usually discarded.

Yet all of the mergansers and the sea ducks can be surprisingly palatable table birds when drawn and skinned—not plucked—before cooking. Skinning and drawing shortly after shooting will not give the bird the flavor of a grain-fed mallard or pintail, but sea ducks can hold their own on the table if cooked correctly.

Sea Duck Stew

Prior to cooking sea ducks, I recommend disjointing and marinating them for 12 hours either in a dry red wine marinade or in tomato juice with chopped onions, garlic, and a touch of soy sauce added. The secret to cooking these ducks is to baste them in a flavorful sauce. I generally use one with plenty of mushrooms, onions, and garlic. The birds should also be cooked fairly slowly so that the sauce has time to flavor the meat.

We came across our favorite sea duck recipe quite by accident. On a one-week vacation, shooting diver ducks in northern Ontario, we ran into particularly bad weather and ended up close to stranded in the northwoods for four days beyond our expected stay. True to form, in the late fall when the north wind was blowing and the thermometer was threatening to freeze us out of our tent, the divers were riding the winds and laughing at the elements.

With our limit of divers in hand, we decided one day on a stew. Now you can make a stew of most anything. Ours was made from floured bluebill legs and breasts, potatoes, carrots, canned tomatoes, onions, powdered garlic, salt and pepper, and parsley flakes. With a topping of boxed biscuit mix, the stew was so delicious that it's been adopted as a household standard.

Duck Curry

Some years ago, we were introduced to a British couple who had spent some time in India. They were living in Zambia when we met them, while we were photographing wildlife for a European airline. The first night we were invited to their home, we were fed an Indian curry made with wildfowl.

There are several tricks to curries. One is not to pepper the dish so much as to overpower the flavor of the birds. The other is not to use commercially available "curry powders", but to mix your own herbs and spices from individual ingredients.

For a superb sea duck curry, start with 2–3 pounds of duck breasts, skinned and split. Shake the duck pieces in salted flour, and fry 3–4 minutes until browned. Transfer to a casserole. Fry separately 2 cups chopped onions, 1 tablespoon chopped garlic, and 2 tablespoons fresh ground ginger root. When the onions are soft, add ¾ teaspoon ground cumin; ¾ teaspoon ground turmeric; 1 teaspoon ground coriander; ½ teaspoon cayenne; ¼ teaspoon ground fennel; 1½ cups chopped, canned tomatoes; 1 teaspoon lemon juice; 3 tablespoons chopped, fresh coriander; and 1½ teaspoons garam masala (a blend of spices available at most stores selling Indonesian food-stuffs). To this sauce, add ¾ cup natural yoghurt.

Pour the sauce over the pieces of sea duck, in the casserole. Garnish with slivers of onion, slivers of almonds, and thin lemon slices. Bake at 300 degrees until the duck is tender.

Serve over a bed of long-grain rice with condiments such as sweet and hot chutneys, raisins, freshly ground coconut, and roasted peanuts.

Roast Goose with Sauerkraut

Geese, in the kitchen, are as versatile as ducks. Again, simple roasting without stuffing can produce superb results. However, the method of cooking depends largely on the species.

Canadas are, of course, the epitome of the goose world. Speckle-bellies fellow a pretty close second. But most geese, throughout the world, are mainly vegetarians and will yield a reasonable dish if handled with a minimum of care in the kitchen.

The Europeans, I believe, head the world with goose dishes. Although I've partaken of very enjoyable feasts of cackling Canadas on the Canadian prairies, Magellan geese in South America, and pygmy geese in Africa, the master chefs of goose cookery, in my opinion, stem from central Europe—from the "Viennese Empire".

For a 10-pound goose, drain and rinse 3 pounds of sauerkraut. In a large saucepan, brown 2 large chopped onions in margarine or butter, and add the sauerkraut. When the sauerkraut is warm, add 2 cups chopped apples, 1½ cups grated raw potato, salt and pepper to taste, and 1 tablespoon caraway seeds.

Salt and pepper the cavity of the goose. Then stuff with the sauerkraut filling. Truss the bird and roast until tender, basting frequently.

If you really want a gourmet delight, serve with potato pancakes, smothered in gravy made from the drippings, and mashed turnips.

Potato and Sausage Stuffed Goose

The first time I shot a goose was on the lichen-rich tundra of

Hudson Bay. It was a memorable occasion. As a botanist, I had spent several days not hunting but admiring the wonders of above-the-tree-line vegetation. As a goose hunter, I had hunkered in a coppice of Labrador tea, amazed by the number of geese in the air and extremely proud of the proper and suiting behavior of my young dog.

The first Canada I shot was delivered to me by my 10-month-old German wirehair. I well remember that goose. It was brought home and stuffed with potatoes and sausages.

To start with, brown a pound of ground sausage meat. Drain and reserve the fat. In the fat, brown the ground giblets and liver of the goose, along with 1½ cups chopped onions, ½ cup chopped celery, and 1 clove minced garlic. Combine all ingredients with 3 cups mashed potatoes, 1½ cups bread crumbs, 1–2 eggs, and salt to taste. Add freshly chopped parsley and stuff the goose. Roast at a moderate temperature until tender.

Odds and Ends

In the midst of my French ancestry appeared an Italian grandfather—a chef by profession and a thoroughly enjoyable man. I cannot think of a person that, as a child, I admired more. Nor can I name a person who performed as many miracles in a kitchen.

From as early as I can remember, I watched my grandfather at the stove. And I must have taken mental notes, because I learned from him the two most important things in creative cookery: a knowledge of foods, and the confidence to experiment.

A couple of years ago, faced with a stack of scoter and eider breasts and wondering what to do with them, I put my "creative genius" to work. The result was sea duck sausage.

For each pound of ground sea duck breast, add ⅓ pound ground uncured pork, 2 cloves crushed garlic, ¼ teaspoon each of salt, pepper, thyme, sage, and allspice, and moisten the resulting mixture with a little warm water and bread crumbs. Then stuff the sausage meat into casings (I prefer the sheep-gut kind if I can get them), and smoke the final product over a "cold" fire overnight. Broil before eating.

But there are so many things you can do with wildfowl; so

many avenues to explore. You need only the wildfowl, a little imagination, and a desire to experiment. With these, epicurean delights can be created from the marsh with each fowling season.

Bon appétit!

14

Wildfowling in Eastern Canada

George Gruenefeld

W ITH THE ARCTIC ARCHIPELAGO and subarctic expanses to the north, as well as balmy wintering grounds to the south, Canada's five easternmost provinces represent an ideal staging area for countless thousands of ducks and geese. Birds of two of the major flyways—the Atlantic and Mississippi—funnel through this immense territory, drawing on ducks and geese not only from Ungava and Baffin Island, but also from breeding grounds as far away as the Yukon.

Roughly 23 percent of the 3½ million ducks and 20 percent of the 420,000 geese taken annually in Canada are killed in the five Atlantic provinces—Newfoundland, Nova Scotia, New Brunswick, Prince Edward Island, and Quebec. A little over a quarter of the country's 115,217 wildfowl hunters are found in this same region.

The major species hunted by these wildfowlers are black ducks, mallards, green-winged teal, common goldeneyes, scaup, eiders, brant, Canada geese, and to a lesser extent snow geese. But many other species show up in hunters' bags as well. Unique to the St. Lawrence

Quebec's Crane Island offers fabulous fast action on teal early in the season.

River region is greater snow goose hunting. Until recently, greater snow geese could be gunned only in Quebec.

Throughout the five Atlantic provinces, the seasons are long and the limits generous. All provinces require a small game hunting permit in addition to a federal migratory bird hunting permit.

Let's take a whirlwind wildfowling tour through Canada's maritime provinces and Quebec, starting with Nova Scotia. Most of the hunting in this picturesque province is done on salt marshes for puddlers and off coastal shoals for divers and sea ducks. The main species hunted are black ducks, green-winged teal, goldeneyes, eiders, and

Canada geese. In the western half of the province, the wildfowl hunting season lasts from the beginning of October to the end of the third week of December. In the eastern part, along the Atlantic coast, there is a split season, the first part lasting from the middle of October to the beginning of November and the second from the middle of November to the middle of January.

Bag limits are generous, with a quota of six ducks and five geese per day. The possession limit is the total of two daily limits. From the beginning of November, hunters may also have two additional scaup in their daily limit, while hunters of sea ducks are permitted to take a total of 10 scoters, eiders, oldsquaws or mergansers per day. The only major restriction is that hunters may not have more than one wood duck in possession.

The eastern shore of Nova Scotia offers mostly sea duck hunting although some green-winged teal, blacks, and geese can be found during the early season. Eiders, scoters, and oldsquaws are the predominant species, but there are large numbers of mergansers available as well. Few hunters, however, bother with the fish-eating sawbills. Brant occasionally turn up in hunters' bags.

The shooting is generally done from brush blinds on shore, camouflaged floating blinds, and to some extent from layout boats or "tubs" as the locals call them. Ideal spots are passes between islands or in narrow channels where a bay opens out to the Atlantic. These areas act as funnels for the flocks, on their way to and from feeding grounds. Blinds are often set up on shoals out in the open water as well.

The gunning is a combination of pass and decoy shooting, since the tollers simply serve to attract the curiosity of the ducks, drawing them close enough for an in-range shot as they fly by. Decoys are mostly hand carved by the hunters themselves, and large rigs are unnecessary. Most hunters from the coastal areas put out three or four sets of decoys, in groups of four blocks.

Since much of the shooting is done in fairly strong winds and at ranges of 40 yards and sometimes more, hunters along Nova Scotia's eastern shore prefer 12 gauge shotguns bored full, loaded with magnum charges of No. 4 shot, and occasionally even No. 2's.

Sea birds winter all along the shoreline, hence the best hunting starts about the end of November and continues right through to the end of the season in January. Hunting conditions are severe at this time. Sleet, snow, or even freezing rain are often encountered. Sea ducks are found almost anywhere along the coast, and many hunters set up their blinds within view of the provincial capital—Halifax.

Pat and Edmond Jewers, of Ecum Secum in Guysborough County, are among the few wildfowl hunting guides available along the entire eastern shore. Their rates are in the $50-per-day range, but of course this varies according to the number of hunters in a party. Included in this price are decoys and blinds.

Around the southern tip of Nova Scotia, most of the hunting also takes place along the coast. However, the emphasis here is less on sea ducks and more on scaup, goldeneyes, and black ducks. Favored spots are points of land or islands where hunters build shore blinds out of brush. Unique to this area is the extensive use of decoys fashioned from clumps of eelgrass, a technique which has been carried up the eastern coast and even onto the stubble fields of the Annapolis Valley. Eelgrass can be found everywhere along the shore, and in the hands of an expert, makes a decoy that effectively fools the birds.

However, the southwestern shore of Nova Scotia has another claim to fame. It was here that the tolling dog originated, and has now become a recognized although little known breed. Avery Nickerson, of Yarmouth, Nova Scotia, deserves a good part of the credit, not only for his work in developing the breed, but also for his successful attempt in having the breed recognized by the Canadian Kennel Club. The Nova Scotia tolling retriever looks deceptively like a red fox, as it attracts the attention and curiosity of ducks, by running up and down the shore. Fascinated by the dog's antics, the ducks swim closer and closer until they are within range of the gunner, who jumps out of hiding to shoot. The Nova Scotia tolling retriever is used widely by hunters along the southern coast.

Probably the best duck hunting in the province is found at the tip of Shelbourne County, notably along Barrington Passage, or in the Yarmouth salt marshes of Yarmouth County. Some field shooting for blacks and geese can be found in the Annapolis Valley, and the Annapolis River offers excellent bufflehead and goldeneye hunting. No guides are available for hire, but local hunters are always ready to give directions to the good spots or do some guiding themselves. Prime time is from the middle of November through to the middle of January.

Canada geese and black ducks are the principal species of northern mainland Nova Scotia, and the best hunting takes place along the Northumberland Strait from Amherst to Tatamagouche. Most of the hunting, especially for geese, is done in fields of oats or corn stubble, over decoys. The hunters conceal themselves in the brush along the hedge rows and set up full-bodied decoys. Pits are rare and unnecessary, since the fields are relatively small (about 25 acres on the average). However, the fields are all private property and it's necessary to get permission to hunt from the farmers. The best time is from the beginning of October to the beginning of November.

Black ducks sometimes come in to goose decoys in the stubble fields, but wildfowlers who want good black shooting hunt over decoys on freshwater marshes, or jump-shoot in saltwater marshes and tidal waters along the coast. Prime time is during the latter part of the season, from the middle of November through to the third week of December. Because the season opens late (the beginning of October) in this area, most of the blue-winged teal have already moved south by the time gunners head for the marshes. But every now and then, when the weather remains warm well into autumn, hunters experience some excellent teal shooting. No guides are for hire, but again, local hunters are generally willing to help newcomers to the area.

The northeastern part of Nova Scotia—Cape Breton Island—is for the most part ignored by wildfowlers, since it offers only passable sea duck shooting. The shoreline offers only marginal habitat for both resident and migrating ducks.

The Tantramar Marsh, situated partly in Nova Scotia and partly in New Brunswick between Amherst and Sackville, offers excellent hunting for blacks, blue-winged and green-winged teal, widgeon, pintails, and ring-necked ducks. In fact, it harbors the greatest diversity of species found anywhere in the maritime provinces. This region, covering some 25,000 acres, was originally a saltwater marsh which was drained by Acadian settlers. Some years ago, Ducks Unlimited of Canada, in cooperation with the provincial governments and the Canadian Wildlife Service, began to revert the area back into marshland. About 9000 acres are now prime waterfowl habitat.

Canada's smallest province, Prince Edward Island, is rapidly gaining a name for its excellent goose shooting. Normally the shooting is good throughout the season, which usually lasts from the first Saturday of October to the first Saturday of December. If conditions are favorable, it's not hard to fill a limit of five birds before lunch. On ducks, the daily limit is six birds, of which no more than four can be blacks. On both ducks and geese, the possession limit is two daily quotas. Only one wood duck is permitted in both the daily and possession limits.

Most of the goose hunting in PEI is done on stubble fields rather than on water, simply because it's much easier hunting. Hunters usually make provisionary blinds along the edges of fields and put out an average of 25 full-bodied standing decoys (although spreads of up to 150 birds are sometimes used). During the first two or three weeks of the season, the geese decoy eagerly. But after they've been shot at often enough, they become wary. For this reason, hunters prefer full-bored 12 gauge shotguns, loaded with 3-inch magnums. No. 2's and BB shot are most popular.

The best goose shooting is along the northern and eastern shore, especially in King's County. The problem is that most of the best stubble fields are leased by hunters many months in advance of the season, and it's extremely difficult for people from the outside to find a hunting area. For this reason, the Prince Edward Island game department has been trying to promote estuary shooting for geese and ducks. Malpeque Bay in Prince County and Hillsborough Bay in Queen's County are considered top prospects.

During the first half of October, the duck shooting is excellent in the estuaries and along tidal rivers for both blue-winged and green-winged teal, pintails, blacks, and some mallards; while after the beginning of October, the bags consist almost entirely of blacks, goldeneyes and scaup. Some shooting can be done from shore brush blinds, but it's best to use camouflaged floating blinds. The Morell, Vernon, and Mill River systems are favorite areas among PEI duck hunters.

No guides are available, but it is possible to make arrangements with local hunters to go both goose and duck hunting. This may be the only way to find excellent goose shooting in the stubble fields of Prince Edward Island. The province's tourism and game departments, located in Charlottetown, are always ready to assist visiting waterfowlers.

In New Brunswick, wildfowlers have a wide choice of species including Canada geese, black ducks, teal, wood ducks, scaup, goldeneyes, eiders, scoters, and oldsquaws along the coastal regions. The season lasts from the beginning of October through to the third week of December, except in a small area west of St. John Harbour, where the opening date isn't until the last week of October. In this latter territory, there is a second season in coastal waters during the month of February. The daily limit is six ducks and five geese, with a maximum possession of 12 ducks and 10 geese per hunter. During the February season near St. John, however, the daily limit is a total of 10 scoters, eiders, and oldsquaws.

Wildfowlers who prefer to hunt freshwater marshes can try the St. John River system. This area holds mainly black ducks and teal, and is the only place in the maritime provinces with a significant number of wood ducks. Most of the shooting is done over decoys from brush blinds. The best time is between the beginning of October and the beginning of November. Later in November scaup become the predominant species, with favored spots on Grand Lake, as well as the lower St. John River.

During the month of October, Canada geese are found in numbers along the coast of New Brunswick, especially in the northern part of the province. Tabusinac Lagoon in Northumberland County is one of the top spots for geese, but most of the small bays along the same stretch of shoreline are good. Pass and decoy shooting are the most common hunting methods.

Blacks and goldeneyes are the most sought after ducks of the coastal areas. Black duck hunting is best when the season opens at the beginning of October, but for goldeneyes wildfowlers must wait until the end of the month. Blinds are located either on shoals, islands, or points where the ducks pass regularly. Open boat blinds are used to a lesser extent. Blacks Harbour in Charlotte County offers some good shooting.

Most of the wildfowling in Newfoundland consists of coastal shooting for black ducks, although green-winged teal are taken early in the season. Eiders, scoters, and goldeneyes are also hunted later on. Due to a shortage of appropriate habitat to attract birds in significant numbers, as well as poor access for hunters, the interior of Newfoundland offers only marginal wildfowling.

Wildfowl hunting in Labrador is even more difficult because of its remoteness. Almost all travel is restricted to either boat or aircraft and during fall even these are often unable to venture out due to the weather.

Newfoundland's season for shore ducks and geese lasts from the beginning of September to the end of November, but there is an added season for scoter, eider, and oldsquaw ducks which closes at the end of February or the middle of March, depending on the area. The limit is six ducks and five geese per day, while the possession limit per person is 12 ducks and 10 geese. In Newfoundland, the limit on sea ducks is 12 per day, while in Labrador, the maximum daily quota is 25 sea ducks. Again, the possession limit stands at two daily limits.

Guides are rare, but it is possible to hire one of the fishermen along the coast to take hunters out for a day's shoot. Sea duck gunning has a great tradition among Newfoundland's hardy fishermen. Information on both Newfoundland and Labrador is available from the Newfoundland Tourist Development Office, Confederation Building, St. John's, Newfoundland.

Last but not least is Quebec. "La Belle Province" offers the greatest diversity of wildfowling in eastern Canada—from teal to Canada geese; from marsh hunting for puddlers to goose hunting on James Bay. Virtually all species are represented in Quebec. The goose hunter's bag can include Canada geese, greater and lesser snow geese, blue geese, and brant. The tidal mudflats of the St. Lawrence River, about 30 miles east of Quebec City, are the major staging area of some 200,000 greater snow geese. The windswept coastline of James Bay, on the other hand, is one of the best areas on the continent to hunt Canadas.

Duck hunters can take blacks, mallards, pintails, blue-winged and green-winged teal, shovelers, wood ducks, redheads, canvasbacks, goldeneyes, buffleheads, scaup, ringnecks, oldsquaws, eiders, and scoters. However, blacks, mallards, teal, goldeneyes, and scaup are by far the most abundant.

The St. Lawrence River system itself, from the Ontario border eastward to the gulf, is the most popular waterfowl hunting area. Starting at the western end of the province, there is Lake St. Francis, where the puddle duck hunting is at its best from the opening of the season (the third Saturday of September) to half way through October. During this time blacks and mallards can be found in shoreline marshes, out in weed beds, and around most of the many islands on the lake. About the beginning of October, the Canada geese and frequently a flock of several hundred snow geese arrive, but these are usually shot over duck hunting rigs. The geese stay in this area for about 3 weeks before continuing southward.

Diving ducks begin to flock into Lake St. Francis between the middle and end of October, remaining well into December when the weed beds start to freeze. Whistlers (common goldeneye) and bluebills (lesser and greater scaup) are the most common divers, but several thousand canvasbacks come in to the lake as well.

The top area on Lake St. Francis is between St. Anicet and the Ontario border. Bernard Hart, of Cazaville, is the major outfitter catering to waterfowl hunters, and has floating blinds, lay-out boats, decoys, and guides available. Normally he remains in operation until the shore ice makes it impossible to get the boats out, some time after the beginning of December. Puddlers can also be hunted with success by jump-shooting the Dundee marshes west of Cazaville.

The situation is much the same on Lake St. Louis, in that puddler shooting is at its best before the middle of October, with diver shooting starting after that. Again, the major species are mallards, blacks, and teal, along with a fair number of shovelers, wood ducks, whistlers, bluebills, and some canvasbacks, redheads, and ringnecks. The majority of the divers remain until December, but there is always shooting either until the lake freezes up or the season closes at the end of December.

Here, the weed beds near Windmill Point off Ile Perrot are the local hot spots. Rene Aumais, of Point du Moulin, has lay-out boats, floating blinds, and some decoys available for hire to wildfowl hunters. As on Lake St. Francis, large spreads of three or four dozen or more decoys are necessary to hunt whistlers and bluebills effectively. There is little jump-shooting to speak of.

Lake of Two Mountains, actually a widening of the Ottawa River where it flows into the St. Lawrence, is a favored spot for early season divers. Whistlers and bluebills usually arrive just after the beginning of October but the hunting is at its peak towards the end of the month. They can be hunted over decoys out of lay-out boats, floating blinds and to some extent from shore blinds. Towards the upper end of Lake of Two Mountains jumpshooting and decoying mallards, blacks, teal and wood ducks can prove productive during the first three weeks of October. Canada geese can be hunted either out of floating blinds or in the fields. The pity is that the lake freezes relatively early, and often by the middle of November duck hunters must look for other spots.

The most popular duck hunting spot in Quebec is Lake St. Peter, noted especially for its diver duck gunning. The third weekend of September, when the season opens, is the best time to hunt blacks, mallards, green-winged and blue-winged teal, and sometimes, if the weather stays warm enough, pintails. Jump-shooting and hunting over decoys are both extremely effective along both shores of Lake St. Peter, but the top spots are Baie de Vallieres, Baie St. Francois, and Baie Maskinonge.

Bluebills and whistlers start pouring in to Lake St. Peter after the beginning of October, followed by canvasbacks and redheads around the middle of the month. The end of October and the first few weeks of November are prime time. Vercheres boats, camouflaged with cedar boughs, are usually used as blinds. Each is surrounded with several dozen decoys—mostly bluebill and whistler blocks, since these are the most abundant ducks locally. Canvasbacks will sometimes decoy to bluebill blocks, but it helps to have half a dozen or so canvasback tollers in the spread.

During the month of October, Canada geese are plentiful on the lake, rising in great clouds off the water. However, most waterfowlers pass-shoot the geese as they come close to the duck decoys. A limited amount of field shooting is also done for geese in the surrounding farm country.

No discourse on wildfowling on Lake St. Peter would be complete without making mention of the famous Desmarais clan of Notre Dame de Pierreville, on the south shore. As veteran duck hunting guides, they are well known throughout Quebec, and it's often necessary to make reservations to hunt with one of the Desmarais brothers far in advance. Although all are excellent guides, Hector Desmarais is regarded as the unrivalled master.

Around the first week of October, the greater snow geese start flocking in to the tidal flats of the St. Lawrence River east of Quebec City. Within a week or so, all 200,000 birds are in the area. Most of the hunting takes place either at Cap Tourmente, where a controlled snow goose hunt is held every year for residents of Canada, or on Ile aux Grues (Crane Island). Prime time is right after the main body of the migration has arrived, and again shortly before the geese leave towards the end of October.

The hunting is done on tidal mudflats out of pit blinds, and both silhouette decoys and sheets of white paper stuck in the mud are used to attract the birds. Greater snow geese respond well to calling, but the commercial calls available on the market are generally too low pitched. It is far better to use your own voice to imitate the "hucc-hucc" of the white geese.

On Ile aux Grues, the farmers have sole rights to all of the tidal flats. During the hunting season most of them cater to wildfowl hunters, offering guiding services, room and board, and blinds. Reservations, however, must be made in advance. Among the better known outfitters operating on the island are the Vezina and Lachance families. The island, incidentally, also has excellent duck shooting for teal, mallards, blacks, and pintails, especially before the geese arrive.

Much of Quebec's Canada goose hunting is done in the James Bay region. Literally thousands upon thousands of Canadas stage

Some of the best goose gunning anywhere is found along Quebec's James Bay coastline.

along the entire James Bay coastline before migrating southward. As a result, the hunting can be simply phenomenal. Prime time is around the third week of September, even though the season in this northern district traditionally opens on the first day of September.

At the beginning of the season, the geese are hunted on offshore islands, where they gather to feed on berries. At that time the hunters simply hide themselves in alder thickets on ridges, and pass shoot the birds as they trade back and forth. Later in the season, when the stock of berries is depleted, they turn to inland marshes.

From then on the hunting is tough, since the blind consists of little more than scrawny twigs stuck in the swampy ground (a more complicated blind would scare off the geese) located out in the middle of large bogs. At this point, it's a combination of pass and decoy shooting, the decoys serving only to draw the birds within gun range. Some of the northern goose hunting areas also offer outstanding duck shooting as a bonus.

There are a number of goose hunting camps along the Quebec shore of James Bay. Quebec Indian Eskimo Outfitters operate five, with locations at Cape Jones, Roggan River, Jack River, and two more around Fort George (the North and South camps). Arctic

Adventures, the tourism branch of the Federation of Nouveau Quebec Cooperatives, has one goose camp situated about 25 miles south of the Paint Hills settlement.

For information and rates on these and other Quebec outfitters and guides, contact the Quebec Department of Tourism, Fish and Game, Parliament Buildings, Quebec City, Quebec.

Although the prime hunting period in northern Quebec is during the final two weeks of September and the first few days of October, the season in the northern zone lasts from the beginning of September to the middle of December. In the central zone, south of 50 degrees latitude, the opening date is usually about the third week of September and the season closes at the end of December. However, the Magdalen Islands in the Gulf of St. Lawrence have a separate season for scoter, eider, and oldsquaw ducks, lasting from the beginning of November to the middle of February.

The limit for ducks during the early part of the wildfowl season is six birds, but after the middle of October hunters may take two additional bluebills and two additional sea ducks (scoters, eiders, or oldsquaws) for a total daily limit of 10 birds. The possession limit is equal to two daily limits. As far as geese are concerned, the maximum daily quota is five birds, including brant, snow geese, and Canada geese. In the northern district, including James Bay, the possession limit is 10 geese. In the central district, 15 geese or a three-day limit are permitted in possession per hunter.

Quebec is one of the few regions where the use of sink boxes is still permitted, and in recent years they have become increasingly popular among the province's waterfowlers. There cannot be any question as to their effectiveness, and hunting from one can be a unique experience. However, it is highly likely that the use of sink boxes may be banned in Quebec in the near future.

Atlantic Canada has a rich waterfowling tradition. Sea duck hunting is almost a way of life in many of the coastal communities; while inland and on salt marshes, dabbling duck gunning has been going on ever since the first French settlers landed at Hochelaga. No greater example of this wildfowling tradition exists than in the cuisine. But that's another story!

15

Wildfowling in New England

Gene Gallagher

THE PHRASE "DUCK HUNTING in New England" resounds with nostalgic memories of market hunting, men in oilskins on huge saltwater bays, giant guns charged with every conceivable type of shot, and hundreds of black ducks in the bag. Then, of course, there were the magnificent blinds, built on the most exclusive of private marshes; live decoys; and tunnels leading to lodges where warm toddies awaited the millionaire hunters.

New England doesn't have the waterfowl populations on its flyways that it did before the turn of the century. But it doesn't have the numbers of duck hunters found in the more southerly areas where the migrating birds winter, either. Despite fewer birds, today's New England duck hunter has some advantages over the duck hunters of yesteryear.

The biggest advantage is access. Any hunter today can pick out a spot that in years past was strictly off-limits, except to well-guided millionaires. The general public has hunting access, yet New England has not become overrun with "skybusters", nor plagued with overharvest. The human population density is too thin for these problems, at least for the moment.

There are places here for wildfowlers with fresh ideas, and plenty of open wetlands on which to experiment with new techniques. That is the beauty of New England waterfowling.

But don't expect an undeserved warm welcome. As you pass north from Long Island Sound toward the shores of Rhode Island and Connecticut, you may begin to notice a stodginess, an aloofness on the part of resident hunters and citizens. It is an affected disdain intended to drive you out of their private world and back to where you came from.

By continuing north, you will find that open areas for waterfowling become much more common; in fact, so common that you may have some difficulty deciding where to hunt. And that's a pleasant thought!

Very few areas in New England are posted or private; habitat is almost ideal; and regulations are minimal, except for federal statutes. With these advantages, all you have to worry about are your own devices and whether the birds are flying.

New England wildfowling usually consists of shooting from blinds,

Greater snow geese have again become legal game in the Atlantic Flyway.

but that's only one option. There are many resident duck hunters who do nothing but jump-shoot birds on potholes and tidal canals. And there are many more who merely pass-shoot near well-travelled migration routes. In addition, a growing number of technical wildfowlers are reviving sneakboat sculling as a way to approach wary flocks.

Another breed of wildfowler in New England shoots nothing but sea ducks. These hardy souls brave the horrendous North Atlantic in early winter. They face high seas and sub-zero temperatures in order to fire a few shots in the direction of scaup, eiders, oldsquaws and harlequins passing over the frigid waves a way out at sea.

Possibilities in New England are almost endless for the dyed-in-the-wool wildfowler. Blacks, mallards, woodies, teal, goldeneyes, ring-necks, scaup, oldsquaws, scoters, mergansers, and lately even a few pintails are all part of the scene. (Where the pintails came from I don't know, but they are becoming more plentiful every year.) And, of course, there are great flocks of magnificent Canada geese.

Hunting seasons and bag limits are very similar in each of the New England states, because of the federal guidelines by which each state must set its rules. Roughly, the puddle duck seasons open near the beginning of October and finish in mid-December, with a pause somewhere in the middle to accommodate the local deer hunting season.

Sea ducks and Canada geese usually open at the same time as puddle ducks, but shooting continues later into the season, sometimes into mid-January. Many New England states have recently reopened the season on snow geese because of the recent comeback of this species on the Atlantic Flyway. The season usually opens in concert with the Canada goose season, but is generally much shorter.

Bag limits, established by federal regulations, have averaged four ducks per day, not including coots, scoters, eiders, and such. Of these, only two may be blacks or woodies. Canada geese usually run three to a daily bag limit and snows are ordinarily two. Of course, a Federal Duck Stamp is required.

The state of Connecticut, bordering Long Island Sound, offers fine wildfowling along its entire coast. But the most productive area is that between Milford and Old Saybrook. Most resident waterfowlers stick to pass-shooting from offshore rocks in this middle portion of Connecticut's shoreline.

There is also superb shooting available in the Connecticut River Valley, from the mouth of the river northward to Cromwell. Not surprisingly, this portion of the state is liberally sprinkled with excellent wildlife management areas. The best of these are Great Island, Lord's Cove, and Ragged Rock near the mouth of the river; Cromwell Meadows and Wangunk Meadows near Cromwell; and Durham Meadows near Durham. On the coast, the best management areas are Barn Island near Stonington, Great Harbor near Guilford, and the Charles E. Wheeler Wildlife Area near Milford.

Licences for non-residents in Connecticut run $13.35 and may be purchased from any town or city clerk. You must, however, show a previous hunting license from another state or province, or possess a certificate of competency issued in Connecticut. Sunday hunting is not allowed, except on privately owned shooting preserves.

For additional information on Connecticut's wildfowling opportunities, contact the Connecticut Department of Environmental Protection, Wildlife Unit, State Office Building, Hartford, Connecticut 06115.

The neighboring state of Rhode Island may be small, but it possesses an enormous amount of shoreline, most of which borders Block Island Sound and the entire Narragansett Bay area. Public boat launching facilities are numerous all along this shoreline, as are many state parks and preserves.

Most Rhode Island wildfowlers concentrate on the bays and nearby salt ponds, shooting either from floating or fixed blinds (a natural preference considering the state's geography). But there is also some fine inland pothole shooting early in the season. Probably the best shooting is found in the upper reaches of Narragansett Bay near Pawtuxet. Two good public launching areas bracket the town, and it's a fairly short haul into prime scaup territory from this point.

Rhode Island's licence fees in recent years have been $10.25 for non-residents, but there is an additional fee of $10.00 if you hunt on a shooting preserve. Licences must be worn on the outside of clothing, and may be purchased from any town or city clerk.

A certificate of competency is required to purchase a licence, unless you have had a prior licence or have been a member of the Armed Forces. Most towns are open to Sunday hunting. Shot sizes larger than No. 2 are outlawed for waterfowling.

Additional information may be obtained by writing the Rhode Island Department of Natural Resources, Division of Fish and Wildlife, 83 Park Street, Providence, Rhode Island 02903.

The waterfowling heritage of Massachusetts can probably be traced to Plymouth Rock and the Pilgrims. The state's sprawling coastline, including the perimeter of Cape Cod, may well be the basis for this heritage. With so much coastline it might seem difficult to pinpoint one area as better than another for wildfowlers. However, such is not the case.

There are at least two very definite hotspots on the Bay State coast; one at the extreme northern end of the state, and the other at the western edge of historic Cape Cod Bay. Strangely, the outstretched arm of Cape Cod itself does not offer any real advantage for wildfowlers.

The Plymouth Bay complex, and in particular Kingston Harbor, is one of the finest wildfowling spots in Massachusetts, especially for blacks, geese, and sea ducks. Farther north, Newburyport Harbor is an excellent area for blacks and a great variety of sea ducks, as is the mouth of the Parker River near Little Neck just to the south. The Parker River Wildlife Refuge encompasses much of the latter, and offers some of the finest goose shooting to be found in the northeast. Shooters here invariably use decoys and well-camouflaged blinds.

Nearby are two other fine duck hunting areas; the mouths of the Ipswich and Essex Rivers. Both offer superb sea duck shooting and occasionally good goose hunting.

Inland, as in most of the other New England states, pothole shooting for dabblers is very productive early in the season. But it drops off rapidly once the ducks have been spooked by too many fusillades of birdshot.

Non-residents need only a small game licence to hunt waterfowl in Massachusetts, plus a $1.25 State Duck Stamp. Proceeds from duck stamp purchases are funnelled into Ducks Unlimited, to be used for waterfowl propagation in the Canadian provinces. The small game licence itself goes for $20.25, and no proof of previous licence or hunter safety certificate is required. The licences and state duck stamps may be purchased from any town or city clerk. Sunday hunting is not allowed.

Massachusetts' recent enactment of an extremely strict gun control law has confused many non-resident hunters, and many have probably turned away from the Bay State for fear of being jailed under the new mandatory one-year prison sentence for violations. In reality, little has changed for the hunter. A non-resident hunting licence is all you need to carry to use a shotgun in Massachusetts.

For additional information on Massachusetts hunting, contact the Massachusetts Division of Fisheries and Game, Field Headquarters, Westborough, Massachusetts 01581.

Gunning for sea ducks from rock blinds offers a challenge to New England wildfowlers.

Of the five New England states, Vermont is the only one which does not have an Atlantic Ocean border. It is, furthermore, a good deal west of the Atlantic Flyway mainstream. Therefore, waterfowling opportunities in this state are fairly limited.

Still, Lake Champlain on the western border provides some reasonably good duck hunting, as does Lake Memphremagog to the north and the Connecticut River Valley on the east. The primary method of wildfowling in Vermont is decoying blacks, mallards, and teal on the larger bodies of water. However, many hunters are turning to sneakboats and floating blinds because of the wariness of these birds. Another popular method is the simple jump-shooting approach on smaller bodies of water. Sunday hunting is allowed in Vermont, another obvious plus for waterfowlers.

There are two excellent management areas on Vermont's side of Lake Champlain; one at Mud Creek in Alburg, and the other at Dead Creek in Addison. The latter is strictly a goose hunting proposition. The number of hunters allowed on these areas is very strictly controlled, and applications must be made well in advance, to the Vermont Fish and Game Department, State Wildlife Laboratory, Roxbury, Vermont 05669.

There is usually a special bonus season on goldeneyes and scaup for Lake Champlain only, but it would be wise to check this out with the Vermont game department during the preseason preparations.

Vermont's non-resident small game licence at $15.50 covers duck hunting, but many out-of-state wildfowlers who also plan on some deer hunting prefer to buy the all-game ticket at $40.50. Licences can be purchased at any town or city clerk's office, but proof of competency must be shown, either with a previous licence from any state or province, or with a valid hunter safety certificate.

For more information on Vermont's waterfowling opportunities, contact the Vermont Fish and Game Department, State Office Building, Montpelier, Vermont 05602.

Of all the coastal New England states, New Hampshire has the shortest coastline, a mere 13 miles. Yet part of that coastline includes the Piscataqua River, outlet for the famous Great Bay.

Great Bay is another of the very best wildfowling places in the northeast, filled constantly with huge flocks of Canada geese, black ducks, and bluebills, not to mention healthy populations of buffleheads and mallards. The big bay offers a constant challenge to every type of waterfowler: the birds are everywhere, but they are so smart that only the experts seem able to bag them.

Well concealed blinds and huge sets of decoys are a must on Great Bay if you expect good results. Sneakboats work well also, but you had better be an expert sculler or you won't get within two hundred yards of the wary birds.

To the south of Great Bay, many shooters stalk the saltmarsh canals near Hampton Harbor, where jump-shooting for blacks and mallards is excellent throughout the season. Further inland, good bags of woodies and blacks are taken earlier in the season on some of the freshwater ponds.

Non-resident hunters in New Hampshire need only buy the small game hunting licence for $20.50, available at most sporting goods stores. A previous licence or certificate of competency is required. Sunday hunting is allowed.

For additional information on New Hampshire hunting, contact the New Hampshire Fish and Game Department, I & E Division, 34 Bridge Street, Concord, New Hampshire 03301.

Maine can probably boast the best wildfowling in New England. The state's 2500 miles of coastline is part of the reason. But the fact that it sits on the doorstep of the Atlantic Flyway also helps. It's no wonder then that Maine wildfowlers enjoy a distinct edge over their more southerly neighbors.

The birds are fresh and unwary, more easily decoyed, and fat. As a result, most Maine wildfowlers use coastal blinds and elaborate decoy sets for attracting the big flocks of blacks, woodies, teal, geese, and a great variety of sea ducks. Maine hunters take over 70,000 puddle ducks annually, and an additional 30,000 sea ducks, not to mention several thousand Canada geese.

To discuss hotspots in this immense coastal area would take more pages than this entire chapter would allow, but there are a couple which must be mentioned, at least briefly. One of these is Merrymeeting Bay near Bath. Merrymeeting has been one of the best producers of waterfowl in the entire northeast for many years, and it shows no sign of slacking off. Over the past 27 years, hunter success on Merrymeeting Bay has averaged around three birds per man-day on the opening day, and slightly less on subsequent days of the season. And that, remember, is just an average. It includes all those guys who can't shoot.

Another great spot is Penobscot Bay, particularly around its northerly reaches near Bucksport and near the islands which dot the huge bay further south. The easterly edge of Casco Bay near Harpswell is also good.

Maine's non-resident licence fees are quite high. Licences now sell for $46.50 and are expected to climb even higher in the future. Sunday hunting in Maine is not allowed.

More detailed information on Maine wildfowling may be obtained by writing the Department of Inland Fisheries and Wildlife, Augusta, Maine 04333.

16

Wildfowling Along the Eastern Seaboard

Bob Gooch

W HEN THE ADVENTURESOME CAPTAIN JOHN
S M I T H, over 300 years ago, led his little band ashore at what is
now Jamestown, he discovered much more than the beautiful Poca-
hontas. He found a land rich in wildlife. Deer abounded in the lush
forests; wild turkeys strutted among the hardwoods; and wildfowl by
the thousands flew the skies. The fertile coastal marshes, rich in
aquatic plants and marine life, were near ideal habitat for ducks
and geese. It's likely that the good captain or one of his men fired the
shot that started the rich wildfowling tradition of the Atlantic Coast.

The early settlers hunted primarily for food. Ducks and geese were
welcome additions to the austere pioneer diet. Then came the market
hunters, hardy men who found a ready market for wildfowl in the
eastern cities. Eventually market hunting gave way to sport hunting,
a grand pursuit in which the monetary value of the kill is of little
consequence. This is the wildfowling we know today.

Virginia, along with Maryland, Delaware, New Jersey, and the
Carolinas, was the setting for this interesting sidelight to the history
of America. As the science of waterfowl management slowly evolved,

the various flyways which marked the major migration routes of our waterfowl resources were established. The old wildfowl states were grouped with New England, New York, Pennsylvania, West Virginia, Florida, and Georgia in what is now well known as the Atlantic Flyway. In many respects, the history of the Atlantic Flyway is the history of wildfowling in America.

The Atlantic is a vast flyway, covering 446,000 square miles of eastern mountains, hills, and coastal regions. But its heart lies in the wetlands—32 million acres of islands, bays, sounds, river estuaries, swamps, marshes, and a 7000-mile irregular coastline. An estimated 90 percent of the best wildfowl wetlands stretch from Maryland south through the Carolinas and into Georgia.

Inland from the rich coastal region, another 29 million acres of freshwater marshes and swamps add considerably to the total water-fowl habitat.

While there is good waterfowl hunting throughout this vast region, the bulk of the migrating flights by-pass the New England states and enter the flyway from New York on southward. Thus the history-rich Atlantic states remain the very heart of the Atlantic Flyway. They are: New Jersey, Delaware, Maryland, Virginia, West Virginia, North and South Carolina, and Georgia.

The two major groups of ducks—puddle ducks or dabblers, and divers—are distributed in about equal numbers in these states. However, the dabblers furnish an estimated 80 percent of the shooting.

The black duck is the top-ranking bird in the bags of Atlantic Flyway hunters. These popular ducks nest from North Carolina northward, but are joined in the fall by migrants from higher latitudes. The tidal areas and freshwater swamps from New Jersey to South Carolina are favored wintering grounds of the black duck (often called black mallard by local hunters and guides).

Perhaps second in importance to the black duck is its close relative, the mallard. Mallards occur throughout the states under discussion, but more than half winter in the wooded bottomlands, marshes, and impoundments of South Carolina. The Delmarva Peninsula marshes and grain fields also offer good shooting. Mallards breed the length of the flyway, yet most migrate into it from the Great Lakes region, Ontario, and Manitoba.

Wood ducks nest in every state in the flyway, with resident birds furnishing most of the shooting. These beautiful little ducks winter mainly in the freshwater swamps and marshes of Georgia and South Carolina. Woodies nest in trees, and the loss of big hollow trees through hurricanes and indiscriminate logging is a major deterrent to greater wood duck populations.

The little green-winged teal rates fourth in the Atlantic Flyway hunter's bag. These popular, fine-eating ducks are produced in the wooded areas of eastern Canada. Most winter in the fresh and brackish marsh areas of North and South Carolina and Georgia.

The American widgeon or baldpate, migrating from the prairie country of Canada, also contributes heavily to the hunter's bag. Widgeon are prominent among the early fall visitors to the Susquehanna Flats, but they winter on fresh and brackish marshes from Long Island south. They are especially abundant in Maryland and South Carolina.

Other important puddle ducks include blue-winged teal, gadwall, pintails, and shovelers. Both the gadwall and shoveler (or spoonbill) winter mostly in South Carolina. However, local colonies of gadwall are found along the coast from North Carolina northward.

The two species of scaup—greater and lesser—are the most popular of the diving ducks. The majority of greater scaup winters from New Jersey north, but severe weather may push them south to the broad Chesapeake Bay. Greater scaup prefer big waters—broad coastal bays, sounds and tidal rivers, and large inland lakes and rivers. Lesser scaup winter in the more southern portions of the flyway, where they favor inland or brackish coastal waters.

The ring-necked duck, although not particularly abundant in the flyway, is a favorite among waterfowlers. It decoys well and is very tasty on the table. This diving duck is most abundant during the winter months, particularly in South Carolina and Georgia, but a few are found as far north as Chesapeake Bay. The wintering ducks prefer fresh or slightly brackish water.

Both canvasbacks and redheads, once among the most popular waterfowl in the Atlantic Flyway, have been fully protected in recent years. But there is some indication that populations may be recovering from their once dangerously low levels.

Canvasbacks winter primarily in Maryland, Virginia, and the Carolinas, where they feed on wild celery and pondweed. The redhead is most abundant along the eastern shore of Maryland and eastern North Carolina.

Other diving ducks include the goldeneye and bufflehead in the more northern parts of the flyways, and the ruddy duck in Maryland and Virginia. Hooded and red-breasted mergansers are taken all along the flyway from New Jersey to Georgia.

Currituck Sound still produces good bags of ducks.

In recent years much eastern waterfowl hunting has been directed toward the huge flocks of Canada geese bred primarily in eastern Canada. An estimated 75 percent of these big birds winter in the tidewater country between Kent County, Delaware, and Hyde County, North Carolina. Concentrations of up to 10,000 birds are common.

The total population of Canadas in this area has averaged between 400,000 and 500,000 birds since the early 1950's. The harvest in the better seasons exceeds 100,000 geese.

The Delmarva Peninsula, a fertile farming area, is the prime hunting ground for geese. In fact, hunters to the south often accuse wildfowl-hunting farmers of stopping the normal migration of geese by providing them with an overabundance of food.

In recent seasons, the expanding goose populations have shown signs of moving inland to the Piedmont and upper coastal plains.

The American brant, once abundant south to North Carolina, suffered a drastic decline in the early 1930's with the disappearance of eelgrass, its favorite food. The comeback of this plant, along with the brant's willingness to accept sea lettuce as a substitute, has brought about a resurgence of brant populations. These birds winter from Cape Cod to North Carolina, but Barnegat Bay is now their prime wintering ground.

The spectacular snow goose, show bird of the Atlantic Flyway and completely protected for many years, appeared again on the legal list for the 1975-76 season. This bird offers an exciting new challenge to the eastern wildfowler. Snows winter along the tidal marshes from New Jersey to North Carolina.

The often-cussed coot is considered a table delicacy by many natives. Wintering primarily in the central and southern states of the flyway, it is usually abundant during the peak of the waterfowl season.

Synonymous with wildfowling in the Atlantic Flyway are such romantic names as Great South Bay, Barnegat Bay, Susquehanna Flats, Chesapeake Bay, Back Bay, Currituck Sound, Mattamuskeet, Pamlico, and Santee River. In the old days hunters from all over the east sought these rich hunting grounds for black ducks, canvasbacks, mallards, redheads, Canada and snow geese, swans, and other abundant species of waterfowl.

Eager New York hunters took the fast Pennsylvania Railroad to Baltimore, boarded a Bay Line steamer for an overnight trip down the Chesapeake Bay to Norfolk, and then took small steamers via the Chesapeake and Albemarle Canal to Currituck. Some hunters travelled the beaches by rail and then horse and buggy to reach plush hunting clubs along the Sound. For many city-dwelling wildfowlers, the excellent shooting at Barnegat Bay was very convenient.

But man and progress turned the tide against this once glorious hunting. River transportation and the resulting canals, channelization, and dredging destroyed prime habitat. The Manasquan Inlet and Bay Canal changed Barnegat Bay from a rich brackish area where aquatic vegetation flourished to a saline body of water which furnished little in the way of food for waterfowl.

Pollution of every conceivable kind was poured into the rivers, and the unrestricted use of pesticides caused high mortality among waterfowl populations, as well as other forms of wildlife. Pest plants such as water hyacinth, waterchestnut, and alligator-weed choked choice waters, eliminating more desirable plants. Thousands of acres of prime wildfowl habitat in New Jersey, Maryland, Virginia, and North Carolina were rendered almost useless to waterfowl by water milfoil. Fortunately, ways have been found to reduce many of these undesirable plants.

The ditching and draining of marshes for resorts; the increased use of the waterways by pleasure boaters; and other demands on the tidewater regions have also hurt the once-rich wildfowling.

Still, much good wildfowl hunting exists along the abused Atlantic Flyway, with much of the better gunning in the more southerly states.

"Duck hunting in South Carolina is equalled in only a few areas," says Tommy Strange, waterfowl biologist with the South Carolina Wildlife and Marine Resources Department. "The state often winters up to 40 percent of the Atlantic Flyway puddle duck population," he adds, "not to mention the divers and sea ducks found offshore." Mallards and blacks on the inland lakes, pintail and widgeon on the coast, and wood ducks in the swamps all provide pleasant memories for those lucky enough to draw a blind in one of the areas managed by the state. According to biologist Strange, the daily harvest per hunter is well above the national average.

Public drawings determine who will hunt the Big Pee Dee, Bear Island, and Santee-Cooper Waterfowl Management Areas. Applications for these drawings are available in early October from the South Carolina Wildlife and Marine Resource Commission, Box 167, Columbia, South Carolina 29202.

The Hatchery Pool Waterfowl Management Area is open on an unrestricted basis on specified days, as is the newly developed Santee-Delta Waterfowl Management Area.

"North Carolina has a long and rich waterfowl hunting tradition," says Joel Arrington, outdoor editor of the state's travel development section. "Its vast coastal sounds attract a great number and variety of divers and puddlers, Canada and snow geese, as well as brant. Hunting lodges and guides are concentrated primarily on Currituck Sound," he adds.

A list of these guides and lodges can be obtained by writing Arrington at the North Carolina Travel Development Section, P. O. Box 27687, Raleigh, North Carolina 27611. Approximately 25 guides operate along the rich Currituck marshes.

The U. S. Fish and Wildlife Service has temporarily suspended hunting at famous Lake Mattamuskeet, in an effort to restore the once fabulous goose shooting.

Public hunting in Virginia is concentrated at the big Back Bay, actually a northward extension of Currituck Sound. Some of the best hunting along this rich, narrow waterway can be found at the state-owned Barbours Hill and Trojan-Pocahontas Waterfowl Management Areas. Applications for blinds can be made by writing the Virginia Commission of Game and Inland Fisheries, Box 11104, Richmond, Virginia 23230. Blind assignments are made in October.

Public blinds are also available at the Hog Island Waterfowl Management Area on the James River. Blinds, boats, and decoys are supplied at Barbours Hill and Hog Island, but hunters must furnish their own at Trojan-Pocahontas.

While some of the very best wildfowling in America is found in the rich coastal region of Maryland, much of it is on private marshes. Still, there is reasonably good hunting on many wildlife management areas. Noteworthy are Sinepuxent Bay, Ernest A. Vaughan, Ellis Bay, Deal Island, Fairmont, Cedar Island, Pocomoke Sound, Fishing Bay, and Taylor's Island.

The hunter is generally on his own, and a boat is needed to reach the better marshes. Managed hunts by permit only are held at Fishing Bay.

"Maryland's eastern shore counties of Kent, Queen Anne's, Talbot, and Dorchester provide some of the nation's very best goose hunting," says Bill Perry, an outdoor writer from Easton, Maryland. "Easton is the hub of all eastern shore goose shooting. Most guides have abandoned water blinds in favor of more productive grain field pits, hedgerow blinds, and shore blinds. A day's shoot averages $100 per two-man blind."

Waterfowlers will find "A Guide to Maryland's Public Hunting Areas" an excellent source of information. This book can be obtained from the Maryland Department of Natural Resources, Tawes States Office Building B-2, Annapolis, Maryland 21401.

Pamlico Sound in North Carolina is a favorite spot for southern goose hunters.

Approximately one-twelfth of Delaware is marshland. Hence wild-fowling has a long and rich heritage in this small Atlantic state. While private lands offer the best shooting, there are also some good public hunting areas. Among them are the Little Creek and Woodland Beach Wildlife Areas, where hunters draw for blinds upon arrival at the checking station; and Assawoman, Augustine, Gordons Pond, and North Little Creek, where they build their own on a first-come basis.

To the south, Georgia offers limited public wildfowl hunting on the Lake Seminole and Altamaha Game Management Areas. However, the best wildfowling in the state is found on private lands.

"More ducks are killed along the coastal fringes than elsewhere. I suppose the best shooting might be around the Savannah National Wildlife Refuge above Savannah; the second best around the state's Altamaha Waterfowl Area near Darien," says Charlie Elliott, well known outdoor writer. "While there's some decoy shooting on the lakes and rivers of the state's interior, most duck hunting there is jump-shooting by guys who float the rivers. A good many gunners shoot the beaver ponds and backcountry lakes where wood ducks come in to roost after feeding in or along nearby streams. Possibly many more wood ducks are bagged in this state than other species," concludes Elliott.

New Jersey, a densely populated state, has good wildfowl hunting. Most of it occurs along the coast from Ocean County south to Cape May, around the Cape, and up Delaware Bay almost to the Delaware River. Ducks and brant make up the bulk of the hunters' bags. Good Wildlife Management Areas include Beaver Swamp, Dennis Creek, Nantuxent, and Tuckahoe-Corbin.

Mountainous West Virginia has "wood ducks and early teal, and lots of them," says outdoor writer Stan Meseroll of Glenville, West Virginia. "And that's about the extent of waterfowling in the state," Meseroll adds. "Most of the birds are taken by jump-shooting around the ponds of the McClintic Wildlife Station at Point Pleasant, and on small streams in the western side of the state. Some blacks and mallards, plus other assorted species are hunted from blinds and by jump-shooters along the Ohio River, usually late in the season."

The waterfowl season in the central Atlantic Flyway states opens in late September or early October for sea ducks. Several states also offer early seasons for coots, but the opening dates for most puddle and diving ducks begins in November. The Canada goose season coincides with ducks. Seasons on snow geese and brant do not ordinarily begin until December. Split seasons are the vogue in several states. West Virginia, for example, has an early October season on ducks and Canada geese, with the second segment of the split in December and early January.

Along with many other wildfowl states, Maryland, North Carolina, and Virginia have adopted the point system for establishing bag limits. Under this system the hunter is allowed 100 points per day, or slightly more if his last bird takes him over the magic mark. High point values are assigned to blacks, woodies, and hen mallards, with the more common and more abundant birds receiving lower numbers. This system permits the hunter to extend his shooting by passing up shots at the high-point ducks and concentrating on the lower valued ones. Geese and coots are not normally included in the point system.

Other states have retained the traditional daily bag limits, with special regulations on woodies, mallards, and some other species.

Non-resident hunting licenses in the waterfowl states are generally not excessive in price. The range centers around $20 to $30 for annual licenses. Less expensive, short-term licenses are available in

North and South Carolina. Some states require a state wildfowl stamp in addition to the Federal Migratory Bird Hunting Stamp.

The great majority of ducks are taken from either public or private blinds located in marshes or over water. Many hunts are guided, with the guides furnishing boats, decoys, and retrievers. But an increasing number of wildfowlers like to run their own hunts, packing boats, decoys, and prized Labrador and Chesapeake retrievers into the marshes.

Field hunting is popular for geese, especially from pits. This method of hunting is particularly effective in the Delmarva Peninsula area.

Sink-box blinds are peculiar to the Oracoke waters of the Pamlico Sound in North Carolina.

Jump-shooting is popular on many inland waters. A pair of hunters in a canoe or light boat can drift slowly down a woodland stream for chance shots at blacks, mallards, and woodies that flush before the boat. This is an exciting and oftentimes productive way to hunt. It is, at times, the only kind of wildfowling available on inland waters.

The Atlantic Flyway's glorious wildfowling history has been marred by man's indiscretions. But it still holds hope for many fowlers living in the crowded east. If we can maintain a healthy respect for wetlands, marshes, and clean waters, the Atlantic Flyway will hold its own with the best of wildfowling across America.

17

Wildfowling the Great Lakes Area

David Richey

W ILDFOWL POPULATIONS in the Great Lakes area have remained relatively unchanged over the past decade. In fact, some species, such as mallards and wood ducks, have increased. But not all is well. Both canvasbacks and redheads have declined noticeably, and are fully protected in some states.

Some states have initiated special scaup-only and teal-only seasons to offer hunters special, extended opportunities to hunt these birds. The teal-only seasons occur prior to the normal wildfowling season, in order to allow a harvest of this early-departing duck. Scaup-only seasons are generous in terms of length, as well as the number of birds available for harvest by hunters. The scaup-only season normally takes place after the general waterfowl season has ended.

Great Lakes duck and goose hunting depends, to a large extent, on the weather in northern Canada. Spring water conditions have a direct bearing on wildfowl populations. In addition, early fall storms in northern Ontario influence the time of migration of the birds into southern Ontario and the Great Lakes states of Michigan, Illinois, Indiana, Ohio, Wisconsin, Minnesota, New York, and Pennsylvania.

I have, indeed, seen instances where heavy migrations of ducks have passed through my area of Michigan before the opening of the season.

On the other hand, I've witnessed years where long, unseasonably mild autumn weather has kept the ducks and geese on the potholes of the Canadian prairies until the bulk of the season had passed. Hunters quibble over such happenings, but there is precious little they can do about them. The ways of weather and wildfowl are never certain.

On the Canadian side of the Great Lakes, the province of Ontario has a very long wildfowling season, extending from mid-September through mid-December. The season varies a little from year to year, and is set by the federal government of Canada.

The mallard is the most abundant duck in Ontario. Approximately one-third of the total duck kill consists of mallards. Game biologists rate the mallard population in southern Ontario as the healthiest in North America. Other ducks in plentiful supply in Ontario marshes and lakes are bluebills, black ducks, blue-winged teal, and wood ducks.

The Great Lakes are best known for their diver duck shooting.

Some of the best duck hunting in Ontario is located along the shorelines of Lakes Huron, Ontario, and Erie. The Thousand Islands area of Lake Ontario is well known among wildfowlers. So are the bays and marshes around Prince Edward County, particularly late in the season when the divers are down from the north. The string of marshes along the north shore of Lake Erie has been famous for duck shooting since the days of market hunting. Many of the marshes are privately owned, but public marshes exist at Long Point and Rondeau. Both of these marshes have controlled hunts, limited to 3 days a week. For more information on duck hunting in this area, write to the Fish and Wildlife Supervisor, Ministry of Natural Resources, District Office, Aylmer, Ontario.

Lake St. Clair is also famous for its duck hunting, particularly on the marshes of the Walpole Island Indian Reserve. A number of Indians guide duck hunters in this area. The local Indian agent arranges the hunts.

The entire coast of Lake Huron has good diver duck shooting late in the season. The Severn River area is particularly well known. But a number of lodges further up the Georgian Bay coastline also offer good duck hunting, including knowledgeable guides with boats and decoys.

Since Ontario is a wetland province with literally over a million lakes, the wildfowling is quite good in many areas, particularly during the early season for local birds. Beaver pond shooting is especially popular. But jump-shooting with canoes on small streams and rivers is also productive.

Non-resident waterfowl hunters require a $35 small game licence plus a $3.50 federal migratory game bird permit.

Canada, blue, and snow geese are the major attraction for Ontario goose hunters. Although many of the big geese are shot by hunters plying the Hudson-James Bay area of northern Ontario, surprisingly good goose shooting exists in widely scattered locations through the south of the province. One of my favorite spots for good Canada honker hunting is in scattered corn fields bordering the Ottawa River near Ottawa. Some blues and snows come into this area as well.

The farm lands around Sarnia on the shore of Lake St. Clair also get good flights of Canadas. Amherst and Wolfe Islands, close to Kingston, are traditional resting spots for south bound geese.

But the holy grail of Ontario goose gunning lies on the west coast of James Bay, from Moosonee northward to Attawapiskat. Blues

Ontario's James Bay coastline.

and snows predominate, but Canadas are abundant east of Moosonee in Hannah Bay. The entire area also offers excellent duck gunning for mallards, pintails, and blacks.

In fact, ducks frequently offer more challenging gunning than geese. Geese can be suckers for the calling skill of the guides. The guides along the west coast of James Bay are Swampy Crees, legendary in their abilities to call goose. It is frequently said that the Crees in this area speak three languages—English, Cree, and goose. The hunting is done out of comfortable camps, and the trips are booked as package hunts, including air transportation, guides, accommodation, and meals. The geese and ducks are plucked and dressed by the Indian women, as part of the package price. Quebec Eskimo

Indian Outfitters, Box 520, Rawdon, Quebec, is a booking agent for a number of government-managed goose camps.

Michigan has a surprising variety of duck and goose hunting. The basic framework of season lengths has remained pretty much unchanged since the mid-1960's. The goose season in zones 1 and 2 (Upper Peninsula and the northern half of the Lower Peninsula) opens October 1. Zone 3 (southern half of the Lower Peninsula) opens the same day as the duck season.

The length of the duck season is dictated by the U.S. Fish and Wildlife Service, and is subject to slight changes from year to year. Michigan operates on the point system. There is no open season on canvasbacks and redheads. Ninety-point ducks include hen mallards, black ducks, wood ducks, and hooded mergansers. Ducks with a 35-point value include drake mallards, ringnecks, baldpate, oldsquaws, scoters, ruddy ducks, common and red-breasted mergansers, goldeneyes, and buffleheads. Scaup, pintails, blue-winged and green-winged teal, gadwall, and shovelers carry a value of 10 points. The point system reads that a daily bag limit for ducks and mergansers is 100 points.

The mallard seems to be the premier duck in Michigan waters, although more and more hunters are leaving the marshes and taking up open-water hunting for the more prevalent diving duck species such as scaup.

The Canada goose is number one in the goose clan, in terms of hunter interest. Several areas have been set aside in Michigan, strictly for goose hunting. Among the favorites is the Seney Goose Management Area in the Upper Peninsula, the Saginaw County Goose Management Area near Saginaw, the Tuscola County Goose Management Area near Sebewaing, and the Allegan County Goose Management Area near Allegan.

Duck hunters have a more diversified area to consider. Some of the most popular spots include Saginaw Bay, Lake St. Clair, Munuscong Bay, the western Lake Erie marshes, Thunder Bay, Squaw Bay, Houghton Lake, Hamlin Lake, St. Martin's Bay, Big and Little Bay de Noc, and many scattered inland lakes, streams, and potholes.

I especially like hunting mallards, blacks, and teal in the marshes of the Nayanquing Point Wildlife Area near Bay City, and scaup or goldeneyes in the offshore waters of Saginaw Bay near Sebewaing. To me, there is a special thrill in watching a brace of blacks circle on cupped wings into a stool of pothole-bound decoys, or in seeing the unafraid splashy entrance of a small bunch of goldeneyes as they pitch, on whistling wings, into the frothy gray waves. These are the thrills that make Michigan duck hunting so enjoyable.

Indiana, although part of the prolific Mississippi Flyway, is not considered an important wildfowling state. There are very few breeding ground areas in the state, with the exception of some fairly good wood duck breeding sites.

The bulk of Indiana's duck gunning revolves around the mallard. The black duck, also an important species in this state, is down drastically in numbers throughout its range. This decline is felt in Indiana's waters.

Indiana has a split season on waterfowl, from late October to early December, and again from mid-December to the end of the calendar year. The goose season runs from late October to early December and again from mid-December to mid-January. A special bonus teal season for bluewings and greenwings takes place in early September.

The state operates a number of waterfowl hunting areas on state lands at Willow Slough, Kankakee, LaSalle, Glendale, Hovey, Pigeon River, Kingsbury, and Tri-County. Hunting blind sites are available at the Monroe, Brookville, and Hardy Reservoirs. Many of these blinds are set aside for goose hunters going after their limit of one Canada goose.

Although much of Indiana's waterfowl gunning takes place on state-owned sites, some hunting can be found on small potholes, inland lakes, and rivers, as hunters work the local populations of ducks.

The duck harvest in recent years has been composed of approximately 39 percent mallards, 19 percent wood ducks, 8 percent black ducks, 8 percent blue-winged teal, 5 percent gadwalls, and 4 percent ring-necked ducks. The remainder is split among various species.

Ohio has a vast reserve of duck hunting along its northern frontier on Lake Erie. The marshes and offshore islands of Lake Erie teem with thousands of waterfowl during the autumn months.

The wood duck is the most common species in Ohio, although blue-winged teal, mallards, and blacks are also abundant. There is some hunting for Canada honkers, blues, and snow geese in certain areas. Ohio has a restriction that redheads and canvasbacks may not be hunted in Ottawa, Erie, and Sandusky Counties.

Many of the shoreline marshes from Toledo east to Cleveland harbor some of Ohio's finest puddle duck hunting. For diver hunting, the offshore waters around the Bass Islands and Maumee Bay near

The Lake Erie marshes offer some of the best duck hunting in the Great Lakes area.

Toledo bear serious investigation by hunters. Some of the best hunting is found in this area.

The seasons on ducks and geese in Ohio vary from area to area. But generally they start in early October, and in some cases run until mid-January.

Illinois is a state rich in wildfowling tradition. Areas such as Crab Orchard Lake, Horseshoe Lake, and a number of spots along the Mississippi River are known world wide as top-notch hunting localities.

Like the time-worn joke, Illinois offers some good news and some bad news. Wildfowl habitat along the Illinois and Mississippi Rivers seems to be declining as a result of siltation. On the plus side of the ledger, Illinois has a number of new reservoirs—Carlyle and Rend Lake—which show great promise for public duck hunting areas. More such areas are being planned. Canada goose hunting also looks bright in Illinois, and the state has plans for expanded hunting over an increasing population.

The Illinois Department of Conservation has a publication entitled *Waterfowl Hunter's Guide to Illinois,* which could be a valuable aid to duck and goose shooters in pointing out wildfowl hunting opportunities. The cost is $2, and the publication can be ordered from the department by writing to 605 State Office Building, 400 South Spring Street, Springfield, Illinois 62706.

Like many other states, Illinois operates under the point system. The season on ducks extends from late October to early December. The goose season in much of the state runs from late October to late December. In Alexander, Jackson, Union, and Williamson Counties, the goose season runs from late November to the end of January.

Southern Illinois continues to show high numbers of wildfowl and hunters. Goose hunters in Illinois harvest about 24,000 birds per year, and enjoy a 49 percent success rate. Only one area of Illinois has special regulations that are mentioned in the federal hunting regulations. This is the Southern Illinois Quota Zone for Canada Geese. Hunters are asked to consult state authorities or hunting regulations for any changes.

Wisconsin offers wildfowlers ample opportunity to sample hunting, from the rough wind-tossed Lakes Michigan and Superior to quiet potholes and state-managed hunting areas. The best waterfowl hunting seems to lie in east-central Wisconsin, within a 50-mile radius of Lake Winnebago, and also along the Mississippi River. The Horicon area, which includes the National Wildlife Refuge and State Wildlife Area, is a heavy concentration point for Canada geese.

The most abundant ducks in Wisconsin are the mallard, the wood duck, and the blue-winged teal. These species are also the primary native ducks produced locally in the state.

Wisconsin's duck season runs from early October to mid-November. The goose season in the Horicon area is open for about 2 weeks in October. The remainder of the state has a goose season extending from early October to early December. The Canada goose is the primary target, although a certain percentage of snows and whitefronts are also taken.

The future of wildfowl hunting in Wisconsin is unclear. Poor hunter attitude and quality are apparent on state wildfowl areas, according to wildlife specialists. They maintain that some hunter control is imperative in the future. Mandatory hunter training and waterfowl identification courses are becoming more and more necessary each year. Wildfowling in Wisconsin will ultimately depend on good habitat and the proper behavior of the hunter.

Minnesota offers some first-rate wildfowl hunting, although the regulations are a bit more restrictive than the federal framework. The best areas are found in the northwestern and west-central portions of the state. Good hunting can also be found on the larger lakes of north-central Minnesota. Some good gunning exists on the many wildlife management areas in the southwest, and on some of the managed game lakes in south-central Minnesota.

The northeastern counties of Cook, Lake, St. Louis, Koochiching, Carlton, and Pine are considered to be the worst wildfowling areas.

Wildfowling regulations in Minnesota have remained relatively unchanged over the past few years. Of particular note to hunters are the following restrictions: there is no hunting from open water; all wildfowl hunting closes at 4:00 p.m.; no bonus teal or scaup are allowed; and a bag limit of only one Canada goose per day is in effect. The general wildfowl season in Minnesota opens at noon on October 1, but some areas have special openings and closings.

Hunters are reminded that no hunting exists in the Voyageurs National Park. Much of this land and water lie in scattered unmarked tracts. Maps are available by writing Box 50, International Falls, Minnesota 56649.

The easternmost Great Lakes state, New York, has enjoyed better-than-average wildfowling in recent years. The brant season has re-opened after an absence of several years, and greater snow geese have become abundant enough to offer the first hunting season since 1930. The upstate area offers a 50-day straight duck season, running from early October through late November.

Liberalized daily bag limits, in the form of two bonus blue-winged teal in addition to the basic bag, have been in effect during the first 9 days of the season in both the upstate and Lake Champlain areas. Scaup are also in excellent supply, and a special scaup-only season is open on certain portions of the Great Lakes and the St. Lawrence River. The limit is 5 scaup per day and 10 in possession. However, wood ducks and black ducks are in short supply, with limits of only one black or 2 woodies per day. Canvasbacks and redheads are completely protected.

The Canada goose season begins in early October and continues through to mid-December. Three Canadas may be taken daily, with 6 in possession. The brant season opens in mid-November and runs to early December, with a bag limit of 4 birds per day and 8 in possession. The same season applies for snow geese, except on Long Island where the season opens and closes a little later.

Long Island has a 50-day duck and a 63-day Canada goose season, opening in mid-November. A special tidal water scaup-only season extends for 2 weeks in mid-January. As before, the limit on scaup is 5 per day and 10 in possession. Long Island also has a special sea-duck season for scoters, eiders, and oldsquaws, running from late September to early January. The daily bag limit is 7, with 14 birds in possession.

New York hotspots for wildfowling can pretty well be pinpointed to Lake Ontario, Lake Erie, the St. Lawrence River west of Interstate 81, Lake Champlain, and the Long Island area. There are, of course, many local areas in addition. The New York State Department of Environmental Conservation, in Delmar, New York, is a good source of wildfowling information.

In neighboring Pennsylvania, duck and goose hunters have a split hunting season, similar to that of several other Great Lakes states. The first half of the season kicks off in mid-October and extends to late November. The second half begins in early December and lasts for 2 weeks. Crawford County has a split season for geese, from mid-October to early December, and again for 2 or so weeks in January. Canada geese, snows, and blues may all be taken. The brant season runs from early November to early December.

Much of Pennsylvania's wildfowl hunting is centered around the marshes bordering Lake Erie. But many duck hunters find fast-paced action on small inland lakes and reservoirs. Jump-shooting with canoes on streams and rivers is growing in popularity. Only two wood ducks may be held as a possession limit in Pennsylvania. Other states in the Atlantic Flyway have a 4-wood-duck possession limit.

Duck hunting in the Great Lakes states can be divided into two classical groups: puddle duck shooting and diver duck gunning. Hunting the ponds and shoreline marshes for dabblers is a favorite sport among Great Lake hunters. Secluded potholes, far back in the marsh, offer the hunter a chance to allow the circling and wary puddle ducks to come in to well placed decoys. Skillful calling can do wonders for duck hunters, although a novice on a call can scare away more ducks than a moving hunter.

Generally speaking, a half dozen to a dozen realistic decoys are sufficient to lure puddle ducks into your pothole. The blocks should be placed so that the ducks, landing into the wind, will pass directly in front of your blind. Blinds should be kept small and covered with natural vegetation such as cattails or local brush, to blend well with the surrounding terrain. Never build a blind from materials foreign to the area.

One regional method of duck hunting is float-hunting a river with a canoe. A small canoe, with one paddler and one shooter, floats downstream with the gunner in the bow. The paddler steers the canoe and sticks to the insides of the river bends. Ducks will usually flush within easy shooting range. Many hunters paint their canoe a drab olive, and outfit the bow with a small blind which can be pushed down when it's time to shoot.

Goose hunting in the Great Lakes region takes place, with few exceptions, on state-operated areas. These goose hotspots are often close to a state or federal refuge. Strict quotas govern the numbers of geese that can be harvested.

Much of the goose hunting in these areas is done from pits dug at strategic locations. Goose decoys are set out, and the hunters wait anxiously for the morning flights to work out of the refuges and into the feeding areas. Pass-shooting is the name of the game in some areas, while in others the geese will come warily into decoys.

I much prefer to watch flights of geese to determine where the birds are feeding, set up a timetable as to their arrival, and get my decoys out at least an hour before the geese are due to come in. Silhouette decoys are ideal for corn field hunting. Silhouettes are light-weight and facilitate easy placement. And they really fool geese.

On the whole, wildfowling in the Great Lakes states and Ontario has a pretty secure future. Wildfowl management has brought back some species of ducks, and the sport is looking reasonably good. The Great Lakes area certainly offers some of the most varied and interesting types of wildfowling known.

18

Wildfowling in the Upper Mississippi States

H. Lea Lawrence

THE UPPER MISSISSIPPI states—Missouri, Kentucky, Arkansas and Tennessee—exhibit wildfowl hunting opportunities that range all the way from superb to minimal. But considering the overall topography of the regions involved, a part of this is easily understood.

Kentucky and Tennessee, for example, each begin on their eastern borders with mountain ranges—hardly ideal wildfowl habitat. From this highland terrain, there is a gradual "ironing out" of the countryside as it progresses westward, with rolling hills in the central portions, then flatter land approaching the Mississippi and Ohio Rivers.

In the past, these rivers and their influences were responsible for the principal amount of wildfowl hunting, and in effect, the fairly narrow bottomland strip was "it" with respect to the concentration of activity by both hunters and birds. With nothing to the east that was particularly attractive, ducks and geese seldom fanned out from the mainline flyway route.

It isn't the same in either of these states today, but it's best to look at their situations individually.

In Kentucky, extensive management in the western part of the state has produced results that have been highly significant, and which have attracted the attention of wildfowl managers all over the country.

A single area has accomplished the big difference: the Ballard County Wildlife Management Area, a model plan that has succeeded in producing an exceptional amount of sport for a great many hunters. It has also proved that through proper management, a substantially improved bag can be obtained.

Snugged up against the Ohio River, the Ballard Area is approximately 35 miles southwest of Paducah, and directly in the flyway pattern. The county has long enjoyed fine duck and goose shooting; however, it wasn't hunting to which the public had access, other than through commercial operations.

The Kentucky Department of Fish and Wildlife Resources developed the Ballard County unit to provide as much public hunting opportunity as possible. The success of the program is unquestionable. Hunters can submit applications for hunts in late September, and each individual is permitted to participate for a certain number of days each season. The small fee required pays for pit maintenance, decoys, transportation to and from the pit, and so on. As a part of the management plan, shooting ends at 12 noon each day, and there is no Sunday or Christmas Day shooting.

Ballard is best known for its goose hunting, but there is also high quality duck hunting on the area, with mallards and blacks the predominant species. In order to obtain maximum results, the two kinds of shooting are separated. Another of the regulations that has increased the efficiency of hunters is the eight-shell limit governing the amount of ammunition that can be taken into the pits.

There are also several commercial goose hunting operations in the county for those who prefer a situation where advance applications aren't required. Visiting hunters can find rooms and meals at La Center, Barlow, Oscar, Bandana, Wickliffe and Paducah.

Another popular Ohio River wildfowl hunting location is the Henderson Sloughs Wildlife Management Area, which lies west of Owensboro. There are three units within this complex, and no special regulations apply beyond the statewide rules. The sloughs represent a somewhat different kind of hunting than the Ballard Area. Most shooting is done from blinds, and the most prevalent game sought are ducks, rather than geese. A greater variety of ducks are found there, both puddle ducks and divers.

Since some of the terrain around the sloughs is swampy, a four-

The area around White River Refuge offers some of the best wildfowling in Arkansas.

wheel-drive vehicle is advisable. Obtaining additional information on the area in advance of a planned hunt is also wise. Guide services can sometimes be secured by inquiring at the small towns near the individual units.

Both the Kentucky Lake and Barkley Lake segments of the public hunting area complex offer considerable opportunity, as well. Kentucky Lake has 3274 acres in Calloway, Marshall and Lyon counties, consisting mainly of islands, mudflats, lowlands at the backs of bays, and a narrow strip of land around much of the shoreline. Access is by boat and by several TVA access points and rural roads. No special regulations apply.

At Barkley, 2400 acres in Trigg, Lyon and Livingston counties are available, primarily on islands. At this location, special regulations are imposed.

Both of these areas provide good goose and duck shooting, and the big water attracts a wide number of species. Pits on the islands are popular for geese, and some hunters favor the use of floating blinds for duck shooting. With several refuges on these lakes, a concentration of birds is assured annually.

The nearby Land Between the Lakes, TVA's model recreational project, has wildfowl hunting that is managed by TVA and the Department of Fish and Wildlife. Statewide season structures usually apply, but there are special area regulations, also.

The central and eastern portions of the state offer less spectacular opportunities, and the successful hunter must be both mobile and imaginative. Yet those who are willing to work at it can end up with respectable bags of birds for their efforts. The problem lies in the fact that there are no major concentrations of wildfowl in these regions, and a number of tactics must be employed that aren't necessary in the western hunting locations.

Floating streams and rivers produces good shooting at times, and there are numerous farm ponds that attract small numbers of ducks. On some riverbottom lands, where mechanical harvesting of corn occurs, field shooting can be good. A few of the lakes in the central-state area also offer hunters some incentive to hunt over decoys. Finally, those who are knowledgeable about specific places along the Ohio River have particular "hot spots" that can keep a limited number of hunters pretty happy. Most of these, however, are on private land.

Information on hunting in this state can be obtained from: State of Kentucky, Department of Fish and Wildlife Resources, Capital Plaza Tower, Frankfort, Kentucky 40601.

Tennessee's wildfowl hunting can't be classed as the best in the Mississippi region, but it can easily qualify as having the most diversified offering. There are reasons for this, and practically all of them are man-oriented in one way or another.

At one time, Tennessee, like Kentucky, had duck and goose hunting of reasonable quality only in the western part of the state. This was either on the Mississippi River, in the seasonally flooded timberlands adjacent to the river, or at the famed Reelfoot Lake, the earthquake-formed wildfowl paradise in the extreme northwestern corner of the state. Of these, only Reelfoot remains as a prime spot.

What created the potential for a comprehensive and widespread wildfowl program was the emergence of the vast network of TVA and U.S. Corps of Engineers impoundments that dot Tennessee from border to border. With these large water areas to attract the birds, the next step was a series of refuges to provide food and resting places to hold the birds.

Actually, the principal amount of intensive management with regard to hunter participation has occurred in the mid-state region where the character of the lakes has permitted use of the sub-impoundment plan. This concept, in which birds are hunted over crops grown at the sites when they are drained, and which are flooded prior to the season, has been tremendously effective. Where at one time only minimal wildfowl hunting opportunity existed, there is now a dependable annual influx and concentration of birds.

There is no single method used in the operation of these various wildfowl units. On some of the reservoirs, the entire lake is open to public hunting without additional fee or permit. At others, certain portions of the lake are designated as wildfowl management areas, with special regulations and requirements. These differ considerably in the way they are handled. At some, individuals make application for hunt dates, and the facilities are constructed by the state. Vacancies that occur are filled on a first-come, first-serve basis on the mornings of the hunt dates. Other areas have a plan which involves hunters drawing for blind sites that they will use for the entire season. And at a few of the areas, hunters simply check in and choose a spot for a single day's hunt.

All of these provide an enormous amount of public hunting opportunity, but there are other choices for those who don't want to become involved in the managed area activity.

Both float hunting and shooting over decoys are very productive on a number of streams and rivers throughout Tennessee, including several places in the eastern region. None of the major lakes is governed in its entirety by the management plan, and on all of these there is fine hunting potential under the statewide regulations. Free permits for blind construction can be obtained from the U.S. Corps on lands around some of the lakes operated under closer regulations.

At Reelfoot Lake, there are abundant wildfowl hunting lodges and guides. This is one of the most picturesque and productive places in the state. Immediately to the south of Reelfoot, Lake Isom provides terrific goose hunting.

Because of the broad expanse and variety of water areas, Tennessee fowlers get a mixed bag of species. Early-season kills usually include many wood ducks, since a large number of native birds are represented. As the season progresses, both puddle ducks and divers are found on the big lakes. Reelfoot Lake is noted for its gadwall (locally called "gray duck") shooting, but mallards form an equally significant part of the bag there. The only quality goose shooting away from the western border lies at Kentucky and Barkley Lakes.

Since the wildfowl program in the state involves so many separate rules and regulations, it is best to get more comprehensive information. Write: Tennessee Wildlife Resources Agency, Ellington Agricultural Center, P.O. Box 40747, Nashville, Tennessee 37204.

Hunters looking toward Missouri will be happily surprised by the immense amount of public hunting opportunity available for wildfowlers. By the same token, they will discover that it exists at the places where the best potential lies.

A solid development program created this bonanza. The Missouri Department of Conservation took full advantage of the magic of the Mississippi River. Operating on lands leased from the U.S. Corps of Engineers and the Bureau of Sport Fisheries and Wildlife, they put together a complex of hunting locations of exceptional quality.

Actually, they obtained an ideal location at which to do this. The riverbottom lands north of St. Louis have long been famed for superior wildfowl hunting. On the Missouri side of the river, a delta formed by the confluence of the Missouri and Mississippi Rivers parallels another delta that is the result of the joining of the Mississippi and Illinois Rivers. Directly in the heart of the flyway, it is like the flanged end of a funnel.

Called the Upper Mississippi River Waterfowl Management Area, it consists of 87 separate tracts on 12,500 acres lying between the Alton Lock and Dam, and La Grange. Included in this are 85 areas that cover a total of 11,175 acres, all of which is open to public hunting. Some of the units require applications for blind sites, which are selected at a drawing; others are hunted from blinds not assigned by the state.

Many of the hunting units are on islands, but there are numerous public launching ramps that serve as access points. As in the case of the mainland areas, some of these islands are classed as "restricted public hunting," and others as "open public hunting."

Faced with the prospects of trying to unravel all the details and locations represented by this complex might seem to be a difficult chore. But a complete guide, including maps, is furnished free of charge by the Department of Conservation. In addition, specific information can be obtained at the area headquarters located at the U.S. Plant Materials Center, one mile south of Elsberry on highway 79.

This area gets a full spectrum of wildfowl species, and with a variety of shooting situations presented—pits and blinds, and potholes, oxbow lakes and the rivers—hunters can select one which is most favorable for the type of gunning preferred.

The Upper Mississippi Area isn't all of Missouri's wildfowl offering, by any means. Through an intensive development program, a series of managed areas have been created to spread the opportunity all across the state. There are six of these, each handled in such a way as to permit maximum public use. This is accomplished by one-day hunts, reservations for which are made by advance application. All shooting is done from blinds provided by the state. Hunters are not limited to a single trip to these areas, and in most cases, reservations not filled, or cancelled, are available by a telephone call. The basic operation of these areas is the same, but there are certain regulations applying to individual locations that should be checked out in advance of a hunt.

The Duck Creek Area southwest of Cape Girardeau, and near Wappapello Reservoir, is a favorite east-state location that provides excellent timber shooting on a part of the area. The Duck Creek site is adjacent to the Mingo National Wildlife Refuge. This location gets a heavy concentration of mallards, sometimes running as high as 90 percent of the 140,000-bird total.

In the western part of the state, between Kansas City and Springfield, the Montrose and Schell-Osage Wildlife Management Areas serve as places where hunters from these metropolitan areas can enjoy wildfowl shooting within reasonable distances from home. On the Montrose area there are about 15 blinds available, while the Schell-Osage area has about 25 blinds and a wade-and-shoot section.

Directly north of Kansas City, the Trimble Wildlife Management Area offers about 10 blinds, and gets plenty of attention from hunters in the nearby city. As with the Montrose and Schell-Osage Wildlife Management Areas, the large number of applications received annually lengthen the odds for being selected.

The two remaining Wildlife Management Areas in this part of the state, Fountain Grove and Swan Lake, which lie side-by-side due east from Chillicothe, attract large numbers of hunters from the western cities. There is good reason for this, because the Swan Lake National Wildlife Refuge gets one of the largest single concentrations of Canada geese in North America, sometimes numbering as high as 130,000 birds. The Swan Lake Wildlife Management Area, which occupies a strip of land adjacent to the refuge, is managed for goose hunting. There are about 55 pits and blinds for hunter use on a reservation basis. Fountain Grove has both duck and goose hunting from assigned blinds.

In the northwestern corner of the state near Mound City, the Squaw

Flooded timberlands along the Mississippi River make for fine duck gunning.

Creek National Wildlife Refuge attracts thousands of blue and snow geese, as well as a large number of Canada geese and ducks. Lands surrounding this location afford prime wildfowl hunting, mostly in the harvested fields. There are several commercial hunting operations, and some private landowners will permit hunting either by permission or for a small fee.

There is plenty of hunting potential in places other than the state-managed sites. Portions of the Missouri River provide good float shooting and field hunting in the bottomlands. The numerous sandbars and islands not under state management that can be found on the Mississippi River are also good bets. A vast complex of farm ponds across the state give mobile hunters chances for some worthwhile shooting at various times.

The majority of Missouri's duck population is mallards, although other species are taken in considerable numbers at the various locations. Some open water shooting is available on the large impoundments, also, and those who favor this kind of hunting have plenty of room in which to operate. In most cases, hunting around the lakes doesn't involve special regulations.

Stuttgart, Arkansas, has long held the title of "duck hunting capital of the world". It lies in the center of the area that is the terminal point in the southward migration of mallards on the Mississippi Flyway. The Grand Prairie region between the White and Arkansas rivers is prime rice and soybean country, and with these foods it has all it takes to attract and hold birds.

The beauty of this situation from the hunter's standpoint is that there is a tremendous amount of public access to this bonanza. So rather than being a place to simply dream about, it offers wide-open possibilities for any wildfowler. The Arkansas Game and Fish Commission, which years ago recognized the need for public hunting lands, has created more public areas than any state in the nation. These extend all the way down the eastern part of the state from the Missouri border to the Louisiana line.

The most extensive of these public locations is in the heart of the Grand Prairie. Bayou Meto is a 35,000-acre tract in Jefferson and Arkansas counties, and each year some 12,000 acres of live timber is flooded for hunters—"greentree" shooting in the pin oak flats that is superb. This is wade-in hunting, and with no assigned blinds or sites. A hunter can move around and choose his own location.

Around Bayou Meto there are 12 parking and access areas as well as 30 miles of weather roads, so getting to it isn't a problem. However, it is a remote, wild and dense area that should be explored before planning a trip. Experienced hunters sometimes get lost. The best advice for a visiting hunter is to make the initial hunt with either a local hunter or a guide.

Bayou Meto represents only one of a broad array of public hunting locations, and there are a great number of choices that can be considered. In total, more than 134,000 acres are available throughout the eastern part of the state. The details on these are best learned by obtaining information from the agency, since maps and other particulars required serve most satisfactorily in this respect.

Mallards are *the* important species in Arkansas, and although other types occur, they are actually incidental by comparison. Goose hunting isn't of particular consequence. In many parts of the state there is no open season on geese.

The principal mallard migrations take place in early November, and the season in Arkansas is normally set as early as the federal guidelines will allow in order to take advantage of this activity. The large flights come down from Saskatchewan in one non-stop movement, completing the journey at the place where they will remain throughout the winter.

Some of the state's large reservoirs serve as resting locations for ducks, and shooting over decoys at these places can be very productive. In addition, some of the rivers and streams are excellent for floating. Because the "greentree" hunting is so popular, there's usually little competition for those employing these tactics.

Hunters visiting Arkansas have the advantage of a wide selection of facilities provided by the state, as well as a full range of accommodations, guides and other services that are tailored for wildfowlers.

19

Wildfowling in the Midwest

Pete Czura

SOME OF THE PRIME DUCK HUNTING spots in Nebraska are no longer available to most sportsmen. For example, access to most of the Platte River—between Scottsbluff and Bellevue —is locked up by private ownership. Most of this fantastic mallard hunting area is restricted to public hunting, with groups and several industries having leased the majority of hunting lands along the Platte. Chances of obtaining permission to hunt along this river from landowners, today, is practically nil.

During the past few years the Nebraska Game Commission has made some inroads in gaining access to the Platte River by purchasing 36 parcels of land between Grand Island and Big Springs, including 17 miles of Platte riverfront. Here a man can build a temporary blind, either facing the river or looking onto one of the 49 lakes set into the Platte Valley wildlife areas, and from that blind the hunter can count on some of the finest wildfowl hunting in Nebraska.

Although the Nebraska Game Commission does list over 100 public shooting areas which offer wildfowl hunting opportunities, the hunting, at best, can be classed as fair.

One of the best public hunting areas for snow and blue geese is the Plattsmouth Waterfowl Management Area. However, the 12 blinds available are simply not enough for the numbers of sportsmen applying for blind permits. And winners of a blind at a public draw can't apply again for two years. However, if a blind is vacant, hunters appearing at the headquarters office can draw for a chance to use the vacant blind for that day only.

There is some controlled waterfowl hunting at the DeSoto National Wildlife Refuge on the Missouri River between Nebraska and Iowa, but again, good hunting opportunities are limited due to the scarcity of available blinds. Hunting dates vary in this area, as Nebraska and Iowa seasons differ.

The small federal waterfowl production management area of Shickley has some areas open to public hunting on a first-come, first-served basis. Blinds vacant at shooting time are available to the first hunter arriving. The hunting for mallards, scaup, gadwall, and teal is excellent here. During migration, occasional flocks of Canada geese provide bonus shooting. But the prime Canada goose hunting area in Nebraska is at Clear Creek, the western part of Lake McConaughy, near Lewellen. Several blind sites are available to sportsmen at a public drawing.

About 2½ miles west of Wilcox, you will find the Sacramento-Wilcox Game Management Area. It serves two functions: a waterfowl refuge and a public hunting area. Hunters have 22 free blinds available on a first-come, first-served basis. Jump- and pass-shooting are permitted if hunters station themselves at least 200 yards from any other party of hunters. An average of 40,000 ducks—mostly mallards and teal—visit the area each autumn. Goose hunting is prohibited in the area.

The best success on Nebraska ducks during the early season is by jump- and pass-shooting. Farm ponds, particularly in the eastern part of the state, offer the best jump-shooting opportunities. Also, the thousands of small lakes in the Sand Hills, central and western Nebraska, offer prime jump- and pass-shooting. However, you must obtain permission from ranchers or farmers to hunt wildfowl on their land. Permission is usually given.

During the later part of the season, when most of the mallards are in, 90 percent of the successful hunting is done by setting out decoys along rivers, streams, or around the perimeter of the large reservoirs—Enders, Swanson, Harlan County—and shooting out of blinds. When creeks and rivers don't freeze up, jump-shooting on private lands can be absolutely fantastic.

Nebraska has some fine commercial wildfowling establishments. Ralph Kohler has great goose hunting from sunken, gas-heated blinds. His rates from October 1 to October 30 are $15 per day. Write to Kohler, Tekamah, Nebraska 68061 (telephone 402-374-2747). Other fine outfitters for Canada geese include: George Rishling, 236 North Chadron Street, Chadron, Nebraska 69337; H. Tolman, Tekamah, Nebraska 68061; and the Taylor Brothers, Taylor Marina, Republican City, Nebraska.

Approximate seasons and bag limits are the same as other states in the Central Flyway. Nebraska usually has a split duck and goose season, because the early flights of geese migrate along the eastern third of the state (particularly snows and blues); and in December, the mallards and Canadas migrate through the western part of the state. Ducks are harvested under the point system.

For additional data, write to the Nebraska Game Commission, Box 30370, Lincoln, Nebraska 68503.

Nebraska's eastern neighbor, Iowa, also has some fine wildfowling. I certainly wish I had a dollar for every time I hunkered in a blind at Iowa's Forney Lake and watched the mallards and geese come zooming into our decoys. No matter what kind of weather—bluebird or a freezing blizzard—the birds appeared in this area like clockwork each autumn.

According to Fred A. Priewert, director of the Iowa Conservation Commission, the best wildfowling areas in the state are: along the Mississippi River, Missouri River, northern natural marshes, Riverton, Forney, Otter Creek, Odessa, Big Sioux, Sweet Marsh, and Big Marsh. But some of the inland streams and rivers also provide excellent jump-shooting for ducks.

Western Iowa, particularly along the Missouri River, is goose country. The best areas for snows and blues are at and around Forney Lake (with 28 controlled blinds) and Riverton (with 20 blinds). Reservations must be made daily, in person, for a blind. This part of the state attracts migrating geese like a magnet each autumn.

Various public natural marshes in the northern and northwestern part of Iowa also provide good weekday waterfowling, although weekend hunters typically find space at a premium at the better hunting spots.

"One of the most overlooked areas for weekend waterfowl hunting is the Keokuk pool on the Mississippi River," says Wilbur Horine, an outdoor writer from Neveda, Iowa. "This area annually attracts a large concentration of diver ducks. Another spot I would recommend is Lake Odessa, in the same area, for some superb duck hunting and fair chances at some Canada geese."

The Big Marsh Wildlife Unit in the north-central region of the state lies in the Iowa-Cedar River Basin. The wildfowl hunting success varies from year to year here, depending upon local water conditions, crop harvest, and migration patterns. Normally, blue-winged teal and wood ducks provide above average hunting success in early October. Mallards generally arrive the last week of October and offer excellent shooting just before freeze-up, which usually occurs about mid-November. Goose hunting is rated as fair in this region. But if crops are harvested late, it can be exceptional.

The Big Marsh Wildlife Unit, which includes a wildfowl refuge, provides excellent hunting. The fringe areas around nearby Ventura Marsh, Big Wall, and Morse Lakes should not be neglected by hunters.

Northeastern Iowa has the Sweet Marsh Wildlife Unit. Wildfowling

The farmlands along the Missouri River attract thousands of geese in early October.

on private lands is mainly associated with the major river systems— Shell Rock, Cedar, Wapsipinicon, Maquoheta, Volga, and Turkey. Extensive backwaters on these rivers provide choice opportunities for the blind-and-decoy hunter, or for the hunter who enjoys floating a river and jump-shooting waterfowl. Several fine private shooting marshes exist in this region. The best are located along the Wapsipinicon River. The abundance of emergent vegetation and lots of open water attracts and holds large concentrations of waterfowl in this area during the migration periods.

The Missouri River Wildlife Unit is tucked along the extreme west-central part of the state. Numerous backwater areas, oxbow lakes, and marshes abound on the Missouri River floodplain. Most of the wildfowling takes place on privately-owned lands, and is superb.

Mallards, along with snow and blue geese, dominate the fall migration; but good flights of teal, woodies, widgeon, and gadwall also occur. Rivers, drainage ditches, and farm ponds offer select opportunities for ducks and an occasional Canada goose. Jump-shooting along the creeks and drainage ditches is very productive. However, many hunters find that stubble shooting for geese and mallards in harvested corn fields also offers prime sport if you have good decoy set-ups.

The Riverton Wildlife Unit is in the extreme southwestern corner of Iowa. Many creeks and streams winding through this fertile countryside attract migrating wildfowl. The tributaries of the Nodaway and the East and West Nishnabotna Rivers provide best action each fall.

First-rate hunting is available here, especially for blue and snow geese. Numerous private hunting clubs have been developed surrounding the Commission's Riverton and Forney Lakes area. These two public hunting areas attract big flocks of snow geese each autumn.

One of the best duck spots is at the south end of the Riverton unit, in the flooded timber section. Among waterfowlers, it is famous as the "ol' mallard hole" of Iowa. In this flood combination of timber, potholes, and open water, the "greenheads" attract many hunters in the midwest.

In the extreme southeastern part of Iowa, the Mississippi River wanders through the entire eastern border of the Odessa Wildlife Unit, melding the waters of the Iowa, Cedar, Skunk, and Des Moines Rivers along its course. This region provides good duck hunting and fair goose success. Although there are many public wetlands available to sportsmen, the private areas, particularly the inland rivers and streams adjacent to farms, offer prime hunting opportunities. In wet years, the low areas in farm fields, or bottomland timber, can be super-great for hunters using decoy set-ups. The state-controlled area has 55 public blinds. Daily fee is $2.

The Big Sioux Wildlife Unit in the extreme northwestern corner of Iowa contains lakes, marshes, and glacial knobs which could not be conquered by drainage and the plow, resulting in superb waterfowl habitat.

Here are four of the state's largest natural lakes—Big Spirit, East Okoboji, West Okoboji, and Silver. Major marshes include Christopherson Slough, Jemmerson Slough, West Hottes Lake, Rush Lake, and a string of potholes known as Spring Run. This entire region hosts good populations of wildfowl each autumn.

The marshes and lakes of Dickinson and Osceola Counties are probably of greatest importance to the wildfowler because of their excellent duck and goose habitat. Potholes still exist on some private lands, and the Conservation Commission maintains several public hunting areas around the marshes and swamps. Some fine jump-shooting can be enjoyed by walking the streams and ditches.

However, Iowa's waterfowl picture encompasses more than the areas mentioned above. The state's 99 counties offer 151 public hunting areas, with the principal game being waterfowl. To find a good wildfowl hunting spot, just stick a pin in a map of Iowa. Wherever your pin lands, you won't be more than one hour away from some excellent wildfowling.

The lack of professional guides and outfitters in Iowa simply illustrates the abundance of public areas available to visiting wildfowlers. However, Ronald DeBruin, Prairie City, Iowa 50228, and John Mullin, Route 1, Box 28, Goose Lake, Iowa 52750, offer accommodation and fine duck gunning at their shooting establishments. Also, check locally for landowners allowing goose hunting on their property along the Missouri River. A good source of information is the Chamber of Commerce, Missouri Valley, Iowa.

No special regulations apply to non-residents hunting wildfowl. Blinds on public hunting areas are obtained on a first-come, first-served basis. Rates are about $3 to $4, per hunter, per day. Only steel shot is allowed on state-controlled waterfowl units. A non-resident licence is $25, plus $1 for a state duck stamp. You must, of course, have a federal duck stamp as well.

Seasons on ducks and geese are generally split, and the waterfowl season usually begins around October 1 to about December 10. Daily duck bag and possession limits are governed by the point system. The goose bag is usually five daily, including no more than two Canadas and two whitefronts. Possession limit is also five geese, with no more than two whitefronts and two Canadas.

For additional information, write to the Iowa Conservation Commission, 300 Fourth Street, Des Moines, Iowa 50319.

Nebraska's southern neighbor, Kansas, also offers some fine wildfowling. If I were asked to pick one spot in Kansas to hunt wildfowl, it would be the Cheyenne Bottoms Refuge, near Great Bend. This, in my opinion, is one of the superlative duck hunting spots of the entire Great Plains states.

Picture this if you will—167 concrete blinds, all free. And ducks! Each autumn this area attracts about 250,000 ducks which tarry for weeks because the refuge offers an excellent food supply and resting area. Blinds are available on a first-come, first-served basis

Cheyenne Bottoms in Kansas has outstanding duck hunting, as well as 167 free blinds for hunters.

each day, upon personal request at the headquarters office. And there have been times when many blinds were empty.

Here is a superb waterfowl hunting spot. It consists of 20,000 acres of marshland devoted to providing excellent free hunting for sportsmen. An ingenious network of gates and dams has created five separate lakes (three are open to hunting, while the other two are sanctuaries), which always contain enough water to attract birds. In addition, hunters are allowed to erect temporary blinds around the perimeter of the refuge for some choice pass-shooting.

However, Cheyenne Bottoms Refuge is not the only fine wildfowl hunting area in Kansas. Far from it. Three federal refuges worth checking out for a go at ducks or geese are: Marias des Cygnes, Neosho, and the Republican Waterfowl Management Area near Jamestown.

According to John King, of Olathe, a veteran wildfowler who has hunted all over Kansas, the following areas of the large reservoirs could provide first-rate hunting: Glen Elder Reservoir, Redmond Reservoir, and Tuttle and Milford Lakes (all with prime duck and goose gunning); Wilson Reservoir (with large populations of big Canada geese and nearby wheat fields for exciting chances for field hunting); the fringe areas around the Quivera National Waterfowl Refuge (with excellent pass-shooting for Canadas); Elk City (a super spot for ducks); Malvern Reservoir (with a few geese but a large population of diver ducks); Pomoma Reservoir (with tough but, at times, rewarding hunting for ducks); Lovewell Reservoir (which can be extremely good late in the season and is generally overlooked by most hunters); and Kanapolis and Cheney Reservoirs (which also offer duck hunting).

The wildfowl management areas west of highway 283—called the High Plains areas—have excellent duck hunting. According to King, if the waters in this region don't freeze over late in the season, the mallard hunting can be fantastic, especially if the hunters hit the open rivers for some jump-shooting.

The most prevalent species in Kansas is the mallard, comprising about half the harvest of all ducks. Snow and blue geese, particularly in northeastern Kansas, account for nearly two-thirds of the goose harvest. The total harvest in recent years has been around 525,000 ducks and 52,000 geese.

A listing of professional guides or outfitters is not available. However, the following persons do occasionally offer guiding services at certain reservoirs: Gary Heidrick, 511 North Walnut, Beloit, Kansas

67420; Jim Kidd, R. R. #3, Junction City, Kansas 66441; and Mike Alton, 201 West Cloud Street, Salina, Kansas. A non-resident licence costs $25.

Veteran waterfowlers in Kansas use big spreads of decoys—3 to 4 dozen—when hunting around the big reservoirs. Using a competent retriver pays off with fewer losses of downed birds.

As in most states in the Central Flyway, seasons and bag limits may vary, depending upon wildfowl production, availability of water for wildfowl, and flight patterns in the fall. Recently, the season on ducks has been split and the point system used for daily bag and possession limits. Kansas has one of the rare goose seasons without split dates. The daily bag and possession limit for snows and blues is five birds, while the limit for Canadas is one bird per day and two in possession. The same applies to whitefronts. The diminutive Ross's goose stands at one per day and one in possession. No Canadas or whitefronts can be taken after December 21.

For further information, contact the Kansas Forestry, Fish and Game Commission, Box 1028, Pratt, Kansas 67124.

Not many hunters think of Oklahoma as a wildfowling state. But that's a mistake. "During the early part of the wildfowl season," says Dean G. Graham, a friend of mine from Oklahoma City, "the best technique to use on the early duck arrivals is jump- and pass-shooting. The jump-shooting requires careful stalks along the quiet waters of the Arkansas, Deep Fork, and Washita Rivers, where hunters can surprise the loafing ducks."

"Later in the season," Graham adds, "the best system is to seek out some of the public hunting areas (which incidentally often go begging for more hunters), set out decoys, and call the ducks in. When hunting some of the larger bodies of water, it's essential to use a capable retriever to fetch cripples or downed birds."

It has been my good luck to experience some of the finest mallard hunting at Fobb Bottom, one of the outstanding mallard areas on Lake Texoma. On several hunts, when accompanied by Jodie Grigg of Denison, Texas, we often filled out by 10 a.m. and then spent the rest of the day calling ducks in for some close-up photography.

The Department of Wildlife Conservation could not provide a specific list of guides or outfitters operating in the state, but did mention that guides are available on Lake Eufaula and near the Salt Plains Federal Waterfowl Refuge.

According to the latest reports from Oklahoma biologists, the annual bag, on the average, includes about 35 percent mallards, 20 percent green-winged teal, and 20 percent gadwall. No statistics were available on the goose harvest.

Carl Lowrance, an avid wildfowler from Tulsa, feels the best areas for wildfowling in Oklahoma include the Arkansas River, from Moffett on the east to Webb City on the north; the Washita River and its watershed at Russett in the south and northwest toward Ryedon, at the Texas border; and the Deep Fork River, between Hoffman and Sparks.

Of the four federal wildfowl refuges in the state, there are above-par hunting areas at Tishomingo, Sequoyah, and Salt Plains. Other excellent public hunting areas include Altus-Lugert; Canton Lake; Chouteau Dam and Lock 17, northwest of Gibson; Eufaula Reservoir; Fort Cobb Reservoir; Hulah Reservoir; Lexington area, with 26 ponds for attracting ducks; Oologah Reservoir; Pine Creek Reservoir; Robert S. Kerr Reservoir (except no goose hunting); Norman Reservoir, east of Norman on highway 9, with best spots at Upper Little River Arm and Hog Creek Arm; and Lake Texoma, with matchless spots at Hickory Creek, Fobb Bottom, Love Valley, and Camp Lands.

Oklahoma has no special regulations for non-resident wildfowlers. In fact, it welcomes the sportsman to enjoy its fine hunting. The non-resident small game licence is $30.

Oklahoma, like most of the states in this chapter (with the exception of North Dakota), uses a point system on ducks. Duck point allocation is as follows: 100 points for canvasbacks and redheads; 70 points for mallard hens, wood ducks, and hooded mergansers; 10 points for blue-winged teal, cinnamon teal, green-winged teal, pintails, gadwalls, scaup, shovelers, and common mergansers. Other species and sexes count for 25 points.

A basic 100-point bag is reached when the point value of the *last* bird, added to the value of birds already taken, reaches or exceeds 100 points. Possession limit is two legal daily bag limits.

Duck and goose seasons are generally split, with openings and closings varying according to area.

For geese, the bag limit is five daily, including no more than two Canadas, or one whitefront and one Canada and one Ross's goose. Possession limit is two daily bag limits.

For detailed information, write to the Wildlife Conservation Department, 1801 North Lincoln, Oklahoma City, Oklahoma 73105.

Another midwestern state with outstanding waterfowling is North Dakota. But moans of anguish were heard from many wildfowlers

last summer when North Dakota announced their new, harsh restrictive regulations aimed at curbing the amount of non-resident
wildfowl hunters allowed to hunt in this state.

According to Pershing Carlson, Chief of the Information and Education Division, North Dakota Fish and Game Department, "Word
of our fine duck and goose hunting has attracted too many non-resident hunters into a few places of our state. The gist of the new law is:

> Non-resident wildfowlers can hunt ducks and geese for only
> a 10-day consecutive period. The hunter selects the days.
> However, the state has issued only 8000 permits for non-resi-
> dent waterfowl hunting during the 1975 season.
>
> The new law requires an additional $5 non-resident wild-
> fowl state licence, in addition to the regular $35 permit and
> 50¢ for the small game stamp."

In defense of the new law, Department Commissioner Russell
Stuart explained, "The limited non-resident waterfowl licences al-
loted is an important tool to spread hunting pressure, and the worst
situation of over-crowding occurs each autumn at Devils Lake,
where throngs of hunters congregate for the fine Canada goose hunting."

North Dakota is recognized as one of the greatest mallard producing and hatching states in the country. To illustrate the fine wildfowl
hunting available, sportsmen have harvested around 400,000 ducks
and 165,000 geese annually during recent years. No wonder resent-
ment against the new law, by the non-resident hunters, is increasing.

According to the latest information available from the North Dakota Fish and Game Department, the top public wildfowl hunting
areas are Rice Lake, Hyatt Slough, and Wolf Creek.

The most popular method of bagging ducks is by jump- and pass-
shooting, especially productive if the rainy weather sets in early and
the crops—corn and wheat—are left unharvested. These unharvested
crops attract many birds, and hunters decked out in camouflage
garb hide along the edges of the fields to nab birds as they either
head for the grain fields, or leave them.

The best goose hunting in North Dakota is unquestionably at
Devils Lake, which finds a huge concentration of Canadas in the
area each autumn. The most successful method of harvesting the
geese is by pass-shooting. Hunters hide around the perimeter of
the lake and nab the birds as they head out each morning to feed,
and again in the evening when the birds return to the lake.

According to Fish and Game officials, no guides or commercials outfitters operate in the state. The most prevalent species of ducks are mallards and teal. Snows, blues and Canadas frequent scattered parts of the state.

Wildfowl habitat has continued to decline on private lands. For example, an estimated 250,000 to 500,000 acres of grasslands were plowed and wetlands drained in 1974 to provide more cropland. High grain prices, no doubt, contributed to this occurrence. But the U.S. Department of Agriculture's continued encouragement for all-out crop production was the biggest reason for the declining wetlands. And these wetlands are absolutely essential for wildfowl production.

North Dakota's bag limits in recent years have been six ducks per day, of which only three can be mallards, one a wood duck, one a hooded merganser, and one a canvasback or redhead. There is a further stipulation that only one of three mallards in a bag can be a hen. The possession limit for ducks is two daily bag limits.

The bag limits for geese are equally complex. A hunter is allowed five snows or blues per day, but only two Canadas or two whitefronts, or one of each. The possession limit, again, is two daily bag limits.

The wildfowl seasons are split. Usually opening in early October, the first part of the season closes in late November. It opens again for a week about mid-December.

For additional wildfowl data, write to the North Dakota Game and Fish Department, 2121 Lovett Avenue, Bismarck, North Dakota 58505.

South Dakota also ranks as an outstanding wildfowling state. But unfortunately, restrictive regulations mar the picture for non-residents.

South Dakota became the first state in the country to place a total ban on non-resident wildfowl hunting. Despite the hue and cry from sportsmen everywhere and the continued loss of revenue from licence sales, South Dakota remained the only state—for 13 years—not allowing out-of-staters to hunt wildfowl.

The state then had a change of heart and opened its door a crack to permit non-residents to hunt waterfowl. But there was a catch. First, the tab was increased, so that today a non-resident needs three hunting licences for waterfowl: general, $1; small game, $25; and a special wildfowl permit, $30; for a total outlay of $56.

In addition, the state wildfowl licence is good for only 10 consecutive days. (To hunt longer requires another $30 permit.) The state is also divided into units, each with a limited number of licences available.

As if this were not enough, non-resident hunters must apply for their permits ahead of the season, for the specific unit in which they want to hunt. For units over-subscribed with non-resident applications, there is a public drawing. Applications for non-resident wildfowl permits are available after September 1.

Actually, South Dakota is ranked as one of the premier wildfowling states in the country, with the following areas considered by veteran hunters to be tops:

Northeast: This area primarily contains a concentration of diver ducks and snow and blue geese. However, due to the decline of redheads and canvasbacks, Day, Roberts, Brookings, Codington, Kingsbury, Marshall, and Hamlin Counties have closed seasons on these species. Many of the lakes in this region also play host to large populations of mallards.

Giant Canadas show up, as do the common and lesser Canadas, on some of the lakes in this area. However, the biggest hunter harvest is of snow and blue geese, which flight into this region during early October. The top spot would be around the Sand Lake National Wildlife Refuge. Pass-shooting is generally the most productive technique.

Missouri River: Along this river system there are four major wildfowl refuges which provide choice hunting around them. These are: Lake Oahe, Lake Francis, Lake Sharpe, and Lewis and Clark Lake. Large concentrations of Canada geese and mallards frequent these areas each autumn. The best hunting success occurs very early in November. Field shooting—hunting in and around crop fields—is best early in the season. Later, hunters using decoys on water score the best.

Here is a brief summary of the four major varieties of Canada geese common in South Dakota:

SHORT GRASS PRAIRIE CANADAS: There are no major stop-off areas in South Dakota. However, small concentrations do occur, at times, around Shadehill Reservoir, near Lemmon.

TALL GRASS PRAIRIE CANADAS: The major concentrations occur in the Sand Lake National Wildlife Refuge. In recent years there has been a marked increase of these small Canadas using the Missouri River system for a stop-over.

EASTERN PRAIRIE CANADAS: The major concentrations of these birds are in the Mud Lake and Lake Traverse areas. These are fairly early migrants, moving through the state in early October, and providing excellent hunting.

WESTERN PRAIRIE CANADAS: These are probably the most important species to the wildfowl hunter in South Dakota. They are known locally as "Missouri River honkers." Band recoveries indicate South Dakota is a major kill and wintering area. As many as 30,000 have wintered on the Fort Randall Reservoir and Lake Andes National Wildlife Refuge in past years. Major hunting areas are along the Missouri River, with Hughes, Brule, Lyman, Charles Mix, and Gregory Counties being the best. Peak concentrations occur around mid-November.

South Dakota's excellent wildfowl populations are partly the result of great planning by its wildfowl experts, and judicious use of the funds by the game department. In the 1950's, the state concentrated on acquiring wetlands, in an effort to place in public ownership and protection as much of the rapidly declining wetlands as possible. Agricultural drainage had made serious inroads on wildfowl habitat and production in the prairie pothole country. Today, about one-third of the lands owned by the game department are wetlands.

Another factor in the improved wildfowl situation has been the acquisition of some 64,000 acres of prime wetlands, marshes, swamps, and sloughs by the U.S. Fish and Wildlife Service, under its small wetlands preservation program. Purchase of such fine wildfowl habitat is financed by sportsmen everywhere—under the Revenue Sharing Act—when they purchase what is commonly called "duck stamps." Portions of these federal wetlands are open to public hunting.

In a recent booklet issued by the South Dakota Game Department, *Guide to State Public Shooting Areas and Federal Waterfowl Production Areas,* some interesting statistics were published. Of the state's 67 counties, the booklet listed 378 public shooting areas under state management, with fair to excellent wildfowling available. Marshall County led the parade with 33 areas. Next was Day with 32. Codington following with 23 areas. The booklet also lists 424 federal wildfowl production areas, with Day County having 42, and Roberts and McPherson having 34 and 27, respectively.

According to Charles Post, Supervisor of the Information and Education Division, Department of Game, Fish and Parks, there are no known commercial outfitters or guides catering to wildfowlers.

The South Dakota wildfowl season generally opens around October 1 and continues into January. Sometimes the season is split. As for bag limits, they are comparable to those of Kansas and Nebraska. The point system is used for both daily bag and possession limits on ducks. Hunters are encouraged to use retrieving dogs to fetch downed birds; however, a non-resident must show a current rabies vaccination certificate for his retrievers. The dog must be free of communicable diseases and have a health certificate signed by a veterinarian.

For more information, write to the South Dakota Department of Game, Fish and Parks, Pierre, South Dakota 57501.

20

Wildfowling on the Canadian Prairies

Bob Scammell

T HERE IS ONE PLACE and type of hunting in North America where the "good old days" still prevail—well, almost. That place is the Canadian prairies, and the hunting is for wildfowl. Perhaps the hunting may even be too good. Certainly the locals take it so much for granted that only under the direst of duress will they think of mentioning the excellence of their wildfowl gunning.

Last season I was in Alberta's prime pheasant area, enjoying excellent sport, when I ran into one of a party of four eastern hunters out to sample the west. Pheasants? Couldn't care less. But they were positively glassy-eyed over the farmers who were pressing them into service, to come in and shoot the clouds of mallards that were feeding on harvested wheat, barley, and peas.

Later in the week I saw the foursome again, in a restaurant in Brooks, Alberta, having a closing celebration before catching a plane home. They had just returned from the field, and two of them had set aside their guns to lay back and revel in wave after wave of mallards coming in at sunset, the big ducks seeming to make the earth shake as they landed.

Canadian prairie farmers are among the best sources of local duck hunting information.

It took a group of non-residents to make me realize how much the stubble or field shoot for wildfowl is king of sports for many hunters on the Canadian prairies; and what a stirring experience each such hunt is for its practitioners, whether they be novices to the experience or locals who have never hunted ducks any other way.

Locating ducks for a prairie field shoot is not difficult. Local hunters generally receive distress calls from farmers who are being eaten out of stand and swath by mallards, or earlier in the season by pintails. Strangers to an area need only go spotting in the early morning and late afternoon. The spotter picks a high point from which a good patch of grain country can be seen, then scans the horizon with binoculars until the typical milling swarm of feeding ducks can be seen buzzing the grain field of their choice. The hunter then drives roads toward the swarm until the exact field is located; and generally makes arrangements with the landowner to hunt the field the next morning or evening.

Under no circumstances should a hunter ever enter a grain field without permission of the owner, even though many farmers consider hunters to be doing them a favor, particularly if the crop has not yet been harvested.

Experienced stubble hunters claim that once you've gained legal access to the field, the next two essentials are finding a way of concealing yourself and a means of decoying the ducks. Some hunters crawl under swath or, if the field is combined, gather up straw under which to hide. Weeds, ditches, and willows at the edges of fields are also often employed. Rarely do duck hunters bother with digging pits. If there is snow on the ground, white overalls are often worn.

Fanatics at the prairie stubble shooting game generally have a fleet of over-sized silhouette decoys, made of metal or plywood and painted a flat black. Other hunters simply keep a roll of tar-paper in the trunk of their car all through hunting season, and use torn up chunks of the paper to decoy ducks onto the stubble. Scotch duck calls are favored for the minimum of calling required to draw the attention of ducks buzzing a big field to the decoy set.

A triumph of modern game management is that goose hunting on the Canadian prairies is generally considered to be better now than it has ever been. Geese are invariably shot on the stubble, but the tactics are much more exacting than with ducks. The spotting must be more precise, including just where in a field the geese are feeding. And sometimes negotiations must be entered with other hunters who are spotting the same flocks and fields. With geese, especially Canadas, concealment must be perfect; the decoy set impeccable. The white geese are considered somewhat less sophisticated than the grays, and I have often seen whites decoy to clumps of crumpled newspaper.

Pits are frequently dug for goose hunts and must always be filled in, unless the landowner specifically requests the pits be left open for a future hunt. One intrepid group of goose hunters I know travels with a backhoe and blade attached to a small tractor, for pit digging and filling.

Hunting wildfowl on water, and hunting diving ducks at all, are practised very little in Alberta and Saskatchewan, because the stubble shoot is regarded as prime sport. Indeed, many local hunters consider it somewhat unethical to shoot wildfowl over water. (However, water shooting, particularly for diving ducks, is a highly developed art in Manitoba.) The rare birds that hunt on water in Alberta prefer the larger lakes of the central and southern portion of the province. Here they have excellent sport for both puddle ducks and divers, and favor over-sized floating decoys and Labrador retrievers. These are the hunters who generally hunt upland game early in the season; then hope to clean up on the huge flocks of so-called "northern" mallards that generally stage early in November on such large central Alberta waters as Gull and Sylvan Lakes, and on the big irrigation impoundments in southern Alberta.

Whether you find him on water or on stubble, disarm any prairie wildfowler and chances are he'll be carrying a 12 gauge shotgun with at least one full-choke barrel. Full-choke barrels are a tradition that dies hard on the Canadian prairies, in spite of modern knowledge of how the shot-protecting plastic wads tighten patterns. However, each year a few more radicals go afield with more open-choked guns, and I even know a few who use improved-cylinder chokes whenever they are shooting over decoys. If I were limited to only one gun for everything on the prairies, it would be a 12 gauge with a modified or improved modified choke.

Hunters who like to take their waterfowl over water can get fouled by the weather on occasion. As Fred Sharp, Alberta Manager for Ducks Unlimited, puts it: "A big storm comes up the end of October, just as the ducks are thinking of moving a little anyway, and they just keep moving or are blown right out of the province." No matter how high the populations, prairie wildfowl hunting is very much conditioned by weather.

The best Alberta wildfowl hunting is in the southeastern quarter of the province, from Edmonton south to the American border, and east to Saskatchewan. The best goose areas are unquestionably around Coronation, Hanna, and Brooks.

An unusual form of wildfowling is practised in the irrigated areas of Alberta, particularly when upland game hunters find the pheasants grounded by high winds. Hunters often drive the banks of wide canals winding through such areas until a flock of ducks is spotted, sheltering on water in the lee of a high bank ahead. Then the car stops and a hunter or two circles out on the prairie below the bank, until waved up and over by a hunter left back at the car. Such jump-shooting in high winds is extremely fast and furious, and at challenging targets.

Saskatchewan is the only one of the prairie provinces that tries to keep track of the wildfowl kill in particular areas. Published figures make it clear that over the past few seasons, the absolutely prime waterfowling areas, for both ducks and geese, are generally around Kindersley and Humboldt.

Ed Begin, Executive Assistant of the Saskatchewan Wildlife Federation, the organized voice of hunters in Saskatchewan, says that the 1975 season was extremely good as a result of abundant water in the province. But this fact also resulted in the high numbers of birds not being quite as concentrated as in drier years. Begin reflects the general optimism on the prairies in his comments on geese: "Western parts of the province enjoyed heavy flights of geese with an upturn in greater Canada populations and an increase in whitefronts. Central Saskatchewan populations through the Quill Lakes and Ponass Lakes seem to be increasing every year, and the proportion of Canadas seems to be building in this area."

Paul Murphy, Executive Director of the Manitoba Wildlife Federation, says that 1975 was "probably our best year ever, due to some extent to heavy rains, contributing to near-flood conditions in some areas." According to Murphy, the prime wildfowl areas in Manitoba are around the Delta Marsh at the southern end of Lake Manitoba, near Portage La Prairie.

There are some general similarities in hunting regulations in Canada's three prairie provinces. All, for example, require that wildfowlers purchase the $3.50 Canada Migratory Game Bird Hunting Permit, in addition to a provincial game bird licence.

The total licence fees payable by wildfowl hunters in the three prairie provinces are remarkably similar. Non-residents of Canada would pay a total fee of $57.50 to hunt wildfowl in Alberta, $53.50 in Saskatchewan, and $45.75 in Manitoba. There is a greater discrepancy in the licence fees charged to Canadians who are non-residents of the province: $12.50 in Alberta, $23.50 in Saskatchewan, and $25.75 in Manitoba.

Wildfowl limits are also similar throughout the prairie provinces. In recent years, the limit on ducks in Alberta has been eight daily, 16 in possession; and five geese per day with 10 in possession (of which not more than two per day and four in possession can be white-fronted geese). Saskatchewan had precisely the same daily and possession limits on ducks and geese, with the proviso that only one duck per day or two in possession could be either redheads or canvasbacks. There was also a limit of two or three white-fronted geese per day in Saskatchewan, or four or six in possession, depending on which part of the province the birds were taken. Manitoba's wildfowl limits were the most complex of the prairie provinces: the daily limit of ducks was six, possession limit of 12 (of which not more than one daily and two in possession could be canvasbacks and redheads, and not more than four daily or eight in possession could be mallards in zones 1 and 2, and not more than three daily or six in possession could be mallards in zones 3 and 4). The daily goose limit was four, with 10 in possession, of which not more than three daily or six in possession could be white-fronted geese. and a limit of two Canada geese per day for the Oak Hammock Managed Hunting Area.

The wheat stubbles of Saskatchewan provide outstanding gunning for ducks and geese.

On the Canadian prairies, only Alberta did not have a season for sandhill cranes in recent years, and only Manitoba did not practise some form of wildfowl hunting discrimination against non-residents of Canada. In Alberta, non-resident aliens are restricted to only 3 consecutive days of goose hunting as described on the Wildlife Certificate in zone 5, probably Alberta's finest goose hunting area. Saskatchewan's regulations provided that in 26 wildfowl zones, all non-residents of Saskatchewan could not hunt any wildfowl until October 6, approximately a month after the Saskatchewan resident had his first crack at the birds.

Manitoba, in recent years, restricted goose hunting to mornings only for a portion of the season in one of its prime areas (W 4—the southernmost area of the province, taking in the southern two-thirds of Lake Winnipeg).

Alberta traditionally divides the province into eight wildfowl zones and opens the season for both ducks and geese in the north approximately September 1st, and centrally about a week later. Ducks in southern Alberta open around mid-September. Goose season generally starts in the south around the 1st of October. In portions of the province, the season on ducks often extends into January. Further and more detailed information on wildfowl and on current hunting regulations in Alberta may be obtained from Alberta: Recreation, Parks, and Wildlife, Natural Resources Building, Edmonton, Alberta.

Saskatchewan sports 37 wildfowl management zones, with the wildfowl season generally opening around the 1st of September and closing around the 20th of December. There are four wildfowl management areas in Manitoba. The season generally opens around the 1st of September and closes about the end of November. Both Saskatchewan and Manitoba employ the same procedure as Alberta in opening the seasons in the northern zones a week to 10 days earlier than in the rest of the province.

Current Manitoba information on wildfowl regulations may be obtained by writing to the Department of Tourism, Recreation, and Cultural Affairs, 200 Vaughan Street, Winnipeg, Manitoba R3C 0P8. In Saskatchewan, the place to write is the Department of Tourism and Renewable Resources, Regina, Saskatchewan.

In Canada, wildfowl regulations are actually passed by the federal government, after consultation with the provinces and with the United States and Mexico. Consequently, people seeking information should bear in mind that the latest info on seasons, bag limits, and so on for wildfowl are generally not available until mid-summer.

Excellent general information on the state of the wildfowl crop, the best hunting areas in each province, and other facts of interest to a prospective visiting hunter is generally available from the head or regional offices of Ducks Unlimited, found in all of Canada's prairie provinces.

21

Wildfowling in the Mountain States

Clair Rees

I T W A S A B L E A K, chill November morning on Utah's famed Bear River Migratory Bird Refuge. Ken Turner and I were huddled on an island blind in Unit 2, watching our decoys—two dozen empty Clorox bottles — slowly materialize in the gray dawn.

We were hunting wildfowling's largest trophy—the whistling swan. Weighing up to 20 pounds, these huge birds are plentiful enough to be hunted on a draw-permit basis in Utah and two other western states. Both Ken and I had been lucky enough to draw one of the 2500 one-bird permits issued, and had carefully planned our hunt to give us the best chance of bagging a pair of these majestic, long-necked wildfowl.

During earlier forays after mallards and pintails on the refuge's public shooting grounds, we had painstakingly noted the flight patterns of the big swans as they traded back and forth across the 65,000-acre marsh. We soon found which of the waterways the birds favored, and had the site of our blind selected well in advance of the hunt.

Arriving at the refuge a full hour before sun-up, Ken and I moored

Some of the best wildfowling in Utah is found around the Bear River Migratory Bird Refuge.

our dull green, flat-bottomed boat among a cluster of cattails, in plenty of time to set out our decoys and find strategic locations for our folding stools. While swans will sometimes change course to investigate Canada goose decoys, they are generally downright intrigued by a group of white plastic bleach bottles. A 4-foot length of stout anchor cord tied to the molded-in handles is all it takes to turn the bottles into effective decoys. (Let a little water into each container before screwing the lids on and setting the bottles afloat. An empty bottle rides too high and moves too much in the wind.)

The Bear River Refuge is federally operated, and is the one public

The whistling swan, a wildfowler's largest trophy, is legal game in Utah, Nevada, and Montana.

hunting ground in Utah where lead shot is outlawed. So, as much as we would have preferred 1⅞-ounce magnum loads with heavy No. 2 shot for these large, tough-to-kill birds, our 12-gauge pumps were loaded with 1⅛ ounces of No. 4 steel-alloy shot. This meant taking our birds at a relatively close range, and concentrating on aiming for the head and shoulders.

Hunting whistling swans—our largest legal wildfowl—is a unique experience currently available in only three western states: Utah, Montana, and Nevada. While these and the other mountain states (Idaho, Wyoming, Colorado, Arizona, and New Mexico) are more famous for their deer, elk, and other four-legged game, they do offer good-to-excellent gunning for ducks and geese. And much of it is unique.

I recall a cliffside blind along the Snake River in southern Idaho, where I was shooting *down* on the fat mallards following the river below me. That experience provided a never-to-be-forgotten lesson in the amount of lead it takes to hit a passing duck. From my overhead vantage point, the patterns my pellets made as they hit the river were easily visible. The first half-box of shells were clean misses, splashing the water 8 to 10 feet astern of the speeding greenheads. Without that graphic evidence to convince me, I might never have learned to give passing wildfowl the surprising amount of lead needed for a fair chance of connecting.

There's another stretch along the Green River in eastern Utah where you can shoot down on wildfowl, except here your targets are apt to be Great Basin Canada geese. This hotspot is known as Browns Park, and is located a few miles downstream of the Flaming Gorge Dam.

If you crave even more variety, you can jump-shoot several species of ducks from beaver ponds high in the Uinta Mountains before the late October freeze-up. Or you can venture south into Arizona and New Mexico for shirtsleeve-weather wildfowling into December and January.

Where are the best places to hunt wildfowl in the mountain states? Let's check on the hotspots, one state at a time.

In Montana, one of the favorite gunning areas west of the Continental Divide is Freezout Lake. This 12,000-acre wildfowl management project is located between Fairfield and Choteau in Teton County, and provides excellent early-season hunting for ducks and geese. It also harbors the major concentration of whistling swans in the state. (The Montana Department of Fish and Game estimates that a hunter applying for a swan permit has approximately an 80-percent chance of drawing one of the 500 or so tags issued each year. Swan hunting is restricted to Teton County.)

Another good Pacific Flyway hunting area is Nine Pipes Refuge, located south of Ronan. Public gunning is allowed near the refuge. This is pothole country and, like Freezout Lake, provides good hunting until mid-November. When the freeze occurs, truly dedicated fowlers head to the Bitterroot River, south of Missoula. The stretch between Stevensville and Hamilton is noted for good late-season shooting for Canadas and mallards.

East of the Continental Divide, Central Flyway birds are hunted, which means learning the point system. In recent years, hunters have been allowed 100 points per day. If you shot a canvasback or redhead, you were through for the day. Hen mallards, wood ducks, and hooded mergansers counted for 70 points each; while American widgeon, mallard drakes, and ringneck ducks carried 20-point tallies. Teal, scaup, pintails, gadwalls, shovelers, and other mergansers counted 10 points apiece.

In eastern Montana, the Malta area offers good Canada goose gunning, while the Bighorn River attracts fair numbers of mallards late in the season. The Yellowstone River is another good bet. Here, the birds tend to concentrate on rivers after the shallow waters freeze over. The key to wildfowling throughout Montana is to hit the potholes and standing water early, usually during the first three to four weeks in the season, and then shift to the rivers where open water is available.

Seasons run from around the first Saturday in October through early January for Pacific Flyway birds. Hunters on the east side of the Divide can expect a split season with a two-week layoff in December, depending on federal guidelines each year.

In Wyoming, duck hunters must also contend with separate regulations for the two flyways—Pacific and Central. Favorite hotspots in this desert-and-mountain state include Ocean Lake near Riverton, and the Springer Wildlife Unit, south of Torrington. At Ocean Lake, standing crops have been planted to keep wildfowl feeding in the area. An aeration unit also operates at the north end of the reservoir, to keep ice clear as late in the season as possible. This is a state-managed hunting unit, with lakeside blinds available on a first-come, first-served basis. Both ducks and geese are hunted at Ocean Lake.

At the Springer unit, public goose pits are available free of charge on leased lands around the area. These blinds accommodate a trio of hunters, and drawings are held for parties of three if more gunners show up than can be accommodated in the pits. Unless you're there on opening day, chances are you'll draw a blind, even though you may have to share it with two other hunters.

Another favorite among goose hunters is the Table Mountain Unit east of Hawk Springs, where public shooting grounds are also available.

While all three of the above areas lie in the Central Flyway, hunters west of the Continental Divide get their share of shooting, too. Most

Idaho's Snake River Wildlife Management Area is a top wildfowling spot in the mountain states.

of the wildfowling in the western part of the state centers around the large rivers that wend their way southward: the Green, Snake, Hoback, and Gros Ventre.

Idaho offers several good waterfowling areas, with generally light hunting pressure throughout the state. At the north end of Idaho, in the Panhandle, the Coeur d'Alene Wildlife Management Area east of Coeur d'Alene offers good shooting for ducks and geese, as does the lower Coeur d'Alene River.

In southwestern Idaho, the lower drainages of the Boise and Payette Rivers attract good flights of wildfowl. The Snake River also provides fair-to-good shooting throughout the southern end of the state. Lake Lowell near Nampa, the C. J. Strike Reservoir, the American Falls Reservoir, and other impoundments in the Snake River drainage make good resting places for ducks and geese. Hunters can generally do well in these areas.

The Market Lake Wildlife Management Area in eastern Idaho, near Idaho Falls, is another good bet, as is Fort Boise at the mouth of the Boise River.

Mallards are the most popular ducks sought by Idaho hunters, but Canada geese attract their share of Gem State nimrods. Good to excellent goose shooting is provided by flights off Lake Lowell near Nampa, and from the American Falls Reservoir.

More than 500,000 ducks are harvested annually in Idaho, along with some 20,000 geese. As with most western mountain states, few (if any) wildfowl guides are available, leaving you pretty much on your own. Good shooting is abundant, but it's up to you to find it.

Colorado is another two-flyway state. Generally speaking, duck, coot, and goose hunting is best along the streams, lakes, and reservoirs found in the eastern part of the state. One top-rated goose-gunning spot is Two Buttes Reservoir near Lamar, in southeastern Colorado.

Several areas in the state are closed to goose hunting. Special one-goose-per-season permits must be drawn to hunt the San Luis Valley and the West Central area comprising Garfield, Mesa, and Delta Counties. Two federally operated areas in Colorado—the Turk's Pond unit in Baca County and the Monte Vista Wildlife Refuge—allow the use of steel shot only.

Hunters in New Mexico usually enjoy warmer temperatures than their neighbors to the north, and birds tend to arrive in shootable numbers some weeks later in the season. Flights are generally governed by weather, feed conditions and hunter pressure in the northern mountain states. Thus, pre-season forecasting is difficult, to say the least.

Good feed and safe resting places for birds are found along the Rio Grande, Gila, San Juan, and Pecos Rivers. There are several lakes boasting similar wildfowl attractions scattered throughout the state, as well.

In the northeast, the Maxwell and McAllister Refuges form the basis for good duck and goose hunting in surrounding areas. Such hunting is mostly over decoys on private lands, and permission to hunt should be acquired in advance.

Top spots in the southeastern part of the state include Lake Sumner and Lake McMillan; ducks are also found in other likely spots in the Pecos River valley.

The Rio Grande Valley provides the best shooting in southwestern New Mexico, although success here is pretty much dependent upon conditions farther north.

The lesser sandhill crane can be hunted from late October to mid-January in Chaves, Curry De Baca, Eddy, Lea, Quay, and Roosevelt Counties, with the area around Artesia providing fair-to-good gunning for these migratory birds.

Again, New Mexico is a mountain state with portions lying in both the Central and Pacific Flyways. Thus wildfowlers must use the regulations appropriate to the area in which they are hunting.

Arizona also depends largely on adverse conditions in the north to bring down its big flights. Wildlife managers are really working for the hunters in that state. For example, an artificial nesting ground was recently established for Canada geese in the White Mountains, from which Arizona hopes to have its own native population of these popular gamebirds.

In northern Arizona, the Colorado River is a favorite gunning spot for ducks and geese alike, while the Topoc Marshes between Needles and Lake Havasu provide public shooting grounds for nimrods in the southwest. To the south, the Imperial Dam near Yuma is a good place to hunt ducks. Gunners, however, must take care to avoid shooting any Mexican ducks, which are "verboten" for hunters throughout the state.

Wildfowlers used to the cold-weather hunting encountered in most northern states will have some adjustments to make the first time they shoot ducks in the 60- to 70-degree temperatures common, even in wintertime, in this desert state. Birds must be drawn and plucked almost immediately to avoid spoilage, and ice chests should be standard equipment.

The best wildfowling in Nevada probably exists on or near the Stillwater Marshes near Fallon. Mallards, pintails, green-winged teal, and spoonbills can be hunted throughout this Pacific Flyway state, while whistling swans are legal game in Churchill County for lucky permit holders. The drawing for these permits is held in the Department of Fish and Game office in Reno in early October.

In my home state of Utah, the Bear River Refuge, near Brigham City, is the number-one spot for gunning ducks or geese, particularly during the early part of the season. A 30-year tally of hunter success rates for this federally managed area shows an average of 3.2 ducks harvested per man-day. That means your chances are incredibly good for bringing something home to show for your efforts when you hunt Bear River.

The other marshlands surrounding the Great Salt Lake in northern Utah also produce excellent gunning for ducks, geese, and whistling swans. Locomotive Springs, Ogden Bay, Howard Slough, Farmington Bay, and Timpie Springs are bywords among Utah wildfowlers.

In central Utah, Powell Slough is one of several good hunting areas on the shoreline of Utah Lake. Pothole jump-shooting is available, or you can rig for lakeshore gunning by using a boat to place several dozen mallard or pintail blocks out to attract the large flocks of diving ducks that live on the lake.

Farther south, Canada geese nest on the Wales, Gunnison, Koosharem, and Piute Reservoirs, and provide good shooting for hunters who wait for them in nearby grain fields.

The mountain states offer wildfowling under a wide range of climatic and terrain conditions, and some highly unusual hunts can be arranged. I've shot ducks from desert water holes, and gunned geese over high mountain passes. I've been known to tote a shotgun along on mule deer hunts, and more than one fisherman stows his pet duck gun in the bow of his boat while looking for late-season trout on wilderness lakes.

You can have your wildfowling plain or fancy in my neck of the woods. Hunters can spend large sums of money investing in airboats, decoys, and duck club fees; or they can head for some river, pothole, or grain field and enjoy some of the finest jump-shooting available anywhere. Don't leave your shotgun at home if you visit one of the mountain states in the fall. You'll regret it!

22

Wildfowling Along the Pacific Coast

Charles C. Adams

B Y MODERN STANDARDS, the Pacific coast wildfowler has the world by the tail. In an age of shrinking duck and goose habitat, increased hunting pressure, and limited land access, the west coast hunter can still take a wide variety of wildfowl species on huge tracts of state, federal, and private hunting lands. To boot, he is allowed fairly large bag limits. And he can still get away from crowds if he works at it; decoying mallards on an isolated pond, pass-shooting snow geese along an icy bay, or sneaking on Canada geese in a muddy rice field.

But at one time there was more. The Pacific coast area (Alaska, British Columbia, Washington, Oregon, and California) is, in fact, a mere shadow of its former self. Biologists estimate that 90 percent of the prime duck and goose habitat once found here has been drained, dammed, dredged, and scraped into oblivion. California, which winters about 65 percent of the Pacific Flyway's ducks and about 80 percent of its geese, once had over five million acres of prime wetlands. Four and a half million of these are now streets, factories, shopping centers, vegetable gardens, orchards, and the like. Man's

The wetlands of California attract thousands of ducks after the north country freezes up in fall.

penchant for so-called progress has taken a heavy toll on western waterfowl habitat. The huge flocks of pintails, mallards, and widgeon of which the early Spanish conquistadores wrote have dwindled considerably in the past couple of centuries. No longer can a man survive nicely by collecting his fill of snow geese, specklebellies, and Canadas with a club and a gunny sack! Those days are gone forever.

But good hunting remains. Through careful game management instigated by various migratory bird treaties between the United States, Canada, and Mexico, western wildfowl populations are monitored from year to year, and seasons set accordingly. Habitat reconstruction and preservation by private groups and government agencies have helped to snatch some wetland species from near extinction, and continue to keep general duck and goose populations at maximum levels. At certain times of the year, areas like the Yukon-Kuskokwim Delta in Alaska, the Columbia Basin in Washington and Oregon, and the Central Valley in California teem with ducks and geese, reminiscent of days gone by.

The Pacific coast offers the sportsman more kinds of wildfowl than any other single area on the continent. Nine major varieties of geese and many species of puddle ducks and diving ducks live here in huntable numbers. Some of these species are found nowhere else in the world. If a shotgunner picks his hunting area carefully, he can enjoy unbelievable mixed bags. For example, in the Sacramento Valley of northern California, the hunter who plays his cards right can legally take five varieties of geese and seven kinds of ducks in a single day — an unlikely feat, but by no means impossible!

Puddle ducks comprise about 90 percent of all ducks found on the Pacific coast. There are many species of these surface feeders; some abundant, some relatively rare. Each type of duck follows its own peculiar nesting and migrating pattern, one tiny piece in the whole coastal waterfowl puzzle.

The mallard is the most commonly harvested duck along the coast, and the second most numerous. It enjoys the widest distribution of any puddle duck in the entire Pacific Flyway, nesting all the way from Los Angeles north into Alaska. However, most west coast mallards nest in Alberta, British Columbia, and Alaska. They winter in Washington, Oregon, and California, migrating relatively early in the year and moving into winter quarters quickly.

The most abundant duck in this area is the pintail. It ranks second in total numbers harvested, chiefly because it prefers open space and is less widely distributed than the mallard. Its breeding area is extensive, but most pintails nest in Alaska and northwestern and central Canada. Pintails begin a drawn-out migration early in the fall, most eventually reaching their favorite wintering area in northern California. More than 75 percent of Pacific Flyway pintails spend the cold months in this state.

The American widgeon, or baldpate, ranks third in both population and birds bagged by hunters. It winters in Washington, Oregon, and California, after a mid-autumn migration from fairly limited nesting grounds in Alaska and northern Canada.

The shoveler is the fourth most numerous coastal duck. This gullible bird often appears in hunters' bags, providing sport for thousands each fall. Most shovelers nest in the prairie provinces of Canada and in central Alaska. They begin migrating into British Columbia and the western United States in early fall, ending up in California late in the year.

Two other species of puddlers are very common along the coast: gadwalls and green-winged teal. Gadwalls nest in California, Oregon, and Washington in fair numbers, although the bulk of the population summers on the Canadian prairies. Most gadwalls are taken en route to their winter range in southern California and the coastal marshes of western Mexico. Green-winged teal likewise winter far to the south in California and Mexico. But here the similarity between the two species ends. Greenwings nest in Washington, British Columbia, and southern Alaska. They prefer heavy woods to open country, leading a secretive summer life on small potholes and lakes.

Other puddle ducks encountered in fair numbers along the Pacific coast include European widgeon, blue-winged teal, cinnamon teal, and wood ducks. On occasion, even a New Mexican duck or Eurasian teal pops up in hunters' bags.

Diving ducks aren't as widely hunted on the Pacific coast as puddle ducks, mainly because their numbers are relatively small. However, a few species are abundant enough to hunt, especially along coastal bays and estuaries.

The lesser scaup or bluebill is the number one diver, both in numbers bagged and abundance. This medium-sized duck nests in the Canadian prairie provinces, northern Canada, and eastern Alaska. Lesser scaup move south across the interior, ending up on the bays and saltwater marshes of California and Mexico.

Canvasbacks are prized along the coast. Most of these large divers nest in Alaska and the Canadian prairie provinces, but a few summer as far south as northeastern California. They are taken incidentally by duck hunters all along the coastline as they migrate to wintering grounds on or near California's San Francisco Bay. Here they are hunted deliberately by a few hard-core saltwater shotgunners until the close of the season in late winter.

Greater scaup are fairly abundant along the southern California coastline late in the year. They stick to coastal bays the year round, breeding on the Bering Sea and the Arctic coasts of Alaska and Canada each spring, and winging south along the ocean's edge come early fall. They are usually taken in fair numbers by hunters along the full extent of their migration route.

The ruddy duck is also important in the Pacific coast area. It frequents both salt and fresh water on its migration south from central Canada and the northwestern United States, giving many hunters fast action early in the fall. This diver winters in California and Mexico.

One other diver is worth mentioning separately. The redhead nests primarily in southern Canada and the northern United States, heading south very early in the fall to wintering grounds on coastal lagoons in western Mexico. During the first part of the hunting season, large numbers of these big ducks are taken by hunters as they vacate nesting marshes in central Canada, Washington, and Oregon.

The white-fronted goose or speckle-belly and the Ross' goose are quite abundant in California.

Several less-important diving ducks nest and/or winter along the Pacific coast. These include ring-necked ducks, American and Barrow's goldeneyes, buffleheads, oldsquaws, three species of mergansers, three species of scoters, harlequin ducks, and king eiders. These are of minor value to sportsmen.

The Pacific coast offers hunters the most diversified goose shooting on the continent. More species are available here than anyplace else; and three kinds of geese — emperor geese, Ross's geese, and black brant — are found nowhere else in the world.

Canada geese are the most widely distributed and numerous. They are split into many subgroups or races, and biologists disagree on some of these subdivisions. However, four major types of Canadas live here: common Canada geese, western Canada geese, lesser Canada geese, and cackling geese. The common Canada nests from Alaska to California, wintering in southern interior valleys like the Central Valley in California. The western Canada, a slightly smaller goose, breeds on the Gulf of Alaska and winters from there south along the coast. The lesser Canada breeds in Alaska and along the Arctic coast, heading south as far as Mexico for the winter. The tiny cackling goose, smallest of the tribe, nests in western Alaska and winters primarily in the Central Valley of California.

Snow and Ross's geese are the two white species found in the Pacific area. Snow geese are the more abundant of the two. They nest on the Arctic coast, the Arctic islands from Alaska to Baffin Island, the Siberian coast, and Wrangel Island. They migrate slowly down the coastline in the fall, stopping in many places before reaching winter quarters in California's Central Valley.

Ross's geese breed in Arctic Canada near the Perry River, and winter in the Central Valley. Hunters take some of these small geese along the coast as they migrate south in early fall, but most are bagged in California late in the year.

The white-fronted goose, alias specklebelly, is the tastiest goose found on the coast. For this reason, it's the favorite of most hunters. Whitefronts are strictly western geese, seldom found east of the Mississippi River. They breed in Alaska and along the Arctic coast of northwestern Canada. West coast "specks" winter almost exclusively in the Central Valley of California.

The black brant is found only in a narrow coastal corridor. This small ocean-going goose provides plenty of action for salt water gunners each fall, as it migrates from its summer haunts in Siberia, Alaska, and western Canada to wintering grounds on southern coastal bays. It lives nowhere else, and is thus a real bonus for first-time west coast hunters.

The emperor goose is a rare species in much of the Pacific coast area, but is fairly common within its range. This goose nests in the coastal regions of northwestern Alaska and Siberia, and winters as far north as possible. Most emperor geese spend the cold months on the Aleutian Islands, but a few stragglers show up as far south as California each winter.

Other geese appear along the west coast from time to time, including blue geese, tule geese, and American brant. However, these are strays seldom taken by hunters.

Waterfowl hunting seasons in the Pacific coast area are regulated primarily by the federal government of the United States, in cooperation with individual states and British Columbia. The United States received this authority from migratory bird treaties signed by the United States, Canada, and Mexico. These treaties stipulate that the waterfowl season may not exceed 105 days in length, and must fall between September 1 and March 10. Working within these basic parameters, federal, state, and provincial technicians keep track of the birds throughout the year, and send survey results and a fall flight forecast to the Pacific Flyway Council during the first week in August. The council, made up of fish and game directors and commissioners from each of the states in the flyway, reviews the wildfowl information and sends season and bag limit recommendations for the coming fall to the U. S. Fish and Wildlife Service in Washington, D. C. After much deliberation between Pacific Flyway Council delegates and U. S. Fish and Wildlife representatives, the annual season and bag limit guidelines are set by the Fish and Wildlife Service. These must be approved by the Secretary of the Interior.

From here the individual states and British Columbia set exact dates for seasons and bag limits. Seasons usually extend from the first Saturday in October to the second Sunday in January. State commissions have the choice of a straight or a split season, and have some options concerning length of season and bag limit. For example, it is usually possible to increase the bag limit by one duck per day if two weeks are cut off the length of the season. Another option involves the reduction of the daily bag limit by one duck in return for a double possession limit. Thus, a state may reduce the daily bag from seven to six ducks to obtain a possession limit of 12 ducks instead of seven.

The state commissioners have no say in things like shooting hours, restrictions on certain species, and hunting methods. These fall within federal jurisdiction. States and provinces may be *more restrictive* than federal regulations, but never less restrictive. Needless to say, with such rigid controls, wildfowling regulations are fairly standard throughout the Pacific Flyway in any given year.

Seasons on the Pacific coast are long and bag limits on both ducks and geese generous. General duck and goose regulations for Oregon's 1975-76 season are typical of the whole area. The season ran from October 11 through January 11; the daily duck limit was seven with 14 in possession, the goose limit six with 12 in possession. Alaska, British Columbia, Washington, Oregon, and California enforce special rules for certain areas and species, but conform closely to federal season and bag limit restrictions.

The west coast is blessed with plenty of public hunting land. This can be subdivided into three categories: national land, state or provincial land, and accessible private land. Also open to the public are coastal waters such as San Francisco Bay in California and the waters off the coast of Vancouver Island in British Columbia.

The National Wildlife Refuge System is well-established in Alaska, Washington, Oregon, and California. There are between 30 and 40 wildfowl refuges along the Pacific coast, offering thousands of acres of prime hunting land to sportsmen. Hunting rules vary considerably, so the best bet for the duck hunter is to write individual refuges to get specific information on blinds, access fees, etc. Refuge addresses are supplied on request by each state game department and the federal Bureau of Sport Fisheries and Wildlife.

State and provincial lands make even more hunting territory available to the scattergunner. Again, the best way to find out about these is to write the game department office of the state or province in which you plan to hunt. Types of land and hunting rules vary tremendously from area to area. In Alaska, for example, "all lands lower than mean high tide level" are state-owned and unrestricted public hunting domain. The California Fish and Game Department now manages eight State Wildlife Areas covering over 50,000 acres of prime wetland habitat. Other states have similar lands. British Columbia recently inaugurated its first cooperative federal-provincial wildfowl project, the Creston Valley Wildlife Management Area. This southeastern public hunting area includes 16,000 acres of huntable wildfowl habitat. So rest assured there's good state or provincial hunting land throughout the Pacific coast area.

Private land in one form or another harbors the majority of west coast wildfowl. In finding good private hunting, the fowler has to "fly by the seat of his pants." State fish and game departments will send out lists of guides and outfitters on request, and in most wildfowl areas it's possible to hire a duck-hunting guide who has access to private property. Guide fees vary from $15 to $100 per day, depending on the services offered.

Private hunting clubs are a big business in Washington, Oregon, and California, and offer the well-heeled hunter some of the best day-in, day-out wingshooting available. Many types of clubs exist on the Pacific coast, offering a variety of services. Some are formally incorporated and own several hundred acres of land managed year-round by a permanent caretaker. Others consist of a few loosely-organized hunters leasing a couple of duck ponds or some harvested grain fields. Some clubs are too expensive for the average working man; others are quite reasonable. If you're interested in club hunting, contact the fish and game department of the state or province in which you are interested. They can point you in the right direction.

If clubs don't appeal to you, don't make the mistake of writing off all private land. Large tracts of top-notch duck and goose habitat go unhunted in the Pacific area each year, simply because no one asks permission to hunt them. A nimrod can go into an area like California's San Joaquin Valley for the first time and have a great hunt, if he takes a couple of days to drive back-country roads looking for wildfowl and asking locals for permission to trespass. A few dollars offered as an access fee have opened more than one locked gate.

Hunting methods used on the Pacific coast are too diversified to be discussed here. Traditionally, calling both ducks and geese over decoys is more popular along the full length of the coastline and in southern Oregon and California; while pass-shooting and jump-shooting are predominant in Alaska, British Columbia, eastern Washington, and northeastern Oregon. But you're likely to run across the "oddball" hunter anywhere — the man who has his own unique decoy set, calling technique, or jump-shooting strategy. Any generalization has exceptions.

The west coast hunter encounters milder temperatures throughout the wildfowl season than do hunters in most other parts of the continent. The reason for this is the balmy marine climate associated with the Pacific Ocean. However, some inland valleys can get pretty nippy in late fall and winter, so it's best to go hunting prepared for the worst.

Wildfowlers will get more birds if they concentrate their efforts in proven duck and goose hotspots. Less than 3 percent of the Pacific coast area harbors wildfowl in huntable numbers, so the hunter who goes afield at random is severely handicapping himself. Likewise, some areas are good hunting grounds at certain times and totally unproductive at others.

Alaska offers good wildfowl hunting early in the fall, before the cold weather sets in. The major quarry here is mallards, pintails, widgeon, and green-winged teal. These ducks are pretty well scattered across the state, but the huge Yukon-Kuskokwim Delta (north of the Alaska Peninsula and south of the Seward Peninsula and Nome) is superb for all species. White-fronted geese and lesser Canadas are thick in the western interior of the state until about September 20, when they begin to migrate south. These are best hunted by pass-shooting and jump-shooting grass and sedge flats. Snow goose hunting is the best on the Stikine Flats, where over 20,000 birds stay until early fall frosts. The mouth of the Ugashik River near Pilot Point is superb for cackling geese. About 150,000 of these little Canadas nest here, lingering until the end of September before heading south. A few lesser Canadas and emperor geese also stay in the Pilot Point vicinity, adding some variety to the hunting.

The whole population of black brant, some 250,000 birds, bunches up on Izenbeck Lagoon at the tip of the Alaska Peninsula from about September 20 to October 20, providing some unbelievable shooting. From here the brant launch their annual coastal migration. Sixty thousand lesser Canadas, and up to 80,000 emperor geese also congregate on Izenbeck Lagoon in October.

The Copper River Delta east of Anchorage and Valdez serves as a breeding area for dusky Canada geese, a type of common Canada, and provides hunting until mid-October.

British Columbia offers spotty waterfowling at best. The whole province freezes up early in the fall, driving local ducks and geese south and holding little appeal for migrants passing through. There is some local pothole shooting for mallards and other puddle ducks in September and October, but the birds are likely to be here today, gone tomorrow. There is very good black brant and snow goose hunting on bays between Vancouver and Vancouver Island in the southwestern corner of the province. Especially good is the eastern shore of Vancouver Island.

One other area is the exception to the rule in British Columbia: the Creston Valley Wildlife Management Area. This southeastern waterfowl hotspot is consistently good for mallards, pintails, widgeon, and Canada geese early in the fall.

Washington State is divided roughly in half by the Cascade Mountains. The western sector offers good hunting for migrating black brant, snow geese, mallards, pintails, widgeon, and green-winged teal. The best area for these coastal migrants is around the tidelands of Puget Sound, especially the Skagit Wildlife Recreation Area on the Skagit Flats. Other good areas include the Willapa National Refuge on Willapa Bay and Grays Harbor. Each of these has an abundant and diversified wildfowl population in the fall.

Eastern Washington has superb hunting for wintering birds in the wheatlands of the Columbia Basin. The Potholes-Winchester Wasteway-Frenchman Hills-Desert Wildlife Recreation Complex provides excellent public hunting. The main species bagged are mallards, widgeon, green-winged teal, lesser Canada geese, and common Canada geese.

Oregon provides fine hunting for both wintering and migrating waterfowl. The southeastern part of the state is the best place to take early-fall migrants, with good hunting for snow geese, whitefronts, and honkers before Thanksgiving. This southeastern section also offers early hunting for pintails, gadwalls, and mallards. The lakes here are hotspots, with Summer Lake, Goose Lake, Malheur Lake, and the many lakes in the Klamath Basin being top choices. Summer Lake is especially famous for its snow goose hunting. Oregon's coastal bays also hold hoards of migrating wildfowl, mostly black brant, snow geese, pintails, and widgeon. After the middle of November, most migrants have moved on down into California, and Oregon hunters turn to the balance of the state, where wintering ducks and geese abound.

The lower Columbia Basin and the Willamette Valley offer the best late-season hunting in Oregon for mallards, pintails, widgeon, and green-winged teal. The main wintering goose here is the Canada. The wheat fields of the upper Columbia River in the eastern part of the state are good for lesser Canadas and mallards.

California is the big wildfowl wintering area on the Pacific coast. All west coast ducks and geese can be taken here from November through the end of the season. The most commonly bagged ducks are pintails, mallards, green-winged teal, shovelers, and widgeon. The major geese are common Canadas, lesser Canadas, cackling geese, white-fronted geese, snow geese, Ross's geese, and black brant. Good early hunting for resident species like Canadas and mallards occurs across the state, but the big time is late. The Tule-Klamath Basin, Central Valley (including the Sacramento and San Joaquin Valleys), Imperial Valley, Salton Sea, and coastal waters like San Francisco Bay and Suisun Bay are best for wintering birds. Puddle ducks and most of the geese are taken inland; black brant and diving ducks like lesser scaup dominate the coastline.

If you like duck and goose hunting, try the Pacific coast area. There are thousands of birds here of many different species, bag limits are liberal, and there's lots of public hunting land. What more could a wildfowler ask for?

23

Wildfowling in the Gulf States

by Tom Gresham

T HE OVERWHELMING IMPRESSION of waterfowl hunting in the Gulf states is one of change. In a way, the past and present of waterfowling in Louisiana gives a good indication of what is happening elsewhere.

For years, wildlife biologists in Louisiana have contended that many, if not most, of the ducks and geese wintering in that state come from the breeding areas of the Central and not the Mississippi Flyway. However, efforts to have Louisiana placed in the Central Flyway for management purposes have failed.

At the same time, short-stopping has drastically reduced the number of geese wintering in Louisiana. In many of the northern states, waterfowl, particularly geese, are fed at refuges, to keep them in the area. This has discouraged the birds from migrating further south, and is known as short-stopping. (*Editor's note*: There can be little doubt that some short-stopping is due to changes in agricultural practices, especially increased corn production, which has provided waterfowl with plenty of feed on stubble fields.)

In 1962, the hunting season for Canada geese was closed, in an

Louisiana's many marshes and bayous offer outstanding duck gunning.

attempt to save the remaining wintering flock. Even after the closure, the years from 1962 to 1975 saw the population drop from about 12,500 to less than 1000 birds. This decline occurred in the face of no hunting pressure. The birds obviously stopped their migration somewhere north of Louisiana.

Unable to find anyone willing to listen to its claims that Louisiana waterfowl should be managed as part of the Central Flyway, or that short-stopping was unalterably changing the migration instincts of geese, the state withdrew from the Mississippi Flyway Council in 1969. They rejoined the Council in 1976.

Since that year, Louisiana has taken its wildfowl management proposals directly to the U. S. Fish and Wildlife Service, bypassing the Council. That year, the state asked the Fish and Wildlife Service to conduct a study concerning its flyway alignment. The Service replied that it had neither the money nor the manpower available for such a study, but suggested that Louisiana might have its own study done by independent researchers.

Frank Bellrose, a noted wildlife researcher, conducted the study and reported that Louisiana was right in its contention. The state made a proposal to the Fish and Wildlife Service that it be switched to the Central Flyway. A counter proposal came back that ran something like this: Louisiana would be divided into an east and a west zone. The thinking was (is) that the west zone falls in the Central Flyway and the east in the Mississippi Flyway. The zoning would last for four years, during which extensive banding, harvest surveys, and other measures could be carried out to determine the flyway alignment of Louisiana. The first season of the four-year study was in 1975.

Other states on the Gulf are experiencing changes in their wildfowl management plans as well. Mississippi and Alabama withdrew from the Mississippi Flyway Council, to protest short-stopping, and rejoined in 1976.

As one hunter put it, "The wild goose has gone the way of the dodo bird as far as Floridians are concerned." Short-stopping is responsible.

It now appears that snow and blue geese are being short-stopped also. It is possible that in a decade this technique of waterfowl management on the part of the northern states will halt the migration of these smaller geese, ending the "dream hunts" on white spreads in Texas. But there is still more.

Mallards are also susceptible to short-stopping. Upon seeing a large flock of their own kind, they will stop for a visit and stay as long as the pond is kept from freezing and food is available. Wildlife managers in the northern states make sure that these conditions are present.

The question then is: what is the future of waterfowl hunting in the Gulf states? The answer depends on what action is taken by the northern states. If they continue to alter the migration patterns of North American waterfowl, and if the Fish and Wildlife Service does nothing to prevent it, the future for the southern wildfowler may be bleak.

The goose hunting situation in Florida is simple—there is none. Short-stopping has eliminated it. Although Florida is frequently not thought of as a duck hunting state, it does provide ample opportunity for those who know where to hunt.

The many potholes on either side of highway 41 in the southern Everglades offer good mallard hunting. However, there are few, if any, hunting guides available and it is not advisable to wander around in the 'glades if you are not familiar with the area.

Over on the eastern edge of the Everglades, there are guides available for duck shooting in the Conservation Pools. These water storage areas are only a few miles from the coast, and the state has granted concession sites to hunting camp operators.

Duck guides are available from the Loxahatchee Recreation Area, on State Road 827, at Deerfield Beach, and from the Sawgrass Recreation Park, which is near the intersection of U.S. 27 and State Road 84, at Andytown, Florida.

Just north of the Everglades is Lake Okeechobee, one of the largest freshwater lakes in the world. The "Big O" is shallow over most of its area, and harbors a lot of ducks.

The St. Johns River in hunted by locals, but the visiting hunter would have trouble locating the birds.

The Merritt Island National Wildlife Refuge may be the best area for duck gunning in Florida. Located near Titusville, the refuge is practically in the shadow of Cape Canaveral's rocket launching pads. For information on hunting in the refuge, write to the Merritt Island National Wildlife Refuge, P.O. Box 6504, Titusville, Florida 32780.

For more information on Florida hunting in general, and the availability of guides, write the Florida Game and Fresh Water Fish Commission, 620 South Meridian, Tallahassee, Florida 32304.

The Alabama duck hunting picture is one of north and south. Mobile Bay has always been thought of as the best area in the state, and it is still good. However, the northern part of the state, around Huntsville and Decatur, probably has more ducks, a few geese, and more opportunity.

The Alabama Department of Conservation operates several management areas for wildfowl, with the best hunting likely in the Swan Creek area near Decatur. This area of over 6000 acres is planted in the spring and flooded in the fall for the wildfowl season.

Between the two areas mentioned, at opposite ends of the state, is a lot of territory that is hunted sporadically. Through the middle of the state, small bodies of water invite ducks to take a break from their migration. Beaver swamps, creeks, and rivers offer a lot of duck shooting potential for the hunter who is at the right place when the ducks are there.

Information on where to hunt, as well as state regulations, can be obtained from the Alabama Department of Conservation and Natural Resources, 64 North Union Street, Montgomery, Alabama 36104.

The State of Mississippi has created about ten wildfowl areas to provide opportunities for duck hunters. Perhaps the best of these is the Indian Bayou Waterfowl Area, in Sharkey County. The Indian Bayou Area consists of 1700 acres of the Delta National Forest, that is flooded to form a green tree area. The shooting is much like the famous timber shooting around Stuttgart, Arkansas.

One spokesman for the Mississippi Game and Fish Commission said that last year's duck season was the best since 1946 for Magnolia State hunters. He attributes this to farming practices, which are changing from an emphasis on cotton to more rice and soybeans.

Of course, the Mississippi River and adjacent potholes and oxbow lakes provide some excellent hunting as well.

For a brochure on the wildfowl areas, and other information on wildfowling in Mississippi, write the Game and Fish Commission, Box 451, Jackson, Mississippi 39205.

Mississippi's southwestern neighbor, Louisiana, must offer some of the best duck hunting in the south. Toledo Bend Lake, on the border of Texas and Louisiana, offered very good duck shooting in its first few years of existence, but has gradually deteriorated. The flooded timber which provided cover for ducks and concealment for hunters has died and rotted off below the waterline, leaving vast areas of open water.

The best areas for duck hunters are the coves which still have some timber and the north end of the lake.

A word of caution is called for when discussing Toledo. The vast open areas are conducive to very rough water when the winds are high. A small boat can become trapped in a cove and not be able to return to its landing across the lake. Keep an eye on the weather, and head in *before* the wind comes up. If caught by a storm, wait it out! It's far better to be wet and cold from sitting out a storm than to capsize trying to get to your landing.

Catahoula Lake has been called one of the most important stopping points in the Mississippi Flyway. Of course, that may be changing due to short-stopping as well.

Catahoula lies about 15 miles northeast of the central Louisiana city of Alexandria. Hunting conditions are almost entirely dependent on the level of the water. One of the interesting aspects of the lake is its hard bottom. Special, big-wheeled vehicles have been built to take hunters across the shallow flats to their blinds.

Of course, the dominant feature of wildfowl hunting in Louisiana is the marsh—the bayou country. The salt, brackish, and freshwater marsh is the largest in the western hemisphere, and serves as a wintering area for innumerable ducks and geese.

White rags are popular "decoys" for gunning snow geese in the rice fields of Texas.

While the casual observer would say that the marsh looks the same all across the state, there are actually differences in water level, in salinity, and as a result, in type of vegetation.

As already mentioned, Canada geese have been eliminated from the Louisiana hunting scene by wildfowl managers in the northern part of the flyways. Though the geese are gone, the Louisiana marsh offers duck hunting on par with some of the best spots in the country. When conditions are right, hunters can have their limit in less than an hour. This is not-at-all unusual.

The visiting hunter would do well to enlist the services of a guide to hunt in the marsh. One place that provides guide services is the Sheraton-Chateau Charles Motor Hotel in Lake Charles. Zack Roush can take care of all the details, from getting you rooms at the hotel to having your birds picked after the hunt. For more details, write Zack Roush, Sheraton-Chateau Charles Motor Hotel, I-10 West and Highway 90, Lake Charles, Louisiana 70601. The telephone number is (318) 882-6130.

Information on duck hunting in Louisiana can be obtained from the Louisiana Wildlife and Fisheries Commission, 400 Royal Street, New Orleans, Louisiana 70130.

Wildfowling in Texas stretches from desert potholes to coastal marshes. Potholes and impoundments are the ticket for the duck hunter in the western part of the state. Over in eastern Texas, however, the use of white spreads is prevalent.

Laying on your back in a dry field, covered and surrounded by white rags, isn't most people's idea of wildfowling. But if you are in the area around Eagle Lake, Texas, it's the thing to do.

From the air, that spread of white rags looks like a flock of snow geese, and can really pull the geese and ducks in. The hunters dress in white coveralls and lay in a field of rice stubble, amidst rags, diapers, newspapers, or whatever is handy, and call in the birds.

The originator of the white spread is probably J.R. "Jimmy" Reel. Reel said the idea wasn't really new; people used chunks of wood and newspaper to decoy wildfowl years ago. When he saw a stack of county fair posters in a printing shop one day, he decided to try it. The posters worked, and the technique of the white spread became popular almost overnight.

Today, Reel uses plastic table cloths because they don't absorb moisture, a property that makes cloth rags very heavy on the way back to the car.

There are several outfitters in the Eagle Lake area that hunt the white spreads. Reel's operation is the oldest and considered to be one of the best. His address is P.O. Box 756, Eagle Lake, Texas 77434.

For further information on hunting in Texas, contact the Parks and Wildlife Department, John H. Reagan Building, Austin, Texas 78701.

24

Wildfowling in Mexico

Nick Covacevich and Gilberto Quiñones

S O M E   W A T E R F O W L E R S from California, Texas, Arizona, and New Mexico already know of the fine goose and duck gunning in Sonora, Chihuahua, Sinaloa, and Baja California. But word hasn't gotten much farther north. Mexico is a big country, and wildfowling in the southern portion has yet to be discovered by visiting sportsmen.

All of the major flyways converge into Mexico, from the Pacific, Central, and Mississippi to the Caribbean. As a result, hundreds of thousands, if not millions, of ducks and geese arrive each year to spend the winter. In almost any section of Mexico, the visiting hunter can find fair to superb duck and goose shooting. There are very few local wildfowlers, largely because of the high cost of ammunition, licence fees, and transportation. Thus the annual wildfowl kill in Mexico is very low compared to that of the United States. Surveys made by several wildfowl authorities from the U.S. have proven that in the days when supposed "mass" killings of ducks were made by "armadas"—local market hunters—the annual duck kill was never above 500,000 birds. This is low in comparison to the millions of ducks killed in the United States and Canada each year. In fact, it

Bag limits in Mexico are generous by American standards, yet the total wild-fowl harvest in that country is small.

is probable that more ducks are killed on opening day in the United States than throughout the year in Mexico.

The season for ducks and geese in Mexico opens annually on November 1 and closes on February 28.

The limit is 10 birds per day, except on Saturdays and Sundays when it is 20 birds per day. One exception occurs in Baja California and Sinaloa, where the daily bag limit is 20 birds from Monday to

Thursday and 25 birds from Friday to Sunday. The possession limit is 50 birds.

Another exception to the national limit is around Mexico City and Toluca. Duck hunting is allowed only on Sundays, and the bag limit is 25 birds per day.

No goose hunting is allowed in Mexico on Mondays, Tuesdays, and Wednesdays. The limit on Thursdays and Fridays is 10 birds per day, while on Saturdays and Sundays it is 15 birds. The possession limit is 30 geese.

The Mexican Wildlife Department—Dirección de la Fauna Silvestre—has, for the past decade, been very active in prohibiting the "armadas". Consequently, there is little or no sale of wild ducks. The establishment of Ducks Unlimited Incorporated in Mexico, a few years ago, has also helped a great deal in the conservation of wildfowl. It should clearly be understood that *Mexico does have game laws,* and while these may not be as rigorous as those of the United States, they must be obeyed by all visiting and other hunters.

Every hunter must have a valid licence, issued by the state in which he is hunting, as well as a game sticker which must be attached to the hunting licence. There are both small game and big game stickers. Small game, of course, includes wildfowl. The cost of a non-resident small game sticker for the entire season is 600 Mexican pesos or about $48 U.S. An 8-day non-resident small game stamp is also available for a cost of 300 Mexican pesos or about $24 U.S. For any hunter, resident or non-resident, with a valid licence, all wild ducks and geese are legal game.

Mexico does not have an army of game wardens looking down shotgun barrels, but relies on the hunter's sportsmanship for self-policing. Non-resident hunters are welcome in Mexico, particularly if they are good and conscientious sportsmen. This is in sharp contrast to the rather unfriendly attitude towards non-resident hunters in many states of the U.S.

Almost all common species of North American ducks and geese are found in Mexico—blue-winged teal, pintails, baldpates, gadwalls, shovelers, canvasbacks, ring-necked ducks, Mexican ducks, Fulvous whistling ducks, mallards, and redheads. Geese, mostly Canadas and whitefronts, winter in large numbers around such well known goose hunting grounds as the Ciudad Cuauhtemoc and Casas Grandes in Chihuahua, around Ciudad Obregón in Sonora, and in the Matamoros-Tamaulipas region across from Brownsville, Texas.

Lesser and sandhill cranes are protected in most areas of the

The pichiguila is a popular duck among wildfowlers in Mexico.

United States, but in Mexico they are legal game. Sandhills are found in most regions where geese abound.

Those seriously interested in learning more about Mexico's varied game should read A. Starker Leopold's *Wildlife of Mexico—the Game Birds and Mammals*, published by the University of California Press. For those who read Spanish, the publication by Arellano and Rojas entitled *Abes Acuáticas Migratorias en México (Aquatic Migratory Birds in Mexico)* is another good reference.

It is recommended that visiting sportsmen make arrangements for hunting trips using the services of a hunting outfitter or guide that has been authorized by the Mexican Wildlife Department. This is particularly true if you don't speak Spanish. If you would like a list of such guides, write to the authors c/o Apartado Postal 1030, Mexico 1, D.F., Mexico. If you enclose $2, we will send you a list of Mexican hunting guides and outfitters, as well as a list of some of the better wildfowling areas in Mexico. All the money we receive will be turned over to Ducks Unlimited in Mexico.

Another excellent way to arrange a wildfowl hunt in Mexico is through a booking agent. There are a number of specialized travel agencies in both the United States and Canada that arrange wildfowling tours into Mexico. Some of these advertise in the major American outdoor magazines.

In the better wildfowling areas, there are "hunting camps" that provide everything the hunter needs in the way of rooms, food, guides, transportation, decoys, and assistance in obtaining permits and other details. In other places, the local hotels or motels know authorized guides who can guide the hunter. These guides generally furnish transportation, cold drinks, and boys to retrieve the ducks and clean them. The hunter makes his own arrangements regarding accommodation at a local hotel or motel.

Most outfitters and guides will arrange to pluck and dress birds and package them for your return trip. The United States Fish and Wildlife Service regulates the numbers of waterfowl that an American hunter can bring back home. At present, it is 10 ducks and 5 geese. One wing must be left fully feathered on each bird for purposes of identification. But since such regulations may change at any time, it is wise to check first by writing to the U.S. Fish and Wildlife Service, Department of the Interior, Washington D.C. 20240.

The United States Customs Service also has regulations regarding the importation of game. At some ports of entry into the United States, customs officials require that the returning hunter submit a customs form number 3315, "Declaration for Free Entry of Game Animals or Birds Killed by U.S. Residents". There is no duty on game imported into the U.S. by a hunter, if the game is for his own use. Customs regulations concerning importation of dead game are described in a publication called *Pets and Wildlife* available free of charge from the U.S. Customs Service, P.O. Box 7118, Washington, D.C. 20044, or from the nearest District Director of Customs.

Most guides and outfitters in Mexico have shotguns for rent at a

The Chiricahueto Lagoon near Culiacan, Sinaloa, harbors thousands of wintering wildfowl.

Air boats are used to transport duck hunters in Mexican lagoons and marshes.

very modest fee. If you don't mind shooting with a strange gun, it is best to come to Mexico "gunless". To bring in your own gun entails considerable red tape.

All firearms in Mexico must be registered with the Defense Secretariat. Once the firearm is registered, a permit for transportation of firearms must be obtained. This can be obtained from the Mexican Target Shooting Federation, by joining this organization, at cost of 310 Mexican pesos or about $25 U.S.

For those who wish to hunt with their own guns, it is imperative to obtain the following:

(a) a "consular letter" issued by the Mexican Consulate nearest to the hunter's place of residence (at a cost of approximately $16), stating that the person in question is a sportsman interested in hunting in Mexico;

(b) three passport-sized, front-view photographs in black and white;

(c) the make, type, gauge or caliber, and serial number of each sporting firearm to be registered (maximum is two) for bringing into Mexico.

With this data, the authorized guide can help to make the necessary arrangements for firearms registration, a firearms transportation permit, a hunting licence, game stickers, and Mexican customs clearance. Incidentally, a hunter is allowed to bring 100 shot shells into Mexico for each registered gun. However, good shot shells may be purchased right in the country, in both field and high-base loads, and in all common shot sizes.

About the only other thing a visiting hunter needs to enter Mexico is a Tourist Card, which may be obtained at any Mexican Consulate or through any travel agent. Proof of citizenship is all that is needed to obtain the card.

All of Mexico's principal cities are well serviced by the major airlines. And for those wishing to drive their own cars or campers, rest assured that the major highways are good. There is even a special service of mobile "Green Angels" units that the Mexican Tourist Department employs to assist all travellers on Mexican highways. Thus, travelling in Mexico presents no serious problems. Finding good hotels and motels, some belonging to the various U.S. hotel chains, is not a problem either. All of the Mexican hotels catering to the tourist trade generally offer good service.

Goose and duck hunting in Mexico is still very much as it was in the United States at the turn of the century. If you want to enjoy wildfowling like your grandfather did in the good old days in the U.S.A., why not come south with the wildfowl?

25

The Future of Wildfowl

Joseph P. Linduska

Currently, the world population stands at about 4 billion. A little over 20 years from now, in the year 2000, a projected 7 billion souls will inhabit this planet. When you consider these demographic figures, along with the fact that two-thirds of today's population is already going hungry, you may gain some insight into where we are headed. With each passing year, the world-wide food situation will become more critical.

What has all this to do with wildfowl? Attempting to forecast the future of wildfowl without considering the future of mankind is foolish —even impossible. Man and wildfowl are intrinsically tied. Since the first time he stalked this earth as a primitive predator; since the first time he drained a marsh to plant his crops, man has had an impact on waterfowl abundance.

Nearly all of the earth's highly arable land is now under cultivation. To produce more food to feed exploding human hordes means just one thing—intensified crop production on the less productive acres. This has several implications, but for ducks they are all bleak.

The future of wildfowling lies in the preservation of wetlands.

It means an even bigger squeeze on our wetlands so that more acres can be salvaged for wheat.

Bear one thing in mind. Wildfowl depend almost entirely on wetlands for their existence. Lowlands covered by shallow water—sometimes temporarily or intermittently—are wetlands, as long as they hold water long enough to grow moist-soil plants. Mountain beaver meadows are wetlands. The river bottoms of the south, the potholes of the northern prairies, and the marshes around the Great Lakes are all wetlands; and all contribute to the existence of wild ducks. Wetlands are the life blood of North American wildfowl populations.

Yet the future of our wetlands is discouraging. Certainly the past offers no reassurance, but perhaps we can learn from what has happened and do something before it happens again.

Wetlands, often regarded as wastelands, have been subject to reckless draining in the United States since the middle of the nineteenth century. The so-called Swamp Land Acts of that era enabled the states to reclaim wetlands for the purpose of controlling floods and eliminating mosquito breeding habitat. More than half of the estimated original 127 million acres of wetlands were patented to the states. By 1953, only 82 million acres of wetlands remained. Of this remnant, less than one-fourth had a significant wildfowl value.

The conflict between drainage for agriculture and the production of wildfowl is most severe in the glaciated section, the "prairie pothole region", of the northcentral United States. Millions of small wetlands, which form the basis for tremendous duck production, are viewed as obstacles to farming in this major wheat-producing section of the country. As early as 1934, drainage of marshes to create more land for wheat in the northern Great Plains was suggested as a major reason for the decline of continental wildfowl populations. Drainage during the period from 1936 to 1963 added 6.2 million acres to agriculture, in the principal duck-producing states of North and South Dakota and Minnesota. About 25 percent of this 6.2 million acres was of significant value to wildfowl.

In one 4-year period (1951 to 55), federally assisted drainage alone claimed more than 250,000 acres of prairie duck habitat. An inventory in 1964 indicated only 2.7 million acres of wildfowl productive wetlands remaining in the prairie pothole regions of the Dakotas and Minnesota. Drainage surveys between 1964 and 1968 in the same area indicated an annual loss rate of nearly 2 percent. With the market price of wheat doubling and tripling, and the nation's commitment to all-out food production, far greater wetland losses appear to be a foregone conclusion. In the face of this drainage, wildfowl production will decline even more.

Wetland drainage in the glaciated prairie pothole region of southern Canada has not been as widespread as in the United States. However, localized drainage efforts have significantly reduced duck production in several key wildfowl areas. With increased prices of wheat on the export market, wetlands losses in the Canadian prairie "bread basket", where nearly 50 percent of all North American ducks are produced, will almost assuredly expand.

The river deltas and flood plains of northern Canada and Alaska are the mainstay for wildfowl production in years of drought on the prairies. Wetland destruction in the far north has, until recently, been limited. However, potential hydro electric projects, such as the James Bay hydro project, as well as developments associated with oil exploration and development, pose serious threats to a number of the most productive areas of the far north.

And there's more. Highway construction on the prairies threatens vast numbers of wetlands. Federal funds go to both county and state governments to help expand road systems. Roadside ditches are a necessary part of highway construction. They are constructed so that runoff waters reaching the right-of-way will quickly move to the nearest creek or river. These ditches provide drainage outlets for fields and wetlands adjacent to the roadway, with the resultant loss of valuable wetlands and problems to highway maintenance crews who must deal with ever-increasing volumes of water.

In addition to *direct* wetland losses from highway construction, there are *indirect* losses resulting from drainage systems on private lands and outletting into roadside ditches. Thus, highways built at public expense for transportation purposes are being used by private landowners to hasten the destruction of wetlands.

Wetland losses from highway construction occur in all the midwestern states. To estimate the extent of these losses, the Fish and

The draining of potholes and other wetlands for agriculture has greatly reduced this continent's wildfowl habitat.

Wildlife Service of the Department of the Interior conducted a sur-vey in 19 western Minnesota counties containing typical prairie wetlands. The results were appalling. In these 19 counties alone, 99,292 acres of wetlands were found to have been drained as a result of road construction. This represents 29 percent of the total wetlands in the area. Clearly, there is a need here to invoke provi-sions of the Department of Transportation Act and the National Enviromental Policy Act, which presumably protect wildlife bene-fits where federal construction funds are involved.

Estuaries and coastal wetlands, particularly those among the mid and south Atlantic coasts and the Gulf of Mexico, are wintering grounds for a major segment of North America's wildfowl. An in-ventory in 1954 indicated that 5,290,000 acres of coastal saline wetlands existed in the United States, of which 1,896,000 acres were of primary importance to wildfowl. During the period from 1922 to 1954, a minimum of 25 percent of the total productive shallow coastal waters and marshes were destroyed.

More recently, a National Estuary Study, completed in 1970, indicated that 73 percent of the nation's estuaries had been modified or severely degraded. During the period from 1950 to 1969, some 642,000 acres of significant fish and wildlife estuarine habitat were lost to dredging and filling operations alone. Besides dredging and filling for housing and industrial development, major coastal wetland losses are caused by ditching and drainage for mosquito control, construction of marinas, use as garbage dumps, and construction of waterways for navigation routes. Coastal wetland losses have been closely correlated with urban sprawl, primarily along the mid and north Atlantic and southern Pacific coasts. Recent estimates place the nationwide loss of coastal wetlands, conservatively, at 0.5 to 1.0 percent annually.

The need for flood control and the economic gain from conversion to agriculture has resulted in the clearing of millions of acres of bot-tomland hardwood forest, and channelization of thousands of miles of streams in the United States, primarily in the southeastern and northcentral sections. Watershed protection and flood prevention projects have been a major stimulating force in channelization and clearing of bottomland hardwoods in the southeast.

Some 20 million acres of wooded and shrub swamps and overflow bottomlands existed along the Mississippi River and its tributaries during the mid-1950's. Ten years later, conversion of hardwood forests to cropland for cotton, rice, and soybeans in the lower half of the Mississippi River basin had resulted in the loss of approximately two-thirds of the overflow timbered bottomlands. The effect was to seriously deplete major wintering grounds of mallards, and critical breeding habit for wood ducks, the two species most important to wildfowl hunters on the Mississippi Flyway.

Bottomland and hardwoods were cleared in the Mississippi delta region during the 1960's at an average rate of more than 200,000 acres per year. Small watershed projects continue, and with them persists a classic conflict between agricultural interests and wildlife habitat.

Another type of habitat deterioration, which appears to be depressing wildfowl production in many areas, is the so-called "clean" farming. This is particularly noticeable in the northcentral United States, where the average wildfowl nesting success has been reduced from 60 to 70 percent in the 1930's, to 30 to 40 percent in the 1960's. The cause is increased predation because of a lack of suitable nesting cover. Agricultural land retirement programs have assisted considerably with the availability of sufficient upland nesting cover. But there will be much less land retirement in this era of world hunger and high wheat prices.

As bleak as the picture seems, there is a ray of hope. Public awareness of environmental values in the United States has grown rapidly, and a special concern is being shown for aquatic ecosystems. Our citizenry is rebelling over events of the past. It is questioning many present-day projects that stand to further deplete our wetlands.

Not all government agencies and private organizations have passively stood and watched waterfowl habitat disappear. The National Wildlife Refuge System had its beginning in 1903. By the early 1930's, during years of severe draught, substantial tracts of wildfowl habitat were being added to the system. In 1934, the authorization of the Migratory Bird Hunting Stamp provided a source of funds for acquisition of migratory bird habitat. Additionally, substantial appropriations of emergency funds were made during the depression years for land acquisition. By 1958, nearly 3.5 million acres of wildfowl habitat had been acquired by the federal government.

An inventory of wildfowl habitats during the late 1950's suggested that 12.5 million acres should be preserved in public ownership. Of this, 8 million acres were to be acquired by the federal government and 4.5 million acres by the states. Acquisition through the 1950's was concentrated on large marshes, reservoirs, and other permanent wetland habitat. A number of partially drained, large marshes were restored to their former productive capacity.

With the initiation of aerial wildfowl surveys in Canada and the northcentral United States, it became evident that continental duck populations fluctuated directly with water conditions each spring and summer, in the prairie regions of the two countries. About 10 million small wetlands exist in Canada and the United States during a wet year. The need to preserve these became evident as the pressure to drain them for agricultural purposes intensified.

The first step in achieving protection for small wetlands came in 1958. In that year, Congress increased the price of the "duck stamp" to $3; earmarked all duck stamp receipts for land acquisition; and authorized a wildfowl production area program. But the increased monies from the duck stamps were still inadequate to reverse the drainage trend. Therefore, in 1961, an accelerated wetland acquisition program was initiated. The accelerated effort was made possible by an advance loan of $105 million from the Treasury. Funds appropriated from the loan are to be repaid with duck stamp receipts beginning July 1, 1976. Currently the duck stamp, required of all waterfowlers, sells for $5. This means that 2 million hunters of ducks and geese are making a $10 million investment in habitat preservation through that program alone.

National wildlife refuge units for wildfowl, in all four flyways, involve relatively large blocks of land. No refuge system can be established unless the area has historically been used by wildfowl, or unless it can be developed through water control or habitat management to provide specific wildfowl needs. The emphasis has been on acquiring refuges which provide nesting habitat, because this appears to be the main limiting factor in waterfowl populations. However, refuges are also acquired for resting and feeding during migration and on wintering grounds.

In contrast, the objective of the wildfowl production area program is to preserve wildfowl breeding habitat by acquiring land or interests in land to prevent destruction of its wetland character, and to provide suitable upland nesting cover. In general, the more permanent types of wetlands are acquired as brooding areas throughout the prairie pothole region. The more temporary wetlands are protected by easements to prevent draining, filling, and burning of cover. Thus far, a total of 5,157,000 acres of upland and wetland habitat has been set aside primarily for wildfowl in the United States. In addition, 4 million acres have been added to the National Wildlife Refuge System throughout the United States, including Alaska and Hawaii, for all migratory birds including wildfowl.

In carrying out provisions of the Alaska Native Claims Settlement Act of 1973, the Secretary of the Interior recommended that nearly 32 million acres of Alaskan wildlife habitat also be added to the National Wildlife Refuge System. Much of this land has a high value to migratory wildfowl.

Also, a substantial number of wetlands have been preserved from federally subsidized drainage through two laws passed in 1962. The first applies nationwide and prohibits the use of Agricultural Conservation Program funds, administrated by the Department of Agriculture, for the drainage of a number of different types of wetlands. The second law, a so-called Drainage Referral Act, requires that no government funds be obtained by an individual for drainage of any type of wetland in North Dakota, South Dakota, or Minnesota, without determination by the Fish and Wildlife Service as to whether wildlife might materially be damaged by that drainage. If significant damage might result, the service or state agency may offer to acquire the wetland for wildfowl. If the landowner refuses to sell, he may not obtain federal assistance to drain for 5 years after the offer is made. If the wetland has little value to wildfowl or no offer is made to acquire it, the owner may receive financial assistance to drain immediately.

Wildfowl management on National Wildlife Refuges is a high priority activity. The 356 refuges, plus more than 100 small wildfowl production areas, produce nearly 1.5 million ducks, geese, and swans in an average year. Although the federal refuge system is extensive, it represents only a small segment of the total habitat base. Therefore, intensive management is necessary. The quality of habitat on refuges is continually improved through establishment of native grasses and legumes, prescribed burning, forest management, water drawdowns, and other management methods designed to obtain habitat and to increase natural food production.

Creation of new water areas and rehabilitation of deteriorated marshes are some of the other management measures used to provide additional wildfowl habitat. Planting of grain crops for wildfowl, once a major management tool, is being scaled down on refuges to prevent unnatural concentrations of wildfowl for long periods of time. On small wildfowl production areas, the emphasis is to secure high quality upland nesting cover for ground-nesting wildfowl.

The United States Congress provided further benefits for wildfowl when it passed the Fish and Wildlife Coordination Act of 1934. Additional consideration for wildlife, and for development and enhancement of wildlife habitat, were provided through amendments to the act in 1946 and 1958. About 4000 federal water projects have been studied, many of which included wildfowl management provisions, based on recommendations by federal and state wildlife agencies. More than a million acres of land and water associated with federal water projects have been added to the National Wildlife Refuge System, primarily for mitigation and enhancement of wildfowl habitat. Federal water projects sponsored by the Corps of Engineers and the Bureau of Reclamation have brought some 600,000 acres of public waters under state management.

In 1937, Congress enacted the Federal Aid to Wildlife Restoration Act, which provides financial assistance to states for financing wildlife restoration and habitat acquisition. Under the act, a federal excise tax on sporting arms and ammunition is apportioned to state fish and game agencies. Over 1600 individual areas, totalling about 1.5 million acres, have been acquired through this program. In many instances, states have supplemented federal aid money for habitat preservation with other innovative fund-raising mechanisms, such as taxes on cigarettes, pari-mutuel race horse wagering, real estate, seafood, and even dog licences. The total of all state-owned wildfowl areas is in the neighborhood of 2.7 million acres.

Of the primary wildfowl producing states, Minnesota has acquired nearly 300,000 acres, thus preventing the drainage of many small wetlands as well as providing tremendous hunting opportunities. South Dakota has acquired some 60,000 acres, most of which contain small wetlands for wildfowl production. Wisconsin has acquired over 200,000 acres of wildfowl habitat; and North Dakota over 28,000 acres. Many other states have added significantly to the nationwide wildfowl habitat preservation and management effort.

Funds made available to the states through the federal aid program are the primary source of revenue for developing and managing wildfowl habitat. State emphasis is generally towards managing wildlife areas for consumptive public use. Since 1938, more than $76 million in federal aid funds have been expended or obligated by the states for development of wildfowl management areas in all states

The burning of grass in spring and summer destroys many duck nests each year.

except Alaska and Hawaii. Development funds pay for planting wildlife food, posting boundaries, fencing, building roads and trails, clearing and controlling undesired vegetation, managing hunts, trapping and restocking game to suitable ranges, and other habitat improvements.

In the late nineteenth and early twentieth centuries, management of state areas was concerned mainly with protection of wildfowl from overharvest. Since 1935, the trend has been toward creating and managing combination public shooting areas and sanctuaries.

Habitat development and management are a large part of state wildfowl programs. Diking of salt marshes to establish water levels for improved duck food production is practised extensively on the Atlantic and Gulf Coast areas. Flooding bottomland hardwoods, which increases the availability of mast crops to wildfowl, is a common practice in the midwest. States in the midwest and the northeast have created numerous small, shallow wildfowl marshes on which water level can be manipulated, to improve food and cover conditions.

Habitat managed to attract wildfowl can, however, change ancestral distribution patterns of the birds. This has occurred on both state and federal areas, resulting in an interstate problem of equitable wildfowl distribution.

In Canada, most public lands are administered by the provinces.

However, the federal government is empowered to establish migratory bird sanctuaries. These may be established on either private or Crown lands (as public lands in Canada are called). Over 100 migratory bird sanctuaries, totalling more than 25 million acres, have been established in Canada. Over 90 percent of these are on Crown land in the Northwest Territories, to provide control over mineral exploitation in major goose-breeding areas. In 1966, the Canadian Wildlife Service established a program to preserve duck breeding habitat. The goal was to safeguard 300,000 acres. Unfortunately, due to fund shortages, the program was active for only 2 years. However, nearly 39,000 acres for waterfowl had been acquired by the federal government of Canada in 1973.

Probably no sportsmen's organization is better known than Ducks Unlimited. Organized in the United States, this body has been dedicated to preserving, restoring, and creating breeding habitat for waterfowl in Canada. A companion Canadian corporation, Ducks Unlimited (Canada), was formed to manage the projects. Ducks Unlimited owns no land; all projects are established by taking flood easements from landowners. By 1975, 1250 projects were completed, leading to the improvement of 2 million water acres. A new affiliate, Ducks Unlimited de Mexico, will dedicate its activities to preservation of wildfowl wintering habitat in Mexico.

Public ownership of all wetlands necessary for producing and maintaining an adequate population of waterfowl is not possible. It must be supplemented by wetland habitat owned by private individuals, groups, and foundations. The Nature Conservancy is a non-profit organization that buys natural areas, including wetlands, with donations. A revolving fund permits the conservancy to acquire lands in imminent danger of destruction, and later sell them to state and federal agencies for management. But the Nature Conservancy retains ownership of many of its smaller purchases. As of 1974, the conservancy has assisted with acquisition of more than 664,000 acres of natural areas, of which about 100,000 are wetlands.

The National Audubon Society, another private organization, owns or leases 250,000 acres, mostly wetlands, in eight states. Habitat of rare and endangered species or strategic breeding areas, such as large rookeries, receive emphasis.

Private duck clubs manage an estimated 3 million acres, on 6000 areas in the United States. Other private refuges throughout the United States and Canada also provide significant habitat. Some of the better known include the Delta Waterfowl Research Station in Manitoba, the Jack Miner Sanctuary in Ontario, Remington Farms in Maryland, and the Kellogg Bird Sanctuary in Michigan.

Development of small ponds and dugouts for watering livestock came into prominence in the western states after the draught of the 1930's. During the period 1936 to 1972, the United States Department of Agriculture provided technical or financial assistance for the construction of more than 2.1 million stock ponds and dugouts. Another 200,000 to 300,000 were built with private funds. About half of these man-made ponds receive some wildfowl use. In southern Canada, some 93,000 stock ponds and dugouts have been constructed with Prairie Farm Rehabilitation Act funds.

Major reservoirs constructed for flood control, irrigation, recreation, and power provide resting sites for waterfowl throughout the United States. However, they furnish little in the way of natural food. A United States Geological Survey study in 1966 indicated that there were 1562 reservoirs, covering 14,831,000 surface acres.

Despite these determined efforts to preserve wetlands, the future does not look good. Not unless the efforts are increased. We must bear in mind that wetland preservation is not creation. With minor exceptions, the wetlands that have been saved were already there. They were not new areas, habitat gained, to offset the high losses of the past. The net losses of wetlands on the northern breeding ground have been substantial.

Also, many wetlands along migration and wintering grounds have been lost to grain and rice culture. But in these cases the standing crops and residues from harvest may equal the food potential of the pre-existing marsh. Many species of waterfowl, but not all, have been quick to adapt to this new food supply. The net result could represent a partial trade-off in terms of damage done and benefit gained.

Yet the intrusion of agriculture has brought other problems. Crop depredation brings high dollar losses to landowners and many headaches to wildfowl managers. Also, drained marshlands along migration routes and on wintering grounds once served as breeding habitat for some species. This value has been lost. Distribution of wildfowl has also been affected. Some species have adapted readily to changes in their habitat; others have not.

Where then is the solution? Perhaps there is none. There is no doubt that natural habitats must be preserved if we are to enjoy wildfowl, and wildfowling, in the future. If we fail in preserving our wetlands, in preserving nesting habitat, wildfowl will perish. And so will the ancient tradition of wildfowling.

Notes on Contributors

CHARLES C. ADAMS is one of the younger and newer names on the outdoor writing scene. A resident of California, Adams has hunted wildfowl along much of the Pacific coast. Wildfowling and bow-hunting are two of his specialties.

NICK COVACEVICH, an outdoor columnist for Mexico City's English newspaper *The News,* is a walking encyclopedia on fishing and hunting in Mexico. An expert wildfowler, Covacevich is the founding president of Ducks Unlimited of Mexico.

PETE CZURA is one of this continent's top free-lance outdoor writers, with credits in all of the major outdoor and travel magazines. Among his colleagues, Czura is even better known as an outdoor photographer. The jacket of this book is one example of his ability with a camera.

GENE GALLAGHER is a New Englander, with waterfowling roots that stretch across nearly all the tidal marshes of the east. When he is not hunting black ducks or gunning sea ducks, Gallagher is the publisher and editor of the *New Hampshire Outdoorsman.*

BOB GOOCH, a quiet southern gentleman, contributes articles to all of the major outdoor publications. But in his native Virginia, he is best known for his lively and interesting syndicated column "Virginia Afield." When Gooch is not earning his living behind the typewriter, he is generally hunting ducks or quail.

TOM GRESHAM grew up in the bayous of Louisiana, and began wildfowling at an early age with his outdoor writer father. Gresham now makes his home in Montgomery, Alabama, where he is the editor of *Southern Outdoors*, a position which enables him to keep a finger on the wildfowling pulse of the Gulf states.

GEORGE GRUENEFELD has hunted wildfowl over all of eastern Canada. What else can be expected from a man who owns two Chesapeakes and earns his daily bread as a freelance writer and outdoor editor of the *Montreal Gazette?*

MALCOLM HART, a gentleman of outdoor sport, spends much of his leisure time hunting ducks and fishing for trout. He has followed both pursuits from Quebec to Argentina.

ALYSON KNAP, a botanist by profession, enjoys game cookery as a major hobby. Her recent outdoorsman's guide to edible wild plants, *Wild Harvest*, was offered by the *Outdoor Life* Book Club.

JEROME KNAP is a wildlife biologist turned free-lance outdoor writer and photographer. A regular contributor to a number of outdoor magazines, Knap has hunted wildfowl on five continents and has authored 10 books on the out-of-doors.

H. LEA LAWRENCE, a Tennessean, is a free-lance outdoor writer and photographer whose articles have appeared in myriads of outdoor publications. An enthusiastic waterfowler, Lawrence's favorite method of duck hunting is jump-shooting on small streams in a canoe.

DR. JOSEPH LINDUSKA, a dedicated wildfowler, is one of America's leading waterfowl biologists. His credits include a long stint with the U.S. Fish and Wildlife Service. Linduska is now Vice-President for Science of the National Audubon Society. He is the editor of *Waterfowl Tomorrow,* a monumental monograph on waterfowl management.

BURTON J. MYERS is a dedicated wildfowler and decoy carver. Myers has hunted ducks since boyhood, and is an exceptionally accomplished duck caller. When not gunning ducks or fishing for muskies, he is the editor of *Ontario Out-of-Doors.*

GILBERTO QUIÑONES, coauthor of the chapter on wildfowling in Mexico, is a waterfowl biologist with the Dirección General de la

Fauna Silvestre. Quiñones is a graduate of the prestigious Escuela Nacional de Ciencias Biológicas del Instituto Politécnico Nacional in Mexico.

CLAIR REES is one of the most prolific gun writers in the business today. His by-line appears regularly in such magazines as *Guns and Ammo, Petersen's Hunting, Shooting Times,* and *Guns.* Although he covers the entire range of gun writing, shotguns are his specialty. Rees is also an ardent wildfowler.

DAVID RICHEY is a fulltime outdoor-travel writer living in Clio, Michigan. He is the author of six books on fishing and the outdoors, and is a frequent contributor to the outdoor press.

BOB SCAMMEL is an all-around outdoorsman. But living in some of the best duck hunting country of the Canadian west, it should come as no surprise that wildfowling rates high on his sporting menu. Scammel is the outdoor writer for the *Calgary Herald, Lethbridge Herald* and the *Red Deer Advocate.* He also contributes regularly to a number of Canadian and American outdoor magazines.

NORM STRUNG, a free-lance outdoor writer, leads an idyllic life. Strung spends the summer and fall months in the wilds of Montana and winters in Mexico. His by-line appears regularly in *Field & Stream* and *Sports Afield.* Strung is the author of several books, including one on wildfowling—*Misty Mornings and Moonless Nights.*

JOHN WOOTERS is a prolific gun and hunting writer, with columns in a number of magazines. Although an enthusiastic and accomplished shotgunner, Wooters is also pretty handy with a rifle. Every year, he makes many wildfowling expeditions in his native Texas and neighboring states.

Index